The Thought of Sangharakshita

The Thought of Sangharakshita
A Critical Assessment

Robert M. Ellis

SHEFFIELD UK   BRISTOL CT

Published by Equinox Publishing Ltd

UK: Office 415, The Workstation, 15 Paternoster Row, Sheffield,
South Yorkshire S1 2BX
USA: ISD, 70 Enterprise Drive, Bristol, CT 06010

www.equinoxpub.com

First published 2020

© Robert M. Ellis 2020

All rights reserved. No part of this publication may be reproduced or transmitted in any form or by any means, electronic or mechanical, including photocopying, recording or any information storage or retrieval system, without prior permission in writing from the publishers.

British Library Cataloguing-in-Publication Data
A catalogue record for this book is available from the British Library.

ISBN-13 978 1 78179 928 4 (hardback)
978 1 78179 929 1 (paperback)
978 1 78179 930 7 (ePDF)

Library of Congress Cataloging-in-Publication Data
Names: Ellis, Robert M., author.
Title: The thought of Sangharakshita : a critical assessment / Robert M. Ellis.
Description: Sheffield, South Yorkshire ; Bristol, CT : Equinox Publishing Ltd., 2020. | Includes bibliographical references and index. | Summary: "This book surveys Sangharakshita's most important and original ideas with an eye that combines appreciation and critical awareness in equal measure. It celebrates Sangharakshita's pioneering syntheses of Buddhist and Western ideas, but warns against the inconsistencies and dogmas that are also found in Sangharakshita's work - dogmas whose negative practical effects can also be traced"-- Provided by publisher.
Identifiers: LCCN 2019035486 (print) | LCCN 2019035487 (ebook) | ISBN 9781781799284 (hardback) | ISBN 9781781799291 (paperback) | ISBN 9781781799307 (ePDF)
Subjects: LCSH: Sangharakshita, Bhikshu, 1925-2018. | Triratna Buddhist Order--Doctrines. | Buddhists--Great Britain--Biography. | Dharma (Buddhism) | Buddhist cults--Great Britain. | East and West.
Classification: LCC BQ984.A255 E45 2020 (print) | LCC BQ984.A255 (ebook) | DDC 294.3092 [B]--dc23
LC record available at https://lccn.loc.gov/2019035486
LC ebook record available at https://lccn.loc.gov/2019035487

Typeset by S.J.I. Services, New Delhi, India

Scrutiny is most helpful for striving, Bharadvaja. If one does not scrutinise, one will not strive; but because one scrutinises, one strives.

Canki Sutta, Majjhima Nikaya 95.23

Acknowledgements

Although he died in October 2018, I would like to record my gratitude to Sangharakshita for engaging in a series of meetings with me during the final year of his life, in which we were able to discuss many of the issues in this book. I'd also like to thank Sangharakshita's carers and secretaries at that time for facilitating these meetings.

Thanks also to many people in the Facebook group 'Art of Truth and Reconciliation (Triratna)' for their comments, encouragement, and perspectives from standpoints that are often critical of Sangharakshita.

I would also like to thank the following people for reading the manuscript of this book and making helpful suggestions before publication: Viryanaya Ellis, Vajrapushpa Brown, Mahamati, Kamalashila Matthews, Michael Chaskalson, and Nina Davies.

Robert M. Ellis

Contents

1.	**Introduction**	**1**
	a. Meeting Sangharakshita	1
	b. A Sketch of Sangharakshita's Life and Work	7
	c. The Practical Standpoint for Assessment	14
2.	**Making Buddhism Universal**	**18**
	a. The Universal Dharma	18
	b. Mind Reactive and Creative	23
	c. Provisionality	33
	d. Integration	42
	e. Individuality	51
	f. The Middle Way	62
3.	**Practice**	**72**
	a. The Eightfold Path	72
	b. A System of Meditation	79
	c. The Ten Precepts	87
	d. Friendship	94
	e. Institutions and Power	102
	f. The Arts	110
	g. Ritual	117
4.	**Interpreting Buddhist Tradition**	**123**
	a. Enlightenment and 'Reality'	123
	b. Conditionality	132
	c. Karma and Rebirth	138
	d. The Buddha	145
	e. The Unity of Buddhism	151
	f. Faith and Going for Refuge	158

5. Controversies — **167**
  a. Sangharakshita's Personal Authority — 167
  b. 'The Bearer of the Archetype' — 179
  c. *Women, Men and Angels* — 185
  d. The Single-Sex Idea — 195
  e. Sex and Scandal — 203
  f. Marriage and Family Life — 216

6. Conclusion — **222**
  a. Review of the Argument — 222
  b. Responses to the Argument — 225
  c. Sangharakshita's Legacy — 233

Bibliography — 242

Reference List of Sangharakshita's Lectures and Seminars — 247

Index — 249

1. Introduction

1.a. Meeting Sangharakshita

It's a pleasant but chilly winter's day as I cycle through the lanes of Herefordshire, England, and leave my bike by the pond at the entrance to Adhisthana, the Buddhist centre where Sangharakshita lives. I pass through the courtyard of this former school, to the old house where he has his apartment, and am asked to wait a few minutes in the office next to it, until he is ready to see me.

As I wait, I reflect on the unlikeliness of the whole scenario: both that I now wish to see Sangharakshita, and that he now wishes to see me. After all, I resigned from the Buddhist Order that he founded ten years ago. Since then I've been developing a different approach – Middle Way Philosophy – and have started a society quite distinct from that Order and from the Buddhist tradition. Anyone breaking free of a religious group that used to play such a large role in their lives will tend to find themselves emphasising the distance at first, in order to establish their independence. They then need to engage themselves in something else that is positive, which I have done, in order not to spend the rest of their lives reacting counter-dependently to the old organisation.

It is important to move on; but it's also important, as I've since discovered, to then look back and to engage with one's roots. Sangharakshita's influence shaped the Western (now Triratna) Buddhist Order and Community, and that Order shaped my thinking in various important ways all through my twenties and thirties. Meditation practice, solitary reflection, deeper friendship, aesthetic appreciation, moral adequacy, transformative social structures, spiritual or integrative development itself – all of these are practical expectations that I learnt in large measure from the Order. I could have learnt about them in theory elsewhere, but the emphasis in the Order was on the frontline of practice. The very idea of an ongoing practice that permeates one's life, that engages ideals fully with actual experience, does not often get the kind of emphasis elsewhere that it does there. All of these things became important to me through that Order and its work, with Sangharakshita as its instigator.

The guide and inspiration of my life has since become a more general principle, the Middle Way, in which one recognises what is positive in all areas of one's experience, whilst avoiding turning them into absolute beliefs. After writing a detailed account of Middle Way Philosophy, it has begun to seem that my next priority is a detailed sorting process of the traditions and perspectives that have meant most to me. In this spirit, I've written recent books about Christianity, about Jung, and about the Buddha, all distinguishing what I find genuinely helpful in those sources from the things that get in the way. However, as a young man, I doubt if I would have become particularly interested in the Buddha if it wasn't for the effects of Sangharakshita's interpretation of Buddhism. I would thus never have even become aware of the Middle Way as a possible approach. So I began to think about the possibility of writing a similar 'sorting' book about Sangharakshita.

At first, I did not expect meeting Sangharakshita himself to form part of the project. I expected it to consist mainly of research and thinking. After all, he was ninety-two, and had been in variable health. Nor had I had any personal contact with him for many years, even though by coincidence he now lived only a few miles from me. However, when I sent an email to Adhisthana asking if they'd be interested in assisting me with the project, the email was passed on to Sangharakshita himself. To my surprise, he immediately asked to see me. His health had been stably good of late. Several discussions followed, of which this was the third.

When I'm shown into the room to see Sangharakshita, he is sitting in a high-backed armchair with a somewhat frail but alert gravity. He is positively interested in being challenged, in a way that one would expect of few leaders, and indeed of few ninety-two-year-olds. He makes a point of explaining, this time, what he gets from seeing me. He says that he sees few people outside the circle of his immediate disciples these days, and still fewer people who challenge him. I am also put in mind of another suggestion made by an older friend of mine: that at this age, people like to take stock.

On this occasion, as on previous ones, we talk of a range of topics: doctrine versus methodology, the nature of objectivity, evolution, the nature of spiritual commitment. I try to strike a balance between listening respectfully, and putting in the occasional question or opinion that pushes the boundaries. Sometimes he gets diverted into anecdote, or his memory fails. However, when offered a critical perspective, he always pauses and weighs it up with awareness rather than reacting too quickly, and sometimes clarifies or adjusts his position. He is also aware of his limitations, for example, in knowledge of recent psychology and neuroscience. But there are also limits to what I could expect in terms of critical discussion. He tends not to follow through the implications of any concessions that he makes, but rather then to head back to more familiar territory.

The ambience of that discussion – of respectful listening, of testing questions, of a degree of admiration tempered by a recognition of limitations – is the one that I would like to shape this book. I am glad that it has been possible for it to be informed by personal contact, because I believe that this will add, not detract, from its objectivity. Objectivity, in my view, is not an absolute, but a quality one can cultivate. It involves, more than anything, the capacity to consider alternatives to one's current beliefs. At a basic level it does require the capacity for distancing, so as to avoid being overwhelmed by the apparent 'truths' one is encountering at present. However, that distancing process can also become too much of an end in itself, and require a return to the personal. As anyone who has ever written a comment online will know, it is too easy to comment unreflectively and on the basis of limited assumptions about someone else from the distance of a wholly abstracted perspective. To meet them in person, in their complexity, is often the best antidote to that tendency.

Before I had completed my planned series of discussions with Sangharakshita in relation to this book, however, I learned of his death on 30th October 2018. This death, at the age of 93, was long expected, but sudden when it occurred. He always seemed to be very straightforward and open about his death, and had apparently discouraged his disciples from building an over-grand stupa to mark his grave. It is because of the timing of his death that I was unable to ask him in detail about much of the material in the final 'controversies' section of this book. It is also due to this particular set of circumstances that he is usually referred to in the present rather than the past tense in this book: on reflection I have decided not to revise this.

Having set out this positive context, though, I should also acknowledge previous more negative views of Sangharakshita. I had met him on previous occasions (that he does not remember), perhaps fourteen or fifteen years earlier. Two memories are dominant. One is joining a meal at the community known as Madhyamaloka in Birmingham, where he used to live, and finding him totally dominant at the dinner-table conversation. My own contributions, which I think involved beginning to question the basis of one of his assertions, were not taken up nor given any space. Another memory is of going for a walk with him round the local park, and listening to his very conservative – and I thought, ill-informed – views on language, but not at that time having the courage to fully challenge him face-to-face.

Both of these occasions illustrate a certain unfortunate dynamic of spiritual leadership: one that can seemingly occur regardless of the leader's best intentions to avoid the crude features of the repressive cult. A person who gains an important position because others recognise their profound objectivity – an objectivity that is partly dependent on their openness to other ideas – can end up discouraging that objectivity in their disciples. This happens because of a self-reinforcing tendency for the leader to always be listened to first, because he has the most insights on most topics, which then prevent others from developing, because they lack either the confidence or the social opportunity to challenge him. It is perhaps this dynamic that led to Stephen Batchelor's past impression of Sangharakshita and his movement: 'They operate as a self-enclosed system and their writings have the predictability of those who believe they have all the answers. They are structured in a rigid hierarchy and do not seem to question the teachings of their leader.'[1]

The Triratna Buddhist Community is a New Religious Movement, but not a cult in the most widely used pejorative sense of the term,[2] and Sangharakshita is not an authoritarian leader. However, that has not prevented others from relating to him as one, whether positively or negatively. Their tendency to do so has then had complex and far-reaching effects. Whether Sangharakshita could possibly

---

1 Quoted in Bunting (1997).
2 The Cult Information Centre offers five defining features of a cult, none of which can be clearly applied to Triratna: http://www.cultinformation.org.uk/question_what-is-a-cult.html

have done more to discourage this tendency is one of the more important questions that I want to examine in this book.

This dynamic has contributed a good deal to the other controversies that have surrounded Sangharakshita: the ones that I will consider in the final section of my book. Perhaps the rawest of these concern Sangharakshita's homosexual relationships with young men: relationships that his critics have regarded as abusive because they have involved the abuse of a power imbalance. Sangharakshita's expressed views about the relative spiritual status of men and women, and about marriage and family life, have also caused substantial controversy. My goal in this book is not to examine the specifics of any particular allegation, for example of Sangharakshita's sexual misconduct, but rather to create a wider context in which these cases might be fairly judged. I want, as best I can, to try to assess the underlying motives and assumptions that created these controversies. Are they in any sense inseparable from a wider set of attitudes that are helpful? Do they just involve a failure to apply his wider values consistently? Or are they indicative of deeper problems in Sangharakshita's teachings as a whole?

To be able to fully contextualise these controversies, we will need to start by exploring Sangharakshita's most universal and widely helpful ideas. These have arisen from a highly creative set of circumstances: those of a Buddhist monk, trained for twenty years in India, widely read in traditional Buddhist sources and embedded in the practices of a variety of Buddhist schools and teachers, returning to England and founding a new Western Buddhist movement. Creativity arises from synthesis: in this case the bringing together of East and West. But we should add to the factors contributing to that creativity Sangharakshita's own breadth of character: a poet as well as a thinker, an organiser as well as a practitioner, a Romantic as well as a pragmatist.

It is not surprising, then, that we should find Sangharakshita looking for elements of Western culture that he could incorporate into a Buddhist vision, whether that means William Blake or Saint Jerome. Nor should it be a surprise that his most pragmatic teachings incorporate elements shared with psychology (the concept of integration), democracy (the concept of individuality), and science (the concept of provisionality). Sangharakshita is also well known for not accepting any of these aspects of Western culture indiscriminately. In his critical selection from Western culture lies a good deal of the interest and innovation of his approach. But it should also not be forgotten that at every stage these innovations were applied in the context of practice: whether that of meditation, the arts, friendship, or new forms of social organisation.

The Triratna view of the world emphasises personal commitment to practice, but the strength of the community required to support that practice also creates a barrier that prevents their discoveries being known more widely. However, you do not need to sign up to a Triratna view of the world to learn from Triratna and from the views that have informed it. It is time that Sangharakshita's thinking, both in its successes and its sometimes creative failures, played more of a part in a wider discourse amongst all those who are concerned with human development.

1.b. A Sketch of Sangharakshita's Life and Work

This book is not a biography, but nevertheless, some understanding of Sangharakshita's life will be helpful for the full understanding of the discussion that follows. Full details of much of his life, at least prior to his foundation of the Friends of the Western Buddhist Order in 1968, can be found in the four substantial volumes of his memoirs.[1]

Sangharakshita was born as Dennis Lingwood, to what are often described as working-class parents in Tooting, South London, in 1925. As a child, he was diagnosed with a heart condition that meant that he spent two years in bed from the age of eight. This episode seems to have strongly set the tone of Sangharakshita's distinctive individuality and autodidacticism. He read voraciously, including the whole of a children's encyclopedia and many classic works of literature. After two years, the diagnosis of a heart condition was overturned, and he had to learn to walk again. After getting overexcited and running on an excursion, he then collapsed and had go back to bed and start the whole process all over again.

The way that he must have learnt determination in the face of setbacks, and of a gradualist attitude to progress, becomes evident from these early episodes. His remarkable ability to remain mindful may well have been influenced by the formative experience of having to relearn how to walk twice as an older child. However, these experiences also seem to have left a negative mark on his relationship with his body, making him cerebral and uninterested in bodily cultivation. According to one friend, he made some efforts later to compensate for this, for example through yoga or Tai Chi, but these could not entirely overcome the effects of such childhood conditioning. Some of his critics also say they have been put off by his idiosyncratic body language and speech mannerisms, which may have been influenced by these early experiences.

After leaving school at fourteen, Dennis worked for a coal merchant and the London county council. His lack of formal education did not prevent him from continuing to read prodigiously, from Kant's *Critique of Pure Reason* to the theosophical writings of Madame Blavatsky. He also developed a lifelong love of the arts, which always tended towards the refined, classical and romantic.

1 Sangharakshita (1991, 1996, 1997a, 2003).

At the age of sixteen he read the *Diamond Sutra*, which is one of the best-known Mahayana Buddhist scriptures, full of soaring paradox. He had a powerful experience in response to it, of which he has written that he then knew that he was a Buddhist. When I asked him face-to-face what that meant to him at that time, he said that he accepted what Buddhism stood for, even though he had little understanding of the text at that time. He was reluctant to accept labels like 'intuitive' or 'spiritual' for the experience because he regarded them as inadequate, but it is clear that this was amongst the first of many powerful experiences of that kind that inspired him. From that point he started to attend the Buddhist Society in London.

On reaching the age of eighteen, he was conscripted into the army and joined a signals corps. Even under military discipline, his inner life continued, and he composed 'Persian-style quatrains' in his head whilst marching on the parade ground. In 1944 he was sent to India. Though delighted to be posted to the land of the Buddha, Sangharakshita at first encountered little Buddhism, but instead met Hindu teachers and practised Hindu meditation whenever his duties allowed. It was only when he was re-posted to Singapore that he met Buddhist monks and took up specifically Buddhist practices. After the end of the war, he was informed that his unit was to be demobilised in England, but he applied for leave in India and then failed to return, technically a deserter.

In India he worked temporarily for three different Hindu religious organisations, but he became disillusioned with their organisational politics and continued allegiance to caste rules. Accompanied by a friend and taking the name Dharmapriya, he thus decided to go forth, renouncing all possessions and social status. This decision tells us much about Sangharakshita's commitment to the intuitive understanding of the spiritual life he had maintained since reading the *Diamond Sutra*, as well as his courage.

For two years he then lived the life of an Indian *sadhu*, wandering around southern India and often staying at ashrams. At one of these he had another strong spiritual experience: a vision of the Buddha Amitabha. Despite his immersion in a Hindu context, his commitment to Buddhism increased, and he sought ordination as a Buddhist monk, which he completed in Sarnath (the place of the Buddha's first sermon) in 1950. It is from his minor Buddhist ordination in 1949 that he took the name Sangharakshita. After a visit to Nepal, Sangharakshita then studied the Pali language and scriptures for seven months with the Indian Buddhist monk, Ven. Jagdish Kashyap. Kashyap then asked him to stay in Kalimpong, in the Himalaya, and work 'for the good of Buddhism', which he did for fourteen years.

During his period in Kalimpong, Sangharakshita increasingly developed the interpretation of Buddhism that would be put to the test when he later returned to the UK. Despite his Theravada ordination, he had contact with a variety of different Mahayana Buddhist teachers – many of them lamas newly fled from Tibet. He was thus able to evaluate by comparison, not only between cultures, but between schools of Buddhism. He produced a flow of writing, including *A Survey of Buddhism*,[2] which many followers consider his *magnum opus*. He engaged with a range of Buddhist scholars and practitioners, partly by editing a magazine, *Stepping Stones*. He also began to show a talent for organisation, developing the YMBA (Young Men's Buddhist Association) to help provide a positive focus for young people in Kalimpong, and assisting the King of Sikkim in the reform of Sikkimese monasteries.

During this period, however, Sangharakshita was not confined to Kalimpong, but regularly travelled in the rest of India. At this time he met the great Indian Dalit ('Untouchable') leader, Dr Bhim Rao Ambedkar, who had become the first Law Minister of India and had headed the commission that drafted the Indian Constitution. After long deliberation, Ambedkar had decided that, due to the oppression of the Dalits within Hinduism, he would become a Buddhist. Just six weeks before his death, he led a mass conversion ceremony of his Dalit followers. By coincidence, Sangharakshita arrived in Nagpur, where the conversion ceremonies had taken place, just after Ambedkar's death was announced, and was able to console and aid the huge numbers of Dalits who had followed Ambedkar into Buddhism on the basis of personal faith in him, but who knew almost nothing about it. Sangharakshita continued to work in this community for several months a year during the remainder of his time in India, and Indian Dalit Buddhists have since become a significant part of the Triratna Buddhist movement. This involvement has equipped Sangharakshita with a strong sense of the social importance of Buddhism, and the ways that it can potentially be a tool of liberation for desperately poor and uneducated people.

2   Sangharakshita (1987a).

Sangharakshita returned to the UK in 1964 at the invitation of the English Sangha Trust (the ruling body of Theravada monks in England) to help resolve disputes with the Buddhist Society. However, Sangharakshita's idiosyncratic approach to Buddhism itself soon caused new controversy. Sangharakshita quickly gained popularity amongst ordinary people in the UK who were interested in Buddhism, for the same reasons that he was unpopular with the Buddhist establishment. He thought that spiritual life in general took priority over monastic tradition, and offered ideas that crossed sectarian boundaries. He initially came to England on a temporary basis, then decided to stay permanently, and returned to India to wind up his affairs. Whilst in India, however, he was informed by the English Sangha Trust that he would not be invited back. In another of the courageous decisions that punctuate his life history, Sangharakshita decided to go back anyway and to start his own movement.

Thus in 1967, the Friends of the Western Buddhist Order (FWBO) was founded.[3] This was followed the next year by the first ordinations into the Western Buddhist Order. From the beginning, then, the idea of adapting Buddhism appropriately to Western conditions was embodied in the name of the new organisation. Sangharakshita encountered a very different society in the UK of the 1960s to either the one he had left behind in the 1940s or the one he had left in India. Norms of traditional society were being questioned at an unprecedented rate as the post-war 'baby-boomer' generation reached adulthood. Sexual, cultural, and political freedom were all central to this. Experimentation and encounter with new cultures and religions provided an atmosphere in which many young people wanted to try out Buddhism. It was, in many ways, a uniquely receptive time, at least amongst the young urban elites of the West, and Sangharakshita was fortunate in being able to harness that zeitgeist.

Some key aspects of Sangharakshita's temperament emerged in this situation. On the one hand, it did not suit him at all, because his tendencies were quite conservative. Traditional society, classical art, conservative politics, and metaphysical philosophy continued to attract him even in the midst of the experimental movement

---

3 Vajragupta (2010) gives a reliable account of the history of the movement from this point.

that he himself was initiating. On the other hand, however, there was also a pragmatic flexibility in Sangharakshita's character, and a great willingness to adopt what Buddhists refer to as 'skilful means'. One story of this time is that, despite a lifetime's abstention from alcohol, he would sit in the corner of a pub and spin out a drink in order to listen to the conversation and get the measure of the society in which he found himself. According to other stories, he was also willing to offer people a few drinks if he thought that would help them loosen up a bit, even though this was a strictly temporary expedient and not at all part of the culture of the FWBO. He grew his hair long, and tried LSD. His sexual experimentation from this time onwards, whilst he continued to wear the orange robe of the celibate monk, is also a particularly controversial aspect of his practice (see 5.e).

The apparent contradictions need to be understood by returning to Sangharakshita's grounding in traditional Buddhism. This provided him with a confidence in the spiritual life that he felt able to adapt to an entirely different situation. The ways in which his experience crossed East and West and crossed different Buddhist schools provided him with a model of Buddhism which was independent of specific cultural contexts to an extent that was unusual amongst Buddhist teachers. However, that independence never seems to have prevented him from remaining stubbornly attached to the features of Buddhism that he considered to be core and non-negotiable (the nature of those will be discussed later in this book). For traditional rule-followers whose experience is narrower and temperament less pragmatic, Sangharakshita's conduct in the early years of the new movement will seem to be a descent into rootless relativism; but for him, on the contrary, it was in harmony with what he considered to be the flexible universal core of Buddhism.

The new movement began with a basement in central London, but by the early 1970s was already beginning to expand to other places, including beyond the UK. At first, Sangharakshita ran everything, but as his followers developed he increasingly passed on responsibilities to them. At the time of writing, fifty years later, the Triratna Buddhist Community (as it is now called) has 65 city centres around the world, 15 retreat centres, and around 1,900 Order Members.[4] As early as 1973, he left the running of the movement to

---

4 See thebuddhistcentre.com for up-to-date information.

others whilst taking an extended retreat, in order to enable them to take responsibility in a space free of his influence. During the 1990s he gradually handed on his responsibilities for running the Order and movement, leaving him free to concentrate on practice, literary work, and supporting others at a personal level.

A large number of books represent the records of Sangharakshita's teachings during the period since the foundation of the movement. Many of these were delivered in oral form in the context of talks and seminars, and then transcribed and edited by others. The oral origins of this material give it a very different flavour to the books he directly composed, such as *A Survey of Buddhism*. It covers a very wide range of topics, but is most commonly based on the interpretation of a Buddhist text from any of the periods or schools of Buddhism. Sangharakshita's goal always seems to have been to bring out the practical and inspirational relevance of these texts for Western practitioners today.

Sangharakshita's connections with India, and particularly with the Dalit communities led by Ambedkar, did not end with his move back to the UK. In 1977, with his encouragement, some Western Order members began to work in India, creating a new wing of the movement there. This was initially known as Trailokya Bauddh Mahasangha, but the change of name to Triratna was largely motivated by a wish to have a common name for both Indian and Western wings of the movement. The movement in India was challenged by quite different conditions from those in the West. Ambedkar's Dalit followers had converted to Buddhism with little understanding of the implications, and they continued to be constrained by poverty and lack of education and opportunity. The FWBO was able to initiate a charity (the Karuna Trust) to help meet some of these people's social and material needs, as well as help develop a form of Buddhism appropriate for them. From the point of view of Western Buddhists in the new movement, this has provided a strong social element to its work that might otherwise be missing.

Sangharakshita was a complex and multifaceted character. This complexity is something he has discussed himself, in identifying two sub-personalities: 'Sangharakshita 1' and 'Sangharakshita 2':

> *Sangharakshita 1 wanted to enjoy the beauty of nature, to read and write poetry, to listen to music, to look at paintings and sculpture, to experience emotion, to lie in bed and dream, to see places, to meet people. Sangharakshita*

> *I wanted to realise the truth, to read and write philosophy, to observe the precepts, to get up early and meditate, to mortify the flesh, to fast and pray.*[5]

These two sub-personalities are hardly unique. They reflect the varying dominance of the right and left hemispheres of the brain, and reflect similar tensions in all of us. However, Sangharakshita's awareness of the tensions they produced and of the difficulties in integrating them form the biographical basis of some of the most important of his ideas. It is only through our practical engagement with our contradictions that we make spiritual progress.

---

5 Sangharakshita (1996) p. 436.

1.c. The Practical Standpoint for Assessment

How is it possible to assess the work of such a substantial yet elusive figure as Sangharakshita? The task is difficult. Anybody undertaking it will have a point of view, and, however great the care with which they proceed, may misinterpret him or be partial in their assessments. But it is also important to attempt an assessment. Discussion about Sangharakshita's ideas has too often been polarised between uncritical insiders and dismissive outsiders, each equipped with an entirely different selection of assumptions and a different set of priorities. For the uncritical insiders to edge towards a fuller understanding of the limitations of Sangharakshita's thinking, and for the dismissive outsiders to recognise more of what it has to offer, some assessment needs to be attempted, however imperfect, that attempts to address both.

To make it clearer from what standpoint I intend to assess Sangharakshita's thought, I will first say a little more about my own standpoint.

My own point of view is formed by commitment to the Middle Way, which I understand as a general principle of integrated judgement that can be followed by anyone in any context or tradition. My understanding of the Middle Way has been profoundly shaped by Buddhism and indeed by Sangharakshita's thinking, but it has also been influenced by many other sources: for example by study of the Western philosophical tradition and its limitations; by the Critical Thinking tradition in education; by the philosophy of science; by psychology – Jungian, cognitive, and developmental; by the neuroscience of brain lateralisation as developed by Iain McGilchrist; by the embodied meaning theory of George Lakoff and Mark Johnson. These other influences, though, are intellectual ones that have helped me to interpret the direction of practice that I originally absorbed from my formative time in contact with the Triratna Buddhist Order.

The Middle Way is a method of judging that implies a motive and direction of life informed by developing awareness. It can perhaps be most immediately experienced in meditation, in the process of distraction from one's intended focus and recovery, where we become aware of our tendency to temporarily slip into entirely different goals and assumptions from the ones we thought we were motivated by. When we do this, we temporarily lose our capacity to hold more than one motive in mind in a wider awareness, and become fixated by the distraction: it becomes the whole story. The recognition of this tendency to believe we have the whole story, and the practice of avoiding it through wider and more integrated awareness, is the Middle Way. It can be applied in almost any situation, because it is a feature of human judgement, and is very obviously not limited to Buddhist contexts of practice.

I have produced a developed body of work, including the four-volume *Middle Way Philosophy* series,[1] which explores this perspective and its application. So, I have my theory, you might say. Am I thus planning to evaluate Sangharakshita solely by judging how far it agrees with or disagrees with that theory? The idea of such an approach conjures up the disagreeable image of the Procrustean Bed, whose occupants are trimmed to fit its pre-existing length. What I hope will save me from such a torturous approach is the recognition of how much these ideas are themselves a development of some of Sangharakshita's.

It is only in retrospect that I have recognised how much I owe some of the central, universal elements of Middle Way Philosophy to Sangharakshita's influence. Taking the Middle Way itself seriously is one of these. The concept of integration, though broadly Jungian, is one that I first understood via Sangharakshita, and, in discussion, Sangharakshita says he largely developed it for himself rather than from Jung. Sangharakshita's 'provisional belief' becomes 'provisionality' – a central theme of Middle Way Philosophy. Perhaps most importantly, Sangharakshita's essay 'Mind Reactive and Creative' is almost certainly the first source of my understanding of open and closed feedback loops – which one can also find in many other places, helping to distinguish a provisional (creative) way of thinking from a dogmatic and absolute one. It is these kinds of universal ideas in Sangharakshita that I will begin with, because in my view they form the basis for a wider understanding of Sangharakshita's importance.

So, no, I am not setting out to fit Sangharakshita's thought to a Procrustean Bed. Rather I will be using the most universal and helpful elements of Sangharakshita's teachings (which happen to be consistent with my own views) as the basis for judging the rest. Of course, the selection of what is most universal and helpful remains

1   Ellis (2012, 2013a, 2013b, 2015).

my own selection, despite the justifications I will give to it. It is not a divinely ordained perfect selection, and I expect some to disagree with it. Nevertheless, this still seems to me the best way to approach a critical reading of Sangharakshita. I would ask those who disagree with it, rather than criticising it only in the abstract, to reflect on what alternative means they would use to accomplish the same end.

Those with a traditionalist allegiance to Buddhism may well respond that it is the Buddhist tradition itself that they would prefer to use as basis of judgement. After all, Sangharakshita's own allegiance to that tradition has been profound since he first read the *Diamond Sutra* at the age of sixteen. In practice, however, I think that this would result in a much cruder Procrustean Bed than any other approach. The Buddhist tradition is a very varied and disputed tradition, and Sangharakshita's approach has always been to try to find the helpful core of that tradition. If you want to limit your evaluation to an appeal to Buddhist tradition, but do not simply accept Sangharakshita's own interpretation of that tradition as an absolute source of knowledge, then you will have to adopt the standpoint of another traditional school of Buddhism to evaluate his interpretation. Sangharakshita has challenged all of these schools, from the hypocrisy created by Theravadin monasticism to the ethical limitations of Zen. Despite drawing on all the Buddhist schools, he does not wholly accept any of them. Some of Sangharakshita's crudest critics, such as the author of the online 'FWBO Files'[2] take the approach that Sangharakshita's teachings are 'not true Buddhism' because they don't accord with a traditional Buddhist school or lineage. Ironically, then, some of the least Buddhist in spirit are the most 'Buddhist' in form. There is no chance of even understanding Sangharakshita's approach fully if you are not willing to move beyond the assumption that one traditional school of Buddhism is the correct one.

Another possible approach would, of course, be a scholarly one based on reference to Buddhist scriptures. The challenge would then be to judge whether Sangharakshita's teachings accorded with those scriptures. However, given that Sangharakshita has already made a lifetime's project of studying and interpreting those scriptures, not only would such a scholarly survey be forbiddingly vast,

---

2 www.ex-cult.org/fwbo/fwbofiles.htm

but it would also have to be based on some other assumptions than his about how those scriptures should be selected and interpreted. The Procrustean Bed would then be applied indeed, with a particular scholarly basis of interpretation merely opposed to his. Such an approach would also be missing a more basic point: that scriptures are there to serve human practical insight, not vice-versa. Your view may be inspired and informed by Buddhist scriptures, but it cannot be entirely justified by them. It must stand in its own right for its practical value.

These traditionalist and scholarly ways of judging Sangharakshita's ideas, then, would in my view not be adequate. They would also be of very limited interest, directed only at a small group of narrowly focused Buddhist scholars. To judge Sangharakshita's ideas in a relevant and helpful way, the criteria for doing so must be practical and universal. I use the term 'practical' here in a broad sense. It does not necessarily mean offering specific instructions for how to act in a specific situation. However, a 'practical' teaching does offer the *potential* to change one's approach to a specific situation in experience, when reflected upon and applied.

In this sense, assertions of a kind that only have an abstract, self-reinforcing significance, and that cannot be applied in this way, can be judged unhelpful because they are not practical. Generalisation by itself is not a bar to practicality – the test being whether a generalisation does in fact apply to a wide range of cases without evident exception. Judgements about which beliefs can be helpfully applied and which cannot of course need to take as much account as possible of the context in which those beliefs are understood. They also need to be provisional – open to comparison and correction.

This book aims to make practically helpful generalisations about the helpfulness or otherwise of Sangharakshita's generalisations about the spiritual life. Its judgements aim to be provisional, and will be made on the basis of listening to both sides of the debate about Sangharakshita, as well as responding to feedback. However, in the end, judgements are needed, and I take responsibility for those judgements. Even if you end up disagreeing with them, I hope that you will feel that I have proceeded in a spirit of provisionality, and that they are practically motivated.

2. Making Buddhism Universal

2.a. The Universal Dharma

Let us begin by considering Sangharakshita's position when he returned to the West from 1964. Having nearly twenty years of practice in various traditional schools of Buddhism, he was now concerned with communicating the practical insights he believed he had found to people with very different cultural assumptions. Those cultural assumptions were not entirely absent from the Indian context, but much less deeply rooted there, and amount to the features of modern Western society as distinct from traditional societies. They included individualism, liberal democracy, secularism, science, and psychology.

Individualism meant that people expected individuals to make the key judgements about their own lives, rather than automatically following family or tradition. Liberal democracy meant that social and political decisions were expected to follow the wishes of the majority, whilst respecting the rights of individuals and minorities and allowing all views to be heard and explored. Secularism meant that no set of religious beliefs could be taken for granted, and the role of religion was seen as a matter of individual judgement. Science provided a formal basis of evidence with an increasing influence over political and social judgements. Psychology provided an increasingly reliable basis of information about the motives and behaviour of human beings (which since then has also been greatly added to by neuroscience, directly investigating the brain's functions).

To communicate Buddhism in this new Western context, and to help people to engage with it and practise it, required engagement with these forces. It required engagement of a kind that the traditional Buddhist schools had so far managed very little. Figures that Sangharakshita admired, such as Dharmapala, the founder of the Maha Bodhi Society in India, had made a start. It would have been a very small minority of people in the UK who would be willing to engage with Buddhism in its traditional forms without substantially addressing these forces of modernity, but instead Sangharakshita began to reach out to a wider audience. That wider audience at the time largely consisted of younger people in whom these features of modern society were most deeply imbued, making it all the more important to address them. Sangharakshita did not bring Buddhism to conservative English Christians – he brought it to those who wanted to listen, and those people for the most part were the radical products of modernity.

To do this, it is clear that he would have to work back to the common ground between traditional Buddhism and modernity. Sangharakshita seemed already well prepared to do this, because his interpretation of Buddhism was already one that depended on a belief in a universal dharma. The Buddhist term 'dharma' can be translated as doctrine, morality, religion, or 'law' in the sense of a natural law.[1] It means 'Buddhist teaching', at the same time as what is referred to by that teaching. This is often conceptualised as some kind of 'truth' or 'reality' (a philosophically controversial point that I will be returning to). What is important in understanding Sangharakshita's basic approach, however, is that the term 'dharma' in most Buddhist use carries a connotation of universality beyond what Buddhism happens to teach. It suggests a path that is available to all human beings.

Sangharakshita's motives for continuing to seek Buddhism when surrounded by Hinduism seem to have been closely related to a search for that universality, as does his openness to a variety of Buddhist schools and teachers. Indeed, his continuing openness to Western art and culture also illustrates the importance of that universality for Sangharakshita. To remain content with one school's way of conveying the insight that he found in Buddhism in general would in some ways have been a betrayal of that insight, which would always go beyond what the people in only one context had made of it. These insights were identified with the Buddha's experience of enlightenment, which Sangharakshita takes as unifying the Buddhist tradition.

In a talk on the Dharma, Sangharakshita said:

The Dharma really represents not this doctrine, not that teaching, but a great current of spiritual life in which we can participate, in which we can help

---

1 See Ellis (2019) 6.f for a fuller discussion.

> others to share and which sweeps us on, bears us on at any rate, eventually in the direction of Enlightenment.[2]

His typical reliance on the concept of Enlightenment here is one that we will have to return to, because it was not automatically meaningful for all his hearers, even when put in the context of the story of the Buddha. What seems more important overall, though, is that his early followers were able to directly experience a portion of what he meant through practice. Meditation was central to that practice from the beginning, but the other elements of the Noble Eightfold Path also received plenty of attention, and put meditation in a wider context: those of personal ethics, right livelihood in economic relationships, and the creation of a social environment that could help individuals to mature into wisdom.

The universal dharma requires a connection to be made between teachings and individual experience in a very wide range of specific situations. It needs to communicate both the inspiration and the technique required to set off in a direction of spiritual development. For modern Western hearers, that is easily disrupted by a presentation that does not address the features of modernity. For example, the emphasis on traditional authority and the role of the guru was, and still is, likely to be an object of great dubiousness for the scientifically educated children of an egalitarian democracy. Sangharakshita needed to 'translate' the way these things had helpfully functioned in traditional Asian Buddhism, to either make them directly relevant in the West or to produce substitutes.

Some aspects of traditional Buddhism were quickly abandoned by Sangharakshita, their function replaced by alternatives. Monasticism was one example of an early casualty, replaced by a non-monastic ordination system and a set of experiments in the creation of centres, communities, and businesses that could nurture the spiritual life. On the other hand, some aspects of traditional Buddhism were already in a universal form that could readily be accessed by anyone. Mindfulness-based meditation practice is an obvious example: everyone, regardless of culture or background, can become aware of their breath and their body.

In the remainder of this first section of the book, however, I will be exploring, not those elements of traditional Buddhism that

---

2 Lecture 2.

clearly did or didn't fit the new presentation Sangharakshita needed to make, but rather the innovations that he added to the traditional Buddhist perspective to address modern conditions. I am going to concentrate on these because they are the most distinctive positive contributions he made to wider Western thought and practice. They do not necessarily require the acceptance of traditional Buddhist doctrines to be helpful, so we do not have to debate those doctrines, and Sangharakshita's presentation of them, just yet. By the time we do come to those aspects of Buddhism that are usually presented as foundational, I hope we will have another angle from which to interpret Sangharakshita's view of these – one that puts more emphasis on Sangharakshita's *method* for engaging with people's spiritual needs in modern society, and less on such doctrines.

Those distinctive responses to modernity can be related to the features of modernity that I summarised above (individualism, liberal democracy, secularism, science, and psychology). Given the profound engagement with psychology that is already present in the Buddhist tradition, it is not surprising that the best starting point for understanding these responses is psychological. Sangharakshita's work on the creative and reactive mind is perhaps the lynchpin of the universal dharma he is offering. It is universal, not just theoretically and as a whole, but through gradual application in everyday experience. Sangharakshita's use of the term integration, which is now widely applied in Triratna, is also hugely valuable and consists in a psychological model for spiritual progress that can be used independently of the appeal to enlightenment. His ideas about 'provisional belief' offer important links between Buddhist method and the best scientific method. His account of individuality is obviously a response to modern individualism – one that accepts its strengths but also challenges its weaknesses. His view of individuality also has great implications for his understanding of the role of religion in society, which needs to involve autonomous judgement without becoming locked in a set of reactions to groups. His support for consensus decision-making (discussed later in 3.e) is also a response to liberal democracy that, again, tries to adopt its strengths but not its weaknesses.

The common feature I can trace in all these responses to modernity is the Middle Way, which will be the final topic of this first section. All these responses involve the practical finding of an effective point of balance between competing absolute assumptions. The

Middle Way is a traditional Buddhist concept that is to some extent developed and emphasised by Sangharakshita, but we will need to assess how far his presentation of it is consistent with the way he actually employs it in his responses to modernity. What is clear is that, whether or not his formal presentation of it is clear and consistent, he makes a good deal of implicit use of it.

2.b. Mind Reactive and Creative

'Mind Reactive and Creative' is the title of a formative lecture given by Sangharakshita in 1967,[1] and also of an undated booklet[2] which makes the same points in different words. In these sources, he succeeds in identifying the key point of universal practical significance in Buddhist teaching about conditionality. To talk of conditionality as a feature of the phenomenal universe, or of enlightenment as the goal of a path that transcends that conditionality, does not by itself necessarily relate to individual experience, but just involves a set of grand and possibly speculative claims. To bring that contrast into focus, though, as two contrasting types of mental state we all constantly experience in every hour of our waking lives: that is where universal practical teaching begins. It also identifies crucial insights that can be confirmed by many other sources working from many other perspectives.

Like many of Sangharakshita's presentations, it takes a while to get to the point, is freighted with presentations of traditional Buddhist formulae (in this case the twelve links of conditionality[3] and the seven factors of enlightenment), and introduces ultimate metaphysical claims that at best distract from the central practical point. However, when the central point comes, it is worth waiting for:

> *The reactive mind is a re-active mind. It does not really act, but only re-acts. Instead of acting spontaneously, out of its own inner fullness and abundance, it requires an external stimulus to set it in motion. This stimulus usually comes through the five senses. We are walking along the street. An advertisement catches our eye, its bright colours and bold lettering making an instant appeal.... Our attention is attracted, arrested. We go and do what the advertisement is designed to make us do, or make a mental note to do it, or are left with an unconscious disposition to do it as and when circumstances permit. We have not acted, but been activated.*
>
> *The reactive mind is, therefore, the conditioned mind. It is conditioned by its object (e.g. the advertisement) in the sense of being not merely dependent on it but actually determined by it. The reactive mind is not free. Since it is conditioned, the reactive mind is, moreover, purely mechanical. As such it can be appropriately described as a 'penny in the slot' mind. Insert the*

---

1 Lecture 31.
2 Sangharakshita (undated).
3 Conditionality is discussed in 4.b below.

> coin, and out comes the packet.... Not only our behaviour but even much of our 'thinking' conforms to this pattern. Whether in the field of politics, or literature, or religion, or whether in the affairs of everyday life, the opinions we so firmly hold and so confidently profess are very rarely the outcome of conscious reflection, of our individual effort to arrive at the truth. Our ideas are hardly ever our own.[4]

The reactive mind is contrasted with the creative mind:

> The creative mind does not re-act. It is not dependent on, or determined by, the stimuli with which it comes into contact. On the contrary, it is active in its own account, functioning spontaneously, out of the depths of its own intrinsic nature. Even when initially prompted by something external to itself it quickly transcends its original point of departure and starts functioning independently. The creative mind can therefore be said to **respond** rather than react....[5]

> The creative mind is above all the aware mind. Being aware...the creative mind is also intensely and radiantly alive. The creative person...is not only more aware than the reactive person but possessed of far greater vitality.[6]

The crucial difference between these two states of mind, then, is that the former involves automatic, unreflective responses to stimuli. The latter, on the other hand, responds to stimuli with awareness, that allows the possibility of alternative responses. The difference between them is one of judgement. A reactive judgement considers only the possibility of responding in one way (or, we might add, the unthinkable, crude negation of that one way). A creative judgement, on the other hand, offers a variety of options, which greater levels of awareness allow us to choose between. If we are able to choose between a variety of options, we have more flexibility and adaptability, and thus have the practical ability to choose *better*, whatever the nature of the judgement involved.

Since Sangharakshita wrote and delivered this material over fifty years ago, a huge amount of corroboration can be offered to this basic perspective using psychology and neuroscience. It must be stressed that to use such scientific sources of evidence is not reductive but corroborative, using external investigation of the sources of our experience to strengthen our understanding of what internal experience can tell us. It does not involve the acceptance of any

---

4 Ibid. pp. 4–5.
5 Ibid. pp. 7–8.
6 Ibid. p. 9.

claim that the mind is 'only material', but rather suggests that the brain processes that some have interpreted as 'only material' complement our apparently 'non-material' internal experience of reactivity and creativity.

If we ask what 'reactivity' is, in neurological terms, it seems to be the motivational operation of the brainstem, or 'reptilian brain', which provides our basic responses to stimuli: for example, to eat food or to run away from danger. This works together with our limbic system or 'mammalian brain', which can be seen as the source of meaning, interpreting those stimuli for us.[7] We only 'know' that one stimulus is a possible source of danger, or that another offers food or reassurance, by interpreting it. So, for example, if I see a tiger charging at me, my limbic system tells me that this is a source of danger, and my brainstem then motivates me to flee. This is an automatic reaction that bypasses any process of reflection or further awareness. If we stopped to consider too long, we would be eaten.

As Sangharakshita indicates, though, this automatic reaction is not merely a matter of unthinking behaviour, but also a matter of thinking in a way that lacks wider awareness. In other words, the more specifically human frontal and pre-frontal areas of our brain are not entirely excluded from it. In particular, the linguistic and goal-oriented parts of the left pre-frontal cortex may form representational beliefs about how the world is and how we ought to act in it, that habitually interact with the limbic system and brainstem so as to reinforce certain patterns of unreflective response. The more we continue in certain patterns of response to what we encounter, the more entrenched that pattern of response becomes, and the more we bypass wider awareness. Synaptic links in our brains that initially may have been occasional and tentative, rapidly become well-worn superhighways. We can see this strongly illustrated in states of addiction, but also in any kind of unreflective habit. I brush my teeth at a certain time of day. I eat certain kinds of food and not others. I respond to a pet's cries by feeding it. As I do all these habitual things, the energies flow through my brain along more or less predictable tracks.

'Creativity', on the other hand, involves a response to stimuli with wider awareness that enables alternative options to be

7 A variety of sources could be used to confirm the information about the brain given here. There is a very helpful and accessible explanation in Siegel (2010) pp. 14 ff.

considered. This will involve the wider awareness of the pre-frontal cortex broadening the meanings made available to us by the limbic system. That wider awareness could take a predominantly conceptual form, encouraging us to think consistently (using the left hemisphere), or a wider non-conceptual form (using the right hemisphere) that enables us to compare different conceptual beliefs, no longer enslaved to one set of conceptual assumptions. This is not opposed to the processes of the reactive mind, but rather it broadens them. Instead of a particular set of deeply entrenched synaptic links being solely relied upon, a wider set of weaker links are opened up, allowing new possible kinds of judgement.

Sangharakshita's claim that the creative person is also more 'vital' (i.e. has more energy) can also be given a coherent explanation, even if it may be difficult to show in scientific terms. First, we have to assume that this applies to the 'creative person' at the time they are being creative, not necessarily at all times. We can then reflect that reactive states of mind close off alternative ways of thinking that involve different synaptic channels. Creative states of mind, in contrast, allow energy to flow down these channels, adding their energy to what is available to us, and interacting with our bodily states in complex ways. Just as the breaking of a dyke allows a release of energy from water that has previously been held back, the widening of the flow of energy through the brain and nervous system from previously narrower channels releases mental energy.

Further corroboration for the basic model of 'mind reactive and creative' can also be found from its relationship to open (or modifying) and closed (or reinforcing) feedback loops. This is a model that is widely used to understand the operation of systems, and can be applied to our mental processes just as it can be applied to, for example, ecological processes. A closed feedback loop is one in which a system maintains itself in a form distinct from what is around it, through the repetition of the same process based on the same assumptions, to the exclusion of outside influence. Very often this can result in the build-up of a particular type of effect until it is disruptive to the wider environment. For example, if a predator is imported to a small island with an abundant food source that has no defences against it, it will rapidly multiply and destroy that food source, in turn then destroying itself. The island can then suffer ecologically with lots of further effects, such as the loss of the prey-species that previously kept other species in check. In a similar way, if a certain set of assumptions in the mind (e.g. that the next heroin fix will solve all my problems) motivates behaviour that reinforces those assumptions (getting and taking heroin, thus increasing the addiction), this is also likely to damage my environment (destroying relationships, preventing productive activity, motivating crime, etc.). 'Reactivity' is another way of talking about such closed feedback loops in our mental states, whether those are seen in terms of addiction, dogma, hatred, obsession, or conflict.

Creative states of mind, in contrast, can be associated with an open feedback loop. That means one in which new energy or information is allowed to come in from outside the loop of our habitual activity and modify its assumptions. The philosopher of science Karl Popper commented on the way that such open feedback loops are the basis of scientific discovery as well as evolutionary advance.[8] An animal develops a certain genetic form, and certain forms of habitual behaviour, that are adapted to a particular environment. However, when that environment changes, frustration, loss, and even death may result. The survivors from such a situation are those that have modified their form or behaviour in a way that is adapted to the new circumstances. Similarly, Popper argued that scientific advance arises from the falsification of a theory, leading a scientist to modify that theory in response to new evidence. In this case, however, that modification also depends on the creativity of the scientist, who needs to able to respond to new evidence with imagination, rather than continuing to insist on the old theory.

In Sangharakshita's writings on mind reactive and creative, however, there is very little of this wider background. Instead he was concerned with showing the relationship of these features of human thinking to traditional Buddhist teaching. The reactive mind is placed in the context of conditioned existence or samsara, which is depicted graphically in the 'Wheel of Life' paintings found in Tibetan Buddhism. The Wheel depicts the 'poisons' (craving, aversion, and delusion), rising and falling figures (representing the ways in which our fortunes are subject to conditions when we merely react to them), six 'realms' representing states we get into through reactivity (such as contentment, jealousy, craving, suffering, or ignorance), and the twelve links offering a scheme of the process by which reactivity occurs.

8   Popper (1994) ch. 3.

Although traditionally the Wheel is represented in terms of rebirth between lives, Sangharakshita's skilful approach was to suggest psychological interpretations, without actually declaring the traditional cosmological ones to be untrue:

> *Although the five or six spheres of conditioned existence are usually interpreted cosmologically, as objectively existing worlds which are just as real, for the beings inhabiting them, as our own world is for human beings, nevertheless it is also possible to interpret them psychologically as representing different states of human life and consciousness, – an interpretation which has some sanction in tradition.*[9]

This is one of many examples we will find of Sangharakshita focusing on the more universal approaches that will be more useful to his listeners, without disavowing traditional Buddhist beliefs. Rather, it could be said that he seeks to put those traditional beliefs in a wider context of interpretation. Buddhist traditionalists will argue that Buddhism is a path to enlightenment that can only be followed by accepting teachings such as rebirth that they believe come from the Buddha. Thus for them, the Wheel of Life can only be correctly understood with an acceptance of rebirth. Sangharakshita perceived correctly that such an attitude would only block many people's understanding of what he felt to be a more important underlying spiritual message: that we need to recognise the self-feeding circularity of reactive states. To recognise and work with that reactivity in no way requires any view to be taken on whether such reactivity is part of a wider cosmological cycle of rebirth fuelled by it. During his first stay back in England, Sangharakshita evidently offended his fellow monastics by being prepared to give priority to that universal spiritual message over its supposed metaphysical basis.

Similar points apply to the way the Sangharakshita relates creativity to the Buddhist tradition. He does this by discussing the seven factors of enlightenment: awareness, investigation of mental states, energy, rapture, tension release, concentration, and tranquility. These factors show the rewards of creative thought, and the ways that they can reinforce each other. They can be closely related to another distinctive emphasis in Sangharakshita's work: the 'positive nidanas', or 'spiral order of conditionality'. These are neglected by traditional Buddhism, but can be found in the Pali Canon and

---

9 Sangharakshita (undated) pp. 11–12.

are discussed in Sangharakshita's *Survey of Buddhism*.[10] The chief point in emphasising these for him is to convey that creativity is an alternative form of conditioning, though one in which gathering levels of awareness help us to increasingly fulfil our human potential. The 'spiral' metaphor can help us visualise the development of creativity in terms of a spatial metaphor: we are still going round and round (reacting), but in a weakening fashion as we ascend the spiral and get closer to enlightenment (which is seen as the top of the spiral).

In his writings on mind reactive and creative, Sangharakshita emphasises that the link between the reactive and the creative forms of conditionality is awareness. However, if we also consider the twelve links of the spiral, we find that the awareness that forms the first stage of that spiral has to be awareness *of* the experience of suffering or frustration (dukkha) on the Wheel of reactivity.[11] We are propelled onwards, not by satisfaction, but by dissatisfaction. Here we have a crucial link between Sangharakshita's teachings on positive conditionality and the open feedback loops mentioned earlier. Similarly, for philosopher of science Karl Popper, the open feedback loop of learning, discovery, or evolution begins with an 'error'. We have to encounter a problem in our current set of assumptions in order to be obliged to change them, and we cannot develop without change, even if many of those changes turn out to be blind alleys.

Sangharakshita's writings on mind reactive and creative also offer another crucial Buddhist insight into the link between the two orders of conditionality: that awareness needs to be applied at the point between feeling (of pleasant, painful, or neutral experiences) and craving.[12] Craving is the basis of reaction, because it is the arising of a desire for a pleasant experience to continue or for a painful one to go away. If we can maintain a wider awareness, even just to put off that reaction by remaining relaxed and open for a little while, we are obviously better able to judge its appropriateness. For example, the desire for a third helping of ice cream involves the wish for a continuation of a pleasant experience. To merely deny that desire would be another form of reactivity, but to hold it in wider awareness may be all that is required to recognise

10 Sangharakshita (1987a) pp. 137 ff.
11 Ibid. p. 136.
12 Sangharakshita (undated) pp. 21-2.

the importance of not indulging it. There are possible arguments, which I will discuss later (4.b), as to whether this is the *only* point at which the creative mind can emerge from the reactive one, but its practical importance as a working point can hardly be denied. Not having that third helping may give us a sense of disappointment or frustration, but one that is quickly made insignificant by the greater good recognised by our wider awareness.

The practical importance of these teachings can hardly be contested. Not only are they at the heart of the most helpful message of Buddhism, but at the heart of all human learning and development, whether in science, ethics, the arts, politics, or any other field. By emphasising them in his presentation of Buddhism, Sangharakshita helped to channel the energy of many Westerners fascinated by the Orient into a fruitful psychological awareness. Many of his other distinctive emphases, as we will see, build on this one in an equally productive way.

However, even at this early stage of presenting Sangharakshita's most universal and helpful teachings, a few cautionary notes need to be struck. Perhaps the first and most obvious is that Sangharakshita was far from unique in offering these teachings, however distinctive and important they may have been in the particular context in which he presented them. The contrast between open and closed (or 'negative' and 'positive')[13] feedback loops was used by the philosophers Popper and Dewey, and is now widely appreciated in systems theory, neuroscience, and a variety of other contexts. Indeed, the idea of the closed feedback loop is also central to the science of climate change, with its recognition that global warming may be multiplied and accelerated by closed feedback loops.

Secondly, we also need to be cautious even in attributing a full understanding of reactivity and creativity to the Buddhist tradition. In practice, it seems clear, people make spiritual progress by cultivating creative rather than reactive states of mind, in Buddhism as elsewhere, and we can also readily see how many Buddhist practices may help to cultivate creative states of mind. However, the lack of wider recognition of the positive nidanas also suggests a conceptual blockage in Buddhist tradition when it comes

---

13 In my own earlier writings I have used the terms 'negative' for open feedback loops, and 'positive' for closed ones (e.g. Ellis 2012 3.e). I have reformed my usage here to try to avoid confusions created by these terms.

to recognising how widespread, and ordinary, the transition from reactive to creative states might be. As we will see later in relation to the issues surrounding monasticism, the monk-lay division tends to provide social conditions that emphasise the discontinuity, rather than the continuity, between Samsara and Nirvana. Lay people are doomed to the Wheel and can only hope for better rebirths within it, whilst monastics aim for enlightenment as a radically different state. Sangharakshita deserves credit here, not so much for telling us any kind of ultimate truth embedded in the Buddhist tradition (even though that's very much how he sees it), as for selecting and interpreting it in such a way as to bring out its most helpful elements for ordinary Western practitioners.

Thirdly, Sangharakshita's own presentation of these issues could very easily create misunderstandings that cause problems further down the line. These potential problems are created by his reliance on absolute metaphysical language in the intellectual context he gives to the presentation. He begins by talking about a 'twofold' mind, but this is not, to begin with, reactive and creative mind, but 'Absolute Mind' and 'relative mind'.[14] Mind reactive and creative is only then introduced as offering two forms of 'relative mind', but 'Absolute Mind' plays no further role in the discussion at all, its introduction completely redundant. Some might presume from this that belief in 'Absolute Mind' is in some way necessary for the experience, or indeed the cultivation, of creative mind, but Sangharakshita does not even seem to be claiming this, let alone justifying it successfully. To call creative mind 'relative' is itself questionable, since it is clearly regarded as better than reactive mind – so an incremental scale of moral and spiritual judgement is at work, regardless of the question of what may lie at its top. If you define 'relative' as simply not positively absolute then it is accurate, but this sense is also often conflated with the assumption that 'relative' things are of equal value.

Some of Sangharakshita's language in explaining the difference between reactive and creative mind may also potentially invite unnecessary assumptions. He describes reactive mind as 'determined' and 'not free',[15] and creative mind as 'functioning spontaneously out of the depths of its own intrinsic nature'.[16] Although

14 Sangharakshita (undated) p. 3.
15 Ibid. p. 5.
16 Ibid. p. 7.

this may connect us helpfully to an *experience* of greater freedom when we are in more creative states of mind, it also seems to be an invitation to view mind reactive and creative through the lens of the freewill-determinism dichotomy that has become so entrenched in Western philosophy. There is much that can be said about the dangers of this dichotomy, which I have explored in depth elsewhere,[17] but for the moment let me focus only on some of the potential practical effects. If we start assuming that we are *absolutely* free when we are creative, this may well be a trigger for another set of reactions, for example feelings of unnecessary guilt based on the assumption that I was 'free' to do something that I found difficult and failed to do. On the other hand, the assumption that reactivity is determined may be used to justify the assumption that those caught up in reactivity have no responsibility at all for their actions. A whole set of polarised positions may ensue, of a kind that can be illustrated by progressive versus conservative positions on crime, with the former often assuming a lack of individual responsibility and the latter its totality.

To work consistently to promote creative states of mind, it is not always sufficient merely to invoke the Buddhist tradition as a source of creativity, because we are always unavoidably working with our interpretations of that tradition. Sangharakshita's presentation of mind reactive and creative shows a necessary boldness in performing that interpretation and helpfully inspiring his listeners to creativity. However, we are also already encountering difficult questions about how much his approach is consistent in doing this, and also how far he encourages others to engage in their own creative interpretations of Buddhism for new circumstances. These are questions that we will need to ask in relation to many of Sangharakshita's other ideas as well.

---

17 Ellis (2015) 3.f and 4.c.

2.c. Provisionality

We now come to an idea that has huge implicit importance in Sangharakshita's work and legacy, but has received very little explicit discussion. To understand the importance of this idea in the context of Sangharakshita's return to the West, we'll need to first consider the broad impact of science on modern society. I've already mentioned that science is one of the factors of modernity shaping the society that Sangharakshita returned to – but one in which he had no training and little direct interest. How, then, does his approach take science into account and relate it to the universal dharma?

The answer to this does not lie in any appeal to the *results* of science, or indeed to some of the narrower accounts that might be given of its method. Though he was willing to make use of scientific theories such as that of evolution, Sangharakshita was clearly opposed to any attempts to reduce Buddhism to something that is interpreted only in the terms of scientific theory, and that would involve 'reductionist' or 'mechanistic' assumptions.[1] He saw the limitation of science as being the assumption 'that the unaided intellect is capable of penetrating to the truth about the subject of its researches'.[2] This interpretation of science assumes that it relies solely on empirical, public observations to confirm theories about causal relationships – and that these theories have been formulated by the 'unaided intellect'.

An investigation of the philosophy of science, however, can offer us a much more subtle view of how it works at its best, and thus of how much further its influence on modernity extends beyond the acceptance of a 'mechanistic' worldview. Far from being developed by the 'unaided intellect', the philosopher of science Karl Popper pointed out that scientific theories themselves can be conceived by any method, including highly intuitive methods,[3] and it is the way they are tested that then makes them scientific. Two further great philosophers of science, Lakatos and Kuhn, have then examined how scientific theory progresses through the rise and fall of confidence in overarching theories that might be called 'paradigms',

---

1 Seminar 137 pp. 1–3.
2 Sangharakshita (1987a) p. 34.
3 Popper (1959) p. 31.

which can never be finally proved or disproved in themselves, but which can be tested together with auxiliary hypotheses.[4] It is when these tests turn out to be negative that relatively clear advances are made towards the refinement of a paradigm. This happens by gradual revision in response to frustration, following the pattern of the open feedback loop discussed in the previous chapter. On this more adequate model of scientific method, there is no reductionist or materialist assumption required. On the contrary, the very assumption of reductionism (that all phenomena can be ultimately and fully explained in terms of the physics of 'matter') should be eliminated, because, since we are limited by our mind and senses from penetrating to any ultimate explanation of phenomena, it is not open to testing of any kind. Nor is the use of this method confined to formal academic science.

It is only in this somewhat more adequate model of science that the full contribution of the quality of *provisionality* to the scientific process is made apparent. If scientists are not open to the falsification of a specific hypothesis, their theories will never develop, and they will be unable to learn from evidence. Instead they will merely select from their observations those elements that support their existing assumptions. If they were not open, also, to the longer-term abandonment of fruitless paradigms from past science (like those of the flat earth, or of phlogiston), we would be stuck in dogmatic adherence to those paradigms. It is the ability to take evidence from experience in this way, as a basis for adjusting our existing views, whether in the domain of formal, experimental science or not, that helps to distinguish modernity from previous more static states of society.

On his return to the UK, Sangharakshita seems to have quickly understood that most people were unlikely to adopt Buddhism merely on the basis of a dogmatic presentation of its supposed truth. Rather, they needed to become gradually convinced of its helpfulness. For these people, then, Buddhism was not so much a doctrine as a theory to be weighed up and considered alongside other theories. The expectation that it should be treated in that way was partly the result of broadly scientific attitudes imparted through Western education, but also the expectation of individuality or autonomy of judgement (which I will discuss later) and the rights to exercise

---

4 Lakatos (1974), Kuhn (1996).

that judgement, offered by liberal democracy. Fortunately, there are important elements of Buddhist tradition that are not dogmatic but investigatory, and can be interpreted so as to support provisional investigation. Whatever the limitations of his explicit view of science, then, Sangharakshita's skill was to give appropriate emphasis to those elements of provisionality when required.

Sangharakshita's argument is that *faith* in the Buddhist context is compatible with *provisional belief*. Such an attitude in general fits an attitude of autonomous investigation that is highlighted in a few places in the Pali Canon, such as the *Kalama Sutta* (*AN* 3.65) and the *Canki Sutta* (*MN* 95). He highlights provisional faith in response to the life and teachings of the Buddha as the basis on which we may then tread the path, to gain confirmation or disconfirmation of that path through direct experience.[5] He also talks of 'provisional going for refuge' as a level of commitment to Buddhist practice:

> One starts taking Buddhism seriously to some extent, starts practising it to some extent; but one has not really committed oneself to it. One hasn't committed oneself to one's own personal, spiritual development. But one is aware of the possibility of so doing, even the desirability of so doing, and one may be thinking of actually committing oneself later on....[6]

He also discusses 'experiment' as one of the 'Pillars of the FWBO' in a way that encourages some rigour as well as provisionality of investigation at an institutional level, into how best to communicate Buddhism to people:

> Not only should all experiments be properly monitored, not only should records be kept, but the results of the experiments, negative or positive, hypothesis verified or not verified, should be communicated to the rest of the movement....[7]

However, there are several apparent limitations in this attitude to how one might approach Buddhism when it is put in the context of scientific culture. Primarily, it seems to be considered only a preliminary strategy. We can be provisional while we are still finding our feet and understanding what Buddhism is all about, but it appears that we give up this provisionality when we reach what Sangharakshita calls 'effective going for refuge' – when we become

---

5 Sangharakshita (1987a) p. 316.
6 Lecture 137.
7 Lecture 174.

fully committed to our spiritual path. This attitude would fit that of other more conservative Buddhist commentators on the *Kalama Sutta*, such as Bhikkhu Bodhi, who argues that the provisionality and autonomy of enquiry suggested by that sutta only applies to uncommitted enquirers, not to those who have joined the Buddhist community.[8] In scientific culture, however, provisionality is a virtue that is developed ever more fully with greater personal development. As Carl Sagan said:

> In science it often happens that scientists say, 'You know that's a really good argument; my position is mistaken,' and then they actually change their minds and you never hear that old view from them again.... I cannot recall the last time something like that has happened in politics or religion.[9]

In the context of Buddhism, do we really expect that more advanced practitioners lack this capacity to re-examine and change their beliefs, especially given the centrality of Buddhist doctrines such as Emptiness, which give us reason to doubt the final truth of any verbal formulation? When questioned on this point, Sangharakshita wanted to make a distinction between knowing the truth of some formulation that we believe in, and maintaining an emotionally committed relationship to a path. Our commitment to the path is a matter of emotional integration in our response, rather than certainty about how that path is described.

The idea that we should not be too certain about how the path is described is supported by Sangharakshita's discussion of 'right view':

> Right view is also a non-view. It is a non-view in the sense that it is not held with the same pertinacity, or the same conviction of its absolute rightness, that false views are normally held (such pertinacity and conviction are themselves unskilful mental states), but as it were provisionally and tentatively as a means to the attainment of Enlightenment and not as an end in itself.[10]

However, it is only in a book review in response to Stephen Batchelor's book *Buddhism without Beliefs* that Sangharakshita expands further on this point to give a fuller account of what he means by provisional belief. In response to Batchelor's transformation of the Four Noble Truths of Buddhism into Four Tasks, he

---

8   Bodhi (1998).
9   Sagan (1987).
10 Sangharakshita (1989) p. 94.

argues that Buddhists can believe both in the Four Noble Truths as facts, and in the way they need to respond to those facts, but that they can do so provisionally:

> *There are occasions when we are not sure – perhaps cannot be sure – either that the goal on which we have set our heart exists or that, assuming it really does exist, that we have adopted the right means for its achievement. Nonetheless, believing that it exists and that the means we have adopted are the right ones, we go on employing those means until such time as experience confirms both our belief in the existence of the one and our belief in the rightness of the other – or does not confirm them. Belief of this kind is relative, not absolute; qualified, not unqualified; provisional, not final; and tentative, not certain. It is on account of this provisional belief – as for the sake of convenience it may be termed – that we accept the four truths as propositions of fact and act upon them in the particular way each requires and according to the degree of our belief.*[11]

So far, this may seem an exception to Carl Sagan's impression of a lack of provisionality in a religious context. Sangharakshita no longer confines this provisionality to an initial stage of the spiritual path, and also seems to recognise that one can have different degrees of confidence in one's beliefs and yet still act on them in a practically committed way. I would add to this that such a provisional type of belief can be recognised by the mental availability of alternative options,[12] for if the only alternatives we are prepared to consider are our current belief and its undifferentiated negation, we can hardly be claimed to be open to any alternatives.

However, in the next sentence to the extract quoted above, Sangharakshita goes on:

> *Actual* **knowledge** *of the four truths comes only with the attainment of the Transcendental Path.*

It becomes evident then, here as elsewhere, that Sangharakshita does limit provisional belief to an unenlightened state, and that he contrasts the provisional path of the unenlightened with a certainty offered only to the enlightened. He also seems to see the path of the unenlightened as in some sense dependent on the certainties of the enlightened. This raises a lot of further issues that will need to be addressed later. Whatever the strengths of Sangharakshita's use of

---

11 Sangharakshita (1997b).
12 See Ellis (2012) 1.c.

the concept of provisionality, then, it does not seem to apply to all circumstances. Like the other adaptations to modernity discussed in this chapter, it could be interpreted entirely in terms of skilful communication rather than philosophical re-examination of the meaning of Buddhist teachings.

A further contrast between the scientific approach to provisionality and the Buddhist one of Sangharakshita lies in the matter of falsifiability. For Popper, falsifiability was the mark of an acceptable theory, and it meant that one could stipulate in advance what kind of evidence would lead one to abandon (or at least modify) the theory. Note that this does not require an absolute proof of the falsity of the theory (which is impossible), but rather a determination to face up to the possibility of it being wrong. Nor does it require precise evidence of a kind that would typically be needed to satisfy a scientist. However, without being able to state any kind of falsifiability, even in the terms of our own experience, we are in danger of falling into endless *ad hoc* rationalisation. An example of this would be that of the contemporary who responded to Galileo observing craters on the moon (craters that would contradict Aristotle's view that the moon is perfectly spherical) by arguing that the craters must be filled with a transparent substance. When faced with evidential challenge, will the 'provisional belief' of Sangharakshita turn out to be genuine enough to help us to avoid such defensive rationalisations?

Several observations need to be added before trying to answer this question. One is that scientists themselves do not always rise to this level, and that Sagan may be idealising. Another is that it is not a fair demand to make of an overarching or framing system as opposed to a specific theory within that system. To ask, for example, under what circumstances Sangharakshita would abandon Buddhism, a response to life that he adopted at the age of sixteen on the basis of an overwhelmingly intuitive experience, and that has shaped his whole outlook ever since, would be rather equivalent to asking a scientist under what circumstances she would give up science itself. We may not be able to easily imagine such circumstances.

A third observation about falsifiability is that in practice we should only be willing to drop a theory *if a better alternative is available*. In the philosophy of science, it was Popper's follower Lakatos who showed that this is the way in which scientific provisionality can actually operate in practice.¹³ If we have a better alternative, we can avoid the *nirvana fallacy*, which rejects beliefs only because they fail to match up to an unrealistic ideal.¹⁴ There is a better alternative to the moon's craters being filled with a transparent substance, which is to accept that Aristotle was wrong and the moon is not perfectly spherical. However, if we are, for example, to challenge Buddhist doctrines about karma and rebirth, which many Buddhists believe to have a moral function, we need not only to show that no possible evidence could falsify the belief in karma and rebirth, but that its assumed ethical role can be better fulfilled in other ways.

Sangharakshita does not offer an account of this aspect of provisionality, but arguably he does offer some examples of it being put into action, at least in his early life. In *Forty-three Years Ago: Reflections on my Bhikkhu Ordination* he recounts a substantial change of view on the subject of monasticism in response to new experiences. When he received his ordination as a Theravadin monk in 1950, he recounts that the ceremony gave him an 'extraordinary sense of peace, satisfaction, fulfilment, acceptance and belonging', and that becoming a bhikkhu 'represented the culmination of a process of spiritual discovery and development'.¹⁵ It is obvious that at this time he fully accepted the value of monasticism, together with the traditional view that this is the prime form of spiritual commitment in Buddhism. However, in 1956, he discovered that his ordination had been technically invalid. To be valid, all the bhikkhus in the ordaining chapter must be pure in their observance of the monastic rules, including celibacy, and he discovered that one of them had had a secret wife and family. To begin with he pushed this to the back of his mind, but after his return to the UK felt more able to recognise it, and face its full implications.¹⁶ He reasoned that, given the strictness of the criteria, not only he but no bhikkhu could be sure that they are 'really' a bhikkhu.

This is the classic type of situation in which many other people would remain subject to the bias of social proof, which would fuel them in *ad hoc* rationalisations of their position. One of these that Sangharakshita mentions is the claim that lay respect 'is shown to

---

13 Lakatos (1974).
14 See Ellis (2015) 3.g.
15 Sangharakshita (1993a) pp. 7–8.
16 Ibid. pp. 8–10.

the robe ... not to the wearer of the robe'[17] – a convenient prioritisation of the institution over individual conduct when the latter is shown to be lacking in integrity. Given that Sangharakshita did not face up to the full implications of this recognition for more than ten years, it would probably be fair to suggest that he himself was also subject to such social biases and rationalisations that led him to 'push it to the back of his mind'.

However, when Sangharakshita does face up to this issue, it is interesting to see how he does so. He is precise about what it is that is falsified by his disconfirmatory experiences: not the whole of Buddhism, nor even the whole of monasticism. Instead, it is monastic formalism that he rejects, and implicitly with it the authority of the Theravadin authorities insofar as they depend on that formalism:

> *Far from rejecting monasticism, I have a very high regard for it, as an expression of commitment to the Three Jewels, not as constitutive of that commitment.*[18]

This distinction between the value of spiritual commitment and the value of formal monasticism also lies behind Sangharakshita's wellknown dictum that 'Commitment is primary, lifestyle secondary'. He always points out that this does not imply that lifestyle is unimportant, but that lifestyle needs to support commitment rather than the other way round.

Sangharakshita's delay in responding to this may possibly be defended on the grounds that he waited until he had a better alternative to challenge the existing institution of monasticism. In his original conception, the Western Buddhist Order had four levels of ordination, but he quickly revised that, too, so that there was only one level of ordination, initially called upasaka/upasika (according to sex) and later dharmachari/dharmacharini. Here he not only defied the tradition of monastic ordination by conferring a non-celibate ordination without the traditional rules of ordination succession, but also defied the Theravadin refusal to fully ordain women (which had developed after the Buddha's time, and was given entirely formalistic justifications).

Another example of Sangharakshita showing provisionality, that he has himself offered, is that of celibacy. On his own account he was

---

17 Ibid. p. 37.
18 Ibid. p. 42.

initially convinced of the value of celibacy at the time he pledged himself to it when becoming a Theravada monk. However, two of the Tibetan teachers he met and was influenced by in Kalimpong – Dilgo Khyentse Rimpoche and Dudjom Rimpoche – were from the Nyingma tradition of Tibetan Buddhism, where it is customary for lamas to be married laymen. Both of these lamas were married with children, which led Sangharakshita to accept that celibacy was not essential to serious progress on the spiritual path.

That Sangharakshita has demonstrated provisionality of this kind is probably of far greater importance than whether his theory of provisionality is intellectually complete, as long as he also encourages others to do so (which is a point we will need to return to). This is one of many possible examples that shows that the style of judgement Sangharakshita has encouraged in Triratna culture is often far more adapted to modernity than is Sangharakshita's rhetoric. Whilst Sangharakshita's theoretical utterances regularly shock sections of his followers with their apparent dogmatic conservatism, his more specific judgements often in fact reveal an ability to re-examine beliefs that is much closer to the spirit of science. In this, despite his superficial opposition to figures like Stephen Batchelor who seek to challenge the dogmas to be found in Buddhism, he is much closer to them than he cares to admit.

2.d. Integration

The concept of integration – in a psychological, not sociological or mathematical sense – can help us to understand how people develop in creative rather than reactive mind over the long term. Most basically, integration is the overcoming of inner conflict. The basic practice of meditation can help to make us aware of how far we are unconsciously conflicted, as we recognise how far we are not actually in charge of our attention. Every distraction from the object of meditation provides evidence that our energies are not entirely under the command of our conscious will, and thus that those energies are in conflict with what we take our overriding desires and values to be. On the other hand, when we do maintain our focus and develop meditative absorption, the resulting gathering and direction of our energies (either in the short term or in the longer term) is integration that has overcome that conflict to some extent.

The use of the concept of integration is one of the distinctive features of Sangharakshita's response to modernity, and is one of the chief ways in which he has incorporated psychological insights into his thinking. It helps to provide answers to a whole set of questions about the relationship between Buddhist insights and negative psychological states like addiction, depression, and obsession, as well as more positive ones such as happiness, wellbeing, and motivation. Although these connections have since been explored by a wide range of Buddhists, Sangharakshita was one of the first people to make them.

The concept of integration can be particularly associated with Jungian psychology, though Jung himself tends to call it 'individuation', and trace it as a development of wisdom partially dependent on maturity in an individual life. The concept is now used more widely in psychology, and Daniel Siegel, for example, suggests eight 'domains' in which integration can take place: integration of consciousness, horizontal integration (between left and right hemispheres), vertical integration (between brainstem, limbic areas, and cortex), memory integration, narrative integration, state integration, interpersonal integration, and temporal integration.[1] However, a strong case can also be made for the interdependence of these different kinds of integration.

---

1   Siegel (2010) pp. 71–6.

Making Buddhism Universal 43

When asked about the origins of his concept of integration, Sangharakshita told me that it did not arise primarily from reading of Jung, but from his own experience of the conflict between 'Sangharakshita 1' and 'Sangharakshita 2' (already mentioned in 1.b above). The traditional metaphors describing the dhyanas (absorbed meditative states) were also an inspiration to him for the development of an account of integration as an aspect of meditation experience. This passage, originally from a seminar, gives a flavour of how he thinks about this:

> *In the case of the simile for the first dhyana, you have the two elements: the soap powder and the water. So what corresponds to which? The dry soap powder corresponds to you in your unintegrated state, and the water corresponds to the higher state of consciousness which is bringing together, so to speak, all those scattered particles, so that in the end there is complete harmony between them. On account of the growth of concentration, all the scattered particles are brought together, so they are in a sense saturated by some higher element, bound together by that higher element; so, in a sense, completely saturated. But what is completely saturated is the previously unintegrated consciousness.*[2]

This shows the way in which he sees integration as stimulated by the higher states of consciousness developed by Buddhist practice. This raises a question of causal and conceptual priorities. How far can integration, a psychological concept, substitute for the spiritual concepts for higher states of mind described in Buddhist tradition, such as dhyana, samadhi, or even nirvana? Are the two distinct, with one causing the other, or are they merely different ways of describing the same things?

How one answers that question will tend to depend on which sources of Sangharakshita's teaching one prioritises. At some points he seems to emphasise that integration is only a preliminary to the deeper insights of the more advanced Buddhist path, but at others he seems to recognise an interdependence between integration and spiritual attainment that would apply through the whole course of the path.

The impression that integration is merely a preliminary stage might well be produced by the four stages of Sangharakshita's 'System of Meditation'. Here Sangharakshita talks of four stages of meditative practice, which each have specific kinds of practice that

---

2 Sangharakshita (2012) p. 247.

are characteristic of them. These are, first, the stage of integration; second, the stage of positive emotion; third, the stage of spiritual death; and finally, the stage of spiritual rebirth.[3] In the context of meditation, he says that integration is particularly achieved by the mindfulness of breathing practice, together with awareness and mindfulness in general.

However, it is unlikely that Sangharakshita intended these stages to be interpreted as entirely distinct from each other, and this is a point that he has confirmed in discussion. This is particularly the case when we could easily interpret any of them in terms of the others, and thus integration in terms of positive emotion, spiritual death, or spiritual rebirth.

Positive emotion can be interpreted in terms of integration because it is only due to conflict with our images of others (incorporating aspects of ourselves) that we develop antipathetic views of them. In Jungian terms, we project the Shadow, unconsciously transferring an evil latent in ourselves onto someone else. When we develop positive emotions either towards ourselves or others, then, we integrate our feelings towards them, and a release of positive energy can result in the release of kindly feelings.

Spiritual death and spiritual rebirth can be interpreted in terms of integration, because spiritual death is the process of letting go of our identification with things that hinder our spiritual development – a potentially painful process – and spiritual rebirth of recognising the new positive potentialities this opens up. But this is merely a magnification of what happens at each point in meditation where we lose our focus on the object, hijacked by an obsession or an anxiety. Every time we manage to let go of that obsession or anxiety and see it in a bigger context, we suffer a little spiritual death, and every time we gain greater integration as a consequence, we celebrate a little spiritual rebirth.

However, in his lecture on the symbolism of the mandala, Sangharakshita discusses integration in terms of the whole spiritual path.

> *Integration is necessary of course not only at the highest level, but all levels and all aspects of the spiritual life.*[4]

---

3   Lecture 135.
4   Lecture 45.

The mandala represents the ideal of enlightenment in a graphical form that clearly brings out the integrative process involved. The centre of the mandala represents enlightenment, or an archetype of 'Reality itself' as Sangharakshita refers to it. The outer segments of the circle that forms the mandala, however, represent the aspects of our psyche that need to be integrated. Sangharakshita describes these, following Jung, primarily in terms of conflicts with unconscious elements:

> ...*a conflict between the conscious and the unconscious. Not just the personal unconscious – it's not just a question of repressed desires which are incompatible with the conscious attitudes – it's something much more than that – it goes much deeper than that. It's a conflict, we may say, between the ego-centred intellect on the one hand and the deeper, the transpersonal even, psychic and spiritual life deep down within ourselves, on the other....*
>
> *So in this sort of situation with this conflict, this split, this chasm, we need some higher, some third, reconciling factor – something which will unite, something will combine the clarity and precision of the conscious mind, the intellect – its sharpness – its crystalline purity if you like, with the richness, the colour, the activity, of the unconscious.*[5]

Sangharakshita's claim that it is 'not just the personal unconscious' echoes Jung's distinction between personal and collective unconscious[6] – a distinction that can arouse unnecessary controversy. However, there is no need to interpret the collective unconscious (or 'transpersonal' as Sangharakshita puts it) in any other terms than those of shared human needs and functions operating in our deep embodied experience. Regardless of the cause of those shared human needs and functions (for example, whether or not they are primarily genetic), we can identify what they have in common with those of others when we experience them in our deeper experiences (for example in meditation, dreams, or art) and seek the universal common patterns in those deeper experiences that Jung called archetypes. The potential conflict between these deeper experiences and our everyday conscious desires can be experienced as a profound challenge, and it is the addressing of this challenge through spiritual practice that enables integration to take place at a deeper level.

5   Ibid.
6   Jung (1960).

Sangharakshita also acknowledges the role of integration in his lecture on non-duality:

> *Well we have to find the entry into Nonduality within the situation. How are we to do this? We have to question the very terms of the situation. That is to say we have to question their absoluteness. We have to realise that it's not enough to try to sustain attention by means of a forcible act of will. If distractions persistently arise within the context of meditation it means that we have not understood ourselves deeply enough.... It means that there are factors at work within us, psychological factors, of which we are not conscious. And what we have to do is to become conscious of them. We have to take them into consideration. In other words...we have to become more integrated. If we are more integrated the different elements of our being will form an harmonious whole. They will all pull or push in the same direction. They'll no longer be in conflict with one another. We'll no longer have to oscillate between them. So in the case of distraction and attention integration is the entry into Nonduality.*[7]

Despite Sangharakshita's capitalisation of Nonduality, he seems to be referring here very much to the continued experience of being confronted by conflicting assumptions and resolving them through critical awareness. We need to 'question their absoluteness' at each point, which will involve not only a meditative process, but also one of cognitive reflection. We can only question absoluteness through an exercise of provisionality – being prepared to consider alternatives to the beliefs that are in conflict. Given that our conflicting beliefs are likely to be inadequate and to some extent deluded, we need to work on the assumption that they can always be improved. In my own work, this is what I have called 'integration of belief' and explored in relation to biases, fallacies, and metaphysical views whose absoluteness holds us back.[8]

Given this acknowledgement of the role of integration throughout the length of the spiritual path, then, there is no need to interpret Sangharakshita as confining it to the early stages, even though he may emphasise it particularly at that point. Integration thus provides a means of talking about the whole of the Buddhist path in a way that is compatible with psychological understanding, and does not require a prior commitment to belief in enlightenment. The fact that Sangharakshita himself obviously puts commitment

---

7 Lecture 148.
8 Ellis (2015).

to the 'Reality' of enlightenment first, on the basis of his personal intuitions, does not mean that his work cannot provide ways for others to engage with the path in a more gradualistic manner. If we approach the path in this way, our experience of each stage of integration increasingly confirms our commitment to the path as a whole rather than such commitment being deduced from an abstract acceptance of enlightenment.

Another way in which Sangharakshita has discussed integration is in his distinction between alienated and integrated awareness. This seems to be a response to encountering people who had learned meditation in the West but practised it in a way not grounded in bodily awareness – but rather a 'wilful' or 'heady' way heavily dependent on the goal-oriented and linguistic centres of the left hemisphere of the brain.

> I remember on one occasion I was taken to a certain meditation centre – I am not going to mention any names – and I was shown some people who were meditating and had been meditating for several weeks. As I said, I had quite a shock, because they seemed to me just like zombies. They just weren't there at all, they were so completely alienated from themselves. And I found quite a number of people in this state in London after having practised mindfulness, awareness and so on in this alienated way. They had just made themselves mentally ill, and some of them had landed up mental hospitals. They had just been not meditating but developing alienated awareness.[9]

Sangharakshita's definition of alienated awareness (which, to be fair, was delivered orally) is not particularly precise: 'awareness of ourselves, especially of our feelings and emotions, without actually experiencing ourselves, without actually experiencing our feelings and our emotions'.[10] How can we be aware of ourselves without experiencing ourselves? This may baffle anyone who has not practised meditation, but for those who have it will probably be obvious enough. One of the first traps one needs to avoid in meditation is substituting an abstract idea of one's focus of attention for the actual experience of it – for example, an idea of the feelings in one's foot for an actual kinaesthetic experience of the sensations in one's foot. These alienated meditators had presumably worked entirely in this way.

9   Lecture 84.
10 Ibid.

This casts a light on another aspect of integration in general, which is its overwhelming dependence on engagement with wider experience beyond intellectualisations. This does not imply that intellectually formulated beliefs should not be an object of attention, for they need integrating too, but it does imply that the integration process is heavily dependent on intellectual reflection being effectively linked to practices that engage aesthetic experience of the body, emotions, and imagination.

The overall value of the concept of integration has been indicated by its very widespread use in Triratna thinking in practice, as a way of understanding and judging spiritual development. When assessing candidates for ordination, for example, one of the prime criteria is 'a degree of integration'. One can observe this to some degree in the consistency of the beliefs and values with which they lead their lives, and how far they maintain equanimity rather than being subject to unexpected negative reactions. Integration is not only the practical goal of meditation, but also of ethical practice and of the practice of friendship. Yet one would not readily appreciate the practical importance of the concept of integration from Triratna ritual, in which its values are meant to be expressed, nor in much of its most influential literature. In the definitive book by Subhuti summarising Sangharakshita's thought, *Sangharakshita: A New Voice in the Buddhist Tradition*,[11] integration gets only one very brief mention in the context of meditation.

However, it's also important to consider the limitations of the concept of integration. The assumption that it is a quality developed by individuals in a linear fashion can be highly misleading, because the evidence suggests that even those who appear highly integrated in some respects may unexpectedly reveal conflicts. I have discussed this elsewhere as the property of *asymmetry* in integration.[12] Some of the recent research on the nature of wisdom by Igor Grossmann and his associates reinforces this point. They have empirically investigated a number of key wisdom traits and tested to what extent particular subjects tend to show them consistently, and they found considerable variability:

> *The observation of variability in wisdom may sound paradoxical: After all, is not 'true wisdom' stable? Indeed, in many cultures virtue-based qualities*

---

11 Subhuti (1994) p. 194.
12 Ellis (2013a) 5.d, (2013b) 7.b, (2015) 6.b.

> *like wisdom are linked to the concept of a morally good 'true self' – a 'robust, invariant tendency to believe that inside every individual there is a "true self" calling them to behave in morally virtuous ways'. Notably, this belief is rooted in psychological essentialism, which is a fundamental cognitive bias assuming that 'all entities have deep, unobservable, inherent properties that comprise their true nature', and which may not at all reflect the empirical reality of a virtuous characteristic. Indeed, in everyday life, people's ability to express wisdom-related epistemic virtues, such as intellectual humility, open-mindedness or the ability to consider a wide range of perspectives on a challenging issue, varies dramatically. As [our research] indicates, the variability within a person across several days is at least as large if not larger than the variability between people in their average tendency to express wisdom-related characteristics. This is not to say that there are no trait-level components of wise judgment. Rather, based on the density distribution perspective of individual differences, traits may be represented through the unique density distribution profiles of individuals, including unique responses to various situational contingencies.*[13]

Sangharakshita himself provides a strong illustration of this point, as his followers have clearly considered him to be highly integrated, and thus the instances of his sexual misconduct have caused much more upset than might be expected of someone without those expectations attached to them. When I asked Sangharakshita about this (in general terms), he agreed that integration reveals itself more in some circumstances than others. The cognitive bias of *domain dependence*,[14] known in psychology, is likely to be operative here, showing that even a quality like integration that is normally judged in terms of consistency between different contexts (or 'domains') may be patchily present, or, due to unknown disintegrative triggers, may not be exhibited in certain domains of experience. If there are marriage guidance counsellors with terrible relationships, it is no wonder that there are 'highly integrated' Buddhist leaders with skeletons in their closets.

The discussion of integration as an immediate state in meditation also needs to be distinguished from integration as a longer-term state in an individual's psyche. The former can be called *temporary integration*,[15] as exemplified by dhyana (meditative absorption), whilst the latter, though not necessarily completely permanent, is

---

13 Grossmann & Brienza (2018).
14 Ellis (2015) 3.i.
15 Ellis (2013a) 5.c, (2013b) 7.a, (2015) 6.a.

at least supported by longer-term changes in the individual's synaptic configuration and thus their thinking. Temporary integration can have effects that build up over time, or can result in greater energy and creativity that can then be invested in longer-term forms of integrative development. This distinction is not really explicit in Sangharakshita's treatment of the term, but he agreed that it was present when questioned, and it could also certainly be implicit in the different ways he uses it in his lecture about mandalas as opposed to his system of meditation.

Despite its practical importance, then, Sangharakshita has perhaps not analysed the concept of integration in all the ways that might have been helpful. In practice much of the weight of what Triratna Buddhists symbolise by 'enlightenment' is represented in experience by integration. Yet this importance has not led to a proportionately important focus on it in writings by or about Sangharakshita. This is perhaps the most important of a number of instances I shall note in this book of Sangharakshita's theory not being up to the level of his practice.

2.e. Individuality

The late 1960s, when Sangharakshita returned to the UK and established the FWBO, were a period of unprecedented individualism in the Western world. It was marked by an upsurge of consumerism, youth culture, political protest, and liberalisation. Homosexual activity and abortion were legalised, even if they were still circumscribed. Experimentation with drugs, alternative lifestyles, and new religions became more common. All of this was made possible by the political and economic environment. Unprecedented economic security, both from rising living standards and from the development of the welfare state, made people feel able to take more risks. Politically, the development of liberal democracy meant that the role of the autonomous individual was increasingly valued. An autonomous individual, with a certain assumed level of education and rationality, could innovate in ways that liberal thinkers (going back to John Stuart Mill in the mid-nineteenth century)[1] had argued could benefit the whole of society. By thinking and acting freely, short of the point where this would negatively disrupt society, individuals could contribute their energies to a public conversation in which the best strategies could emerge from a wider range of options.

These new conditions also allowed the flowering of a new focus on the development of individuality, not only in society at large, but as a matter of personal practice and cultivation. After all, it is only if individuals succeed in developing individuality that they can make good use of the opportunities that liberal democracy offers them. It is here that Sangharakshita's new approach could be of profound interest to a certain section of the population. Once again, his skill was to tune into the zeitgeist and present Buddhism in a way that would address people's needs. However, Sangharakshita's training in the Buddhist tradition also made him critical of the more superficial aspects of individualism: the consumerism that might lead to states of obsessive craving, and the negative reactions to the community that it might indulge.

His interpretation of individuality, then, applies the Middle Way (which I will discuss later) to the issue of the status of the individual, uniting the importance of the spiritual path in Buddhism to the

---

1 Mill (1972, originally 1859).

importance of individual autonomy in Western thought. He made a distinction between 'true' and 'false' individuality which was also dependent on the notion of integration:

> We can now see the basis of the distinction between the good and the bad usages of the words: 'individuality', 'self', 'person', and 'ego'. 'Good' refers to a higher degree of unification and integration; 'bad' refers to a lower degree of unification and integration. A true individuality is a more integrated individuality – a false individuality is that which is less integrated.[2]

This individuality is presented as dependent on the development of self-awareness,[3] and takes for granted the Buddhist teaching of *anatta* (non-substantiality or 'no self'). Though the use of the word 'true' may confuse the issue, Sangharakshita is not referring to a 'true self' in a metaphysical sense.[4] Instead, the way in which he bases the development of the individual on integration puts it in harmony with psychological models of the gradual development of maturity and autonomy through the resolution of internal conflicts arising in successive new environments. In particular, the outstanding work of Robert Kegan on adult psychological development can provide a detailed corroboration of Sangharakshita's overall view of individuality.[5]

Sangharakshita's model of individuality is linked to Buddhism through the exemplification of the Buddha. The Buddha's seeking of the Middle Way in his early life, moving on successively from the palace and from his teachers in the forest, is presented as the development of individuality by moving beyond the constraints of the group.[6] However, the effectiveness of such a model of individuality in inspiring us to be more individual depends very much on how far we identify it with ourselves as opposed to projecting it or worshipping it as other. Sangharakshita seems to take little account of the ways in which the Buddhist tradition has idealised its founder as fundamentally different from other human beings, and thus often failed to nurture individuality in its followers. Both the level of social conformity in traditional Buddhist countries and the stress on monastic discipline in traditional Buddhist practice

2 Lecture 85.
3 Sangharakshita (1990a) p. 24.
4 Lecture 85, also Sangharakshita (1992) p. 34.
5 Kegan (1982).
6 Sangharakshita (1990a) pp. 32–3.

may be seen as working against the development of individuality. It requires a society that actually values individuality more widely, such as Western society, to nurture 'true' individuals more effectively by offering them a genuine range of options for discriminating judgement.

Sangharakshita's model of individuality is also apparently inspired by the Western source of Friedrich Nietzsche, and Sangharakshita devoted a lecture of his 'Higher Evolution' series to discussion of *Thus Spake Zarathustra*. He wants to interpret Nietzsche's *Übermensch* or 'overman' as a true individual. However, Nietzsche's language is entirely that of combat directed against oneself: the individual develops through 'self-overcoming':

> *Oh no, says Nietzsche, it's yourself that you must negate, it's yourself that you must overcome. It is with oneself that one must be ruthless, with oneself that one must be uncompromising.*[7]

This emphasis in Nietzsche raises serious questions about the compatibility of his whole approach with Sangharakshita's view of the developed individual as increasingly *integrated*. One does not become more integrated by fighting oneself, but rather by accepting and working skilfully with those parts of oneself that one wishes to change. Sangharakshita makes positive use of Nietzsche's combativeness by pointing out that a discontentedness with oneself is needed: 'Without this dissatisfaction, there's no self-overcoming and no spiritual progress.'[8] However, Nietzsche's emphasis on combat, with even the most subtle kinds of technique being turned into tools for struggling against oneself, goes far beyond this basic starting point of dissatisfaction. Its application in Nietzsche's own life (the last eleven years of his life being lost to mental illness) is also hardly encouraging. Robert Morrison, inspired by Sangharakshita's use of Nietzsche, has written a whole book-length study on the 'ironic affinities' between Buddhism and Nietzsche,[9] but even he fails to deal satisfactorily with this basic incompatibility between Nietzsche's attitude and a psychologically effective, integrative form of individual development.[10] Sangharakshita's use

7 Lecture 82.
8 Ibid.
9 Morrison (1997).
10 See Ellis (2001) 4.g.iii for a fuller argument on the limitations of Morrison's treatment.

of Nietzsche as a source either of instruction or inspiration is thus probably best treated as an aberration.

The 'true' individual is able to develop beyond the pressure of the group, not by merely reacting against the group (which would be 'individualistic'), but by maintaining balanced, autonomous judgement in relation to it.

> The individualist is a sort of broken-off fragment of the group, reacting, even rebelling, against the group; he is a sort of group writ small, a sort of one-man group – which is really a contradiction in terms, like a one-man band. The individual, on the other hand, has passed, or begun to pass, beyond the group, beyond group consciousness; he is no longer limited by group consciousness.[11]

Sangharakshita's view of the negative effects of group consciousness on the creativity of the individual can be corroborated by psychological findings, particularly recent research by Bowker et al.[12] Cognitive psychology also identifies four types of group biases: ingroup bias, social proof, groupthink, and false consensus. Ingroup bias leads us to judge people outside the group differently from those inside it.[13] Social proof leads us to take the views of others in a group as the criterion for judgement regardless of the evidence.[14] Groupthink discourages us from speaking up against a group judgement.[15] False consensus leads us to think that our group's way of thinking is normative for everyone else.[16]

None of these tendencies, however, is an inevitable effect of groups as such, nor do they make all association in groups intrinsically deluded. Rather, they are an effect of a lack of awareness in the way we interact with groups, so that we allow our desire for social affirmation to assume an absolute form, overriding our awareness of alternative perspectives. The solution to them, then, lies not in complete isolation, but rather in awareness. Temporary periods away from the group, such as solitary retreats, however, may have the effect of boosting that awareness, and have become part of widespread practice in Triratna.

Central to Sangharakshita's doctrine of the individual is the idea that the spiritual community is made up of individuals, and

11 Sangharakshita (1990a) p. 41.
12 Bowker et al. (2017).
13 Taylor & Doria (1981).
14 Asch (1956).
15 Janis (1982).
16 Ross, Greene, & House (1977).

that this is what distinguishes the spiritual community from mere groups. The individuals in a community are depicted as avoiding absolute views of themselves, either positive or negative, and as not being unnecessarily attached to the procedures of the group (these are the first three fetters, which I will return to in the next chapter). The individual is also self-conscious and independent.[17] He identifies the spiritual community made up of individuals with the Arya Sangha of Buddhist tradition, the community of people who are regarded as inevitably on their way to enlightenment.

There is an important insight here about the ways that individuals and groups need to relate, with the individuality of individuals being valued by the group. In many ways this insight is compatible with that of John Stuart Mill, Karl Popper, John Dewey, and other thinkers who have inspired liberal democracy by pointing out the value of those individual perspectives in providing a critical check on group assumptions. In many ways, liberal thinkers would like the whole of society to become what Sangharakshita would call a spiritual community, even if that is unrealistic in practice. However, there is also a conflict between their perspective and the way in which Sangharakshita presents the spiritual community – a conflict that is not only about the importance of Buddhist practice in developing individuality:

> *If you want to have a spiritual community, then you have to have individuals first, and it's quite hopeless and quite useless to try and have a spiritual community unless you have your individuals first.*[18]

Here Sangharakshita implies that there is a complete discontinuity between a 'true spiritual community' made up of genuine individuals, and one that is just a group pretending to be a spiritual community. As with many assumptions about absolute boundaries, we really need to question this. I have already noted in the previous chapter that integration may be temporary or asymmetrical, and it is also incremental – one develops more or less integration rather than stepping up discontinuously to a fixed quantum of it. Since, as Sangharakshita has also noted, individuality is based on integration, we also need to see individuality as a matter of degree rather than as a fixed quantum. All the qualities that Sangharakshita identifies as features of individuality, such as self-consciousness

17 Lecture 91.
18 Ibid.

and independence, are also matters of degree. How, then, could we possibly identify a fixed quantum of these qualities that makes one a 'true individual', who then qualifies as a member of the Arya Sangha, and who will make a spiritual community genuine rather than fake?

Added to these problems of the complexity and incrementality of individuality, we have one of judgement in practice. How can we possibly judge when a genuine individual is present, and thus when a genuine spiritual community is present? Because a judgement is approximate and uncertain, of course, that does not make the judgement impossible or unhelpful, but in this case our best guess is compounded in its ignorance by the likelihood that the features of individuality are asymmetrically and perhaps impermanently present. Sangharakshita's ideal account of the spiritual community is a mere abstraction if we don't have any way in practice of reaching a conclusion about whether it is present or not. We can try to judge levels of individuality approximately, but the notion of an absolute spiritual community is too conceptually precise to match the approximations of our experience. It's like making an appointment to meet someone in a cafe at 2.37 and 34 seconds – the precision of the idea does not appropriately match the lack of precision in our experience.

It is easy to see why Sangharakshita may have been motivated to present the idea of the spiritual community in this falsely precise form. The idea of the Arya Sangha is important in traditional Buddhism, because it is theoretically the basis of the Sangha Refuge to which Buddhists commit themselves. The Arya Sangha is said to be made up of the enlightened, the stream-entrants, the once-returners, and the non-returners, all of whom are certified to be on the way to enlightenment. However, given the uncertainties of identifying who is enlightened, let alone who is inevitably destined for enlightenment, the false precision of this doctrine makes it a ripe and obvious candidate for being gently set aside and ignored in any transmission of Buddhism to the West. It seems that Sangharakshita may have been too attached to the traditional Buddhist terminology to be prepared to do this.

Despite these problems, however, the much bigger and more relevant practical point in Sangharakshita's teaching about the individual and the spiritual community is simply that the spiritual community should value and promote individuality and try to avoid supporting group biases. Not only the qualities of the individuals participating in the group, but also the way the group itself functions, need to support the scope of the individual to think for themselves. In my experience, this way of operating is often evident in the culture of Triratna. People do accept that individuals may dissent from group positions, and this is normally tolerated as long as they do not go so far out as to be grossly unethical or 'place themselves beyond' the community.

So far, then, in general terms, Sangharakshita's account of individuality is tremendously helpful in synthesising the most helpful insights in Buddhism with those of Western liberal democracy and psychology. When he starts to relate this view of the group to history and religion, however, he does so with some highly questionable generalisations.

His historical sketch of the origins of the relationship between the group and the individual begins with the Palaeolithic and then Neolithic individual submerged in the group. However, in the 'Axial Age', a term which he takes from Karl Jaspers and places in approximately 800–200 BCE, the 'true' individual or 'New Man' begins to emerge.[19] As evidence for this, following Jaspers, he cites the many great thinkers, including the Buddha, Confucius, Isaiah, and Aristotle, who emerged in different areas of the world during this period. These figures were unparalleled up to this point in their individuality and creativity of thought, and thus had a tremendous effect on the culture of their time. However, Sangharakshita puts a lot of discontinuous emphasis on this period, when it seems obvious that its achievements must have built on an incremental development of awareness throughout previous human history, and the developments begun during it continued after it.

It is when Sangharakshita starts to discuss more recent history, however, that his assumptions become even more highly questionable. He claims that there was an on the whole 'lively and healthy' relationship between the individual and the group until about two hundred years ago (presumably referring to the effects of the Enlightenment and the Industrial Revolution), when 'a serious imbalance' began to prevail between the individual and the group.[20] He attributes this imbalance to population increase (which makes

19 Lecture 76.
20 Sangharakshita (1990a) pp. 26–7.

it harder to get away from others, he says), the increase in power of 'the corporate state' (which he describes as 'the group *par excellence*'), the growth of technology, and the rise in standards of living (making us dependent on society to provide worldly goods). The effect of this imbalance, he says, is that 'the true individual is dissatisfied' and might even turn to violence.[21]

This is an instance of a tendency that we will come upon periodically in considering Sangharakshita's thought, which is a tendency to idealise traditional society and underrate the achievements of modernity, despite all the ways in which modernity had presented him with the very opportunities to start a Buddhist movement in the West that could not previously have existed. Any survey of the evidence even of widely available basic statistics on these points is likely, if anything, to lead one in the opposite direction. In particular, a reading of Steven Pinker's carefully substantiated work on the decline of violence (along with oppression and many other accompanying evils) in world history[22] will make it clear just how wide of the mark Sangharakshita's assumptions are.

The medieval period hardly offers a 'lively and healthy' relationship between the individual and the group, but rather a highly repressive society by modern standards, in which deviation from social norms was unlikely to be tolerated in most contexts, those from other cultures were routinely enslaved and demonised, and violence was far more common than it is today. For example, the annual homicide rate per 100,000 people is estimated to have been 110 in fourteenth-century Oxford, but was less than 1 in mid-twentieth-century London.[23] The past two hundred years in the West have increasingly offered previously unparalleled levels of human freedom: the rights of lower classes, women, children, and the disabled gradually coming to be respected; the spread of universal education; the development of free media; and a great increase in leisure time, together with wealth to make use of it, for many people. This massive development of the (potentially creative) freedom of the individual has largely happened precisely *because* of the very things that Sangharakshita blames. Population increase has supported economic development, which has in turn made many

21 Ibid. p. 30.
22 Pinker (2011).
23 Ibid. pp. 72–3.

other freedoms for the individual possible. The state has provided a stable, safe environment in which individuality can develop. The growth of technology and standards of living have freed up individual leisure time and multiplied opportunities for education, travel, the arts, and contact with new people and ideas.

Far from being newly dissatisfied in ways in which he (or she) was not before, the person with greater levels of individuality and integration is likely to have a far more fulfilled life today than ever before, and is also far *less* likely to engage in violence than ever before. This is especially evident for previously oppressed groups – lower classes, women, or ethnic and religious minorities – the very possibility of whose individuality was not considered important before the development of modernity with its 'expanding circle' of sympathy.[24] The modern developments that Sangharakshita points out as interfering with individuality, such as state surveillance and economic dependence,[25] are neither entirely new, nor particularly important in their effects compared to the boost to overall conditions favourable to individuality in the modern era.

Sangharakshita's poorly informed historical theorising can offer a cautionary tale for those offering spiritual teaching of any kind. Not only is your limited view of history likely to be insufficient to make well-founded and helpful observations of sufficient relevance for spiritual development, but *any* dependence on historical claims is likely to become a hostage to fortune. Historical phenomena are extremely complex and highly subject to confirmation bias, so although the broad-brush interpretation of history is a fascinating enterprise, it is most unlikely to yield the kind of generalisations that we can conscientiously offer as a basis for universal practical conclusions. At most one can offer historical parallels or illustrations, but to seek to support arguments for individual practice from broad generalisations about the historical relationship between individuals and groups is an extremely risky enterprise. In Sangharakshita's case, the doubtfulness of that enterprise has had the unfortunate effect of undermining the more basic and helpful case he makes about individuality.

When, in the same book, Sangharakshita comments on the relationships between religions and individuality, the results are

24 Ibid. part 7.
25 Sangharakshita (1990a) pp. 27–9.

similarly unfortunate, offering a crude idealisation of Buddhism and an equally crude dismissal of Christianity. Both of these religions are complex and multifaceted, having numerous different schools and interpretations, but Sangharakshita's tendency (despite his emphasis on the avoidance of absolute assumptions elsewhere) is to distil them to a few essential features based on definitive beliefs.

Buddhism, he claims, is highly hospitable to the development of the individual because of its spirit of tolerance. 'This is why, in the whole of its 2,500-year history, Buddhism has never persecuted anyone for their beliefs. There is no such thing as heresy in Buddhism.'[26] For a clear counter-example of the first sentence here, Buddhists can be recommended to watch Martin Scorsese's film *Silence*, based on a novel by Shusaku Endo, which dramatises the historical persecution of Christians, explicitly *for their beliefs*, by Japanese Buddhists during the seventeenth century. It may be the case that Buddhism has *generally* been more tolerant, but Sangharakshita's absolute claims here set him up for easy falsification.

On the other hand, he goes on,

> Christianity cannot help us correct the imbalance between the individual and the group. The first of these is that Christianity is on the side of the group. That Christianity has no respect for the individual is amply demonstrated by its history.[27]

Sangharakshita then gives a list of well-known examples of Christian intolerance, starting with the Inquisition. The second reason, he then says, is that 'Christianity believes in God', and 'God is simply the most powerful member of the biggest conceivable group'. Thirdly, he then says, 'People are encouraged to fear God', leading to irrational guilt.[28] All of this, like his treatment of Buddhism above, is both absolute in its expression and highly selective in its evidence. One could just as easily pick out evidence from the vast canvas of Christian tradition of ways it has supported individuality, for example through the mystical tradition of individual experience, or from Luther's Reformation galvanising individual reading of the Bible and thus individual theological judgement. God, indeed, can be a symbol of despotic power, but also a symbol of love. When

26 Ibid. p. 35.
27 Ibid. p. 36.
28 Ibid. p. 37.

such sweeping absolute claims are made, it only takes one falsification to puncture them.

We have come a very long way here from Sangharakshita's lecture on non-duality quoted in the previous chapter, where he said 'We have to question the very terms of the situation. That is to say we have to question their absoluteness.' The problem is not just that Sangharakshita got his facts wrong, but rather that he is so inconsistent in the application of his own spiritual method. At one and the same time, he offers inspiring and relevant ways of making the Buddhist tradition practically relevant for people in the West, but on the other hand sabotages this approach through quite unnecessary historical speculation, together with absolutising language that creates big distractions from it. Ironically, these inconsistencies in the presentation of individuality are themselves a result of Sangharakshita's individuality, in the sense of his confident assertion of his individual beliefs. In the wider sense of 'true' individuality that he offers, though, equivalent to integration, they are not very individual, but rather an indication of a lack of awareness where it needed to be applied, to question the inner voices that promoted these absolute assumptions. Such is ever the mixed legacy of this contradictory figure.

2.f. The Middle Way

To complete this section of the book, we now come to the question of what draws together the distinctive approaches that enabled Sangharakshita to adapt Buddhism to modernity. We have so far considered his ideas about mind reactive and creative, about provisionality, about integration, and about individuality. In all of these areas he managed to bring together the Western insights implicit in science, psychology, and democracy and relate them to aspects of Buddhist teaching, and thus allow people to make use of Buddhist practices to fulfil values that they would already appreciate to a large extent from their upbringing in the West. If we ask what these adaptations have in common, however, and again how the common factors relate to Buddhist teachings, I think we can offer a further, more general, principle that in turn casts light back on the others. That more general principle is the Middle Way.

I have already mentioned in the introduction that the Middle Way encapsulates some of the most important and positive ways I have been influenced by Sangharakshita, and the reason why it is so central to the views I have developed since I left his Order. If you want to read my own account of it, I have given that in many other books. However, what I want to do in this chapter is to show how many features of a practically helpful Middle Way can be found in Sangharakshita's teaching (despite there being a great many issues with his most explicit statements of it). All the practically helpful teaching we have considered so far in fact reflects it.

Some of the most interesting evidence for this comes from a lecture given in 1987, entitled 'Twenty Years on the Middle Way'.[1] Early in this lecture Sangharakshita mentions his formal account of the Middle Way: the one also given in his *Survey of Buddhism*, and which I will return to later in this chapter. However, he then goes on to discuss the Middle Way 'in more directly practical terms, ... which moreover have particular relevance to us here in the West'. He then explains how the FWBO follows the Middle Way in three important respects: in relation to monasticism, in relation to parents, and in relation to Western culture. All three of these examples show the centrality of the Middle Way to Sangharakshita's distinctive approach to the adaptation of Buddhism to the West.

1 Lecture 168.

In relation to monasticism, Sangharakshita discusses the 'commitment is primary, lifestyle secondary' approach already discussed in 2.c above, concluding:

> So we can now begin to see in what way the Western Buddhist Order as such follows the middle way, in what way it is on that middle way. It is on the middle way in the sense that it avoids the extreme of rigid, perhaps formalistic, monasticism on the one hand, and lax laicism, as we may call it, coining a term, on the other.[2]

In relation to our attitude to parents, Sangharakshita recommends a Middle Way between submitting to parents' wishes on the one hand, and rejecting parents on the other. He explains that even if we have basic disagreements with our parents, a great deal of our emotional energy is unconsciously tied up with them, and that rejecting our parents may thus have many further negative effects on our relationships with everyone else.

His third example of our attitude to Western culture is subsumed into a wider point about our attitude to 'the world' in general – by which he seems to mean the group pressures towards the social norm that we find in the world, together with its accompanying culture. Sangharakshita recommends that we neither accept the world in its own terms, nor do we reject it. Instead, the Middle Way consists in transforming the world, making use of those aspects of it that aid spiritual development, but seeking to change those aspects that do not. In this respect he clearly disagrees with those Buddhists who seek to purify themselves of all worldly culture.

> The FWBO seeks to create a new society, a society which is conducive to the spiritual development of the individual in the fullest sense of the term.[3]

These three examples effectively cover a great deal of the practice of what is now Triratna, and my own experience is that they are generally put into practice and mark what is most distinctive about Triratna. The Triratna Order is compatible with a wide range of lifestyles, even though the monastically imbued texts of earlier forms of Buddhism are often used for inspirational or devotional purposes. People are generally encouraged to maintain a positive relationship with their parents without sacrificing their autonomy. Western culture (such as the fine arts) is often positively appropriated, but not

---

2 Ibid.
3 Ibid.

necessarily used and interpreted as it was in the context that it was produced.

Sangharakshita does not analyse here what these three examples have in common as expressions of the direct and practical Middle Way he is speaking of, or how exactly they relate to the more formal expressions of it. However, it is clear that in all three of these cases, the opposing extremes consist in rigid, unreflective beliefs and attitudes identified with opposing groups: monastic formalism v 'lax laicism', belief in parental authority v rebellion as an end in itself, and belief in the value of 'worldly' culture v its puritanical rejection. In between these extremes are found more adequate alternatives which link all three of the values discussed in the last three chapters: provisionality, integration, and individuality. In not reacting to either of the extremes, but rather maintaining a more open awareness, we are remaining provisional, working towards their integration, and maintaining an individual response to opposing group pressures.

This practical Middle Way is also explored in relation to the first three fetters of Buddhist tradition in Sangharakshita's lecture on 'The Individual, the Group, and the Community'.[4] These three fetters are the ones that he identifies as needing to be broken to produce a 'true individual', as discussed in the previous chapter. The first fetter is the belief in a fixed personality, that 'I am what I am and I can't be changed.' The second fetter is 'doubt' in the sense of inability to commit oneself to a course of action because of lack of integration. The third fetter is dependence on moral rules and ritual observances as ends in themselves.

At the end of his exposition of these three fetters, their relationship to the Middle Way becomes clearer when Sangharakshita adds:

> Now, this doesn't mean that one should go to the opposite extreme. This doesn't mean that one should discard all these sort of helps whatsoever. This is sometimes an extreme that people go to. They think that they can get along without religious observances, and so on, and maybe they can, but one must be very careful that one doesn't discard these traditional helps before one is really ready to discard them.[5]

The idea of the Middle Way in relation to moral rules and religious observances is an extension of the Middle Way already mentioned

4 Lecture 91.
5 Ibid.

in relation to culture. However, Sangharakshita could perhaps have said more here about the Middle Way in relation to the first two fetters (rather than just 'and so on'). Belief that one has absolutely no personality and could turn oneself instantaneously into anything, like Proteus, would be just as unhelpful as belief in the fixed personality. Similarly, rash overconfidence could be just as much an effect of a lack of integration as an inability to commit oneself to a course of action. The individuality achieved by breaking (or at least weakening) these fetters can be understood rather more clearly with the Middle Way in mind.

Arguably, this implicit and practical Middle Way can be found in all sorts of places in Sangharakshita's thinking, just as his neglect of it in other places can sometimes be associated with insufficient awareness or perspective in his thinking. I will offer one more example of that implicit Middle Way here, which comes from his discussion of the radical view of Christianity offered by John Robinson, the Bishop of Woolwich, in his book *Honest to God*.

> He's quite aware that the traditional conception of Christ as the incarnate second person of the Trinity must go. That's one extreme. But he doesn't go to the other extreme, as some liberal Christians do, of regarding Christ just as a very good man. He doesn't go to the extreme of thinking, as it were, well there are lots of good people in the world and Christ was just a bit better than most, perhaps a bit better than all of them, but essentially just a good man; he doesn't go to that humanistic extreme…we don't say that on the one hand the Buddha is God, nor on the other that he is merely man, but an Enlightened man, a man become one with Reality, so that the two are interfused. You can't see which is the human being, which is the reality.... So that is neither a sort of supernaturalistic assessment of the Buddha nor a purely humanistic one, and it seems to me that the Bishop of Woolwich is as it were working his way, almost struggling towards, a similar conception of Christ.[6]

There is a debate to be had here about whether or not the Middle Way in our view of Christ or the Buddha necessarily implies a view that is in some sense 'humanistic', or whether, as Sangharakshita assumes, the 'humanistic' view is in some way reductionist. This depends very much on exactly what is meant by 'humanistic'. The way in which Sangharakshita uses the term 'reality' here, as elsewhere, also needs further discussion. However, what I'm more concerned to note in this passage is Sangharakshita's Middle Way

6 Lecture 6.

method. He expects to find a more adequate view in the ambiguous zone between the extremes, with the extremes being marked by opposing absolute views supported by different groups. Once the method is employed, there is always room for further debate to refine one's understanding of the nature of the extremes, and of what is implied by the intermediate position.

Having considered these examples of the Middle Way in application, then, it is now necessary to consider the way that Sangharakshita explains the Middle Way in theory – which he does in his *Survey of Buddhism*. He prefaces this by pointing out that the definition of the Middle Way is 'a matter of exceptional difficulty',[7] which may provide an indication that even from the beginning we should not set too much store by the specific claims made in his account of it.

Sangharakshita takes the 'highest sense' of the Middle Way to be

> *A middle position between, or better still 'above' the two extreme conceptions of existence and non-existence.... Metaphysically this amounts to a repudiation of eternalism and nihilism and their respective progenies of wrong views. Doctrines and methods which adopt an intermediate position between conflicting extremes are the manifestations, within their own more or less limited fields, and at their own higher or lower levels of application, of the Middle Path in its highest, transcendental aspect. All extreme or one-sided views and practices are manifestations of either eternalism or nihilism, the two basic errors.... At every stage of the spiritual life we are faced by the necessity of making a choice between either of two opposites, on the one hand, and the mean which reconciles the opposition by transcending it, on the other.*[8]

Sangharakshita takes this overriding view of the Middle Way as lying between 'existence' and 'non-existence' both from Nagarjuna and from the discourse with Kaccanagotta in the Pali Canon:

> *'"All exists": Kaccana, this is one extreme. "All does not exist": this is the second extreme. Without veering towards either of these extremes, the Tathagata teaches the Dhamma by the middle....'*[9]

At the same time here he evokes our experience of making a choice between opposites (already illustrated by the many examples above) and makes claims both about the 'metaphysical' status of those choices and that all extremes are those of eternalism and nihilism. So the question is not whether the Middle Way applies helpfully to

---

7 Sangharakshita (1987a) p. 159.
8 Ibid. p. 160.
9 Nidanasamyutta, *Samyutta Nikaya* 12.15, Bodhi (2000) p. 544.

experience, but whether his theoretical account of it is adequate to that practical application.

The issues involved in Sangharakshita's problematic use of the term 'metaphysics' can no longer be avoided here. On the one hand, the extreme views avoided by the Middle Way are metaphysical views – of the kind about which the Buddha remained silent,[10] but on the other, Sangharakshita (along with many other Buddhists) seems to regard the Middle Way itself as metaphysical. Metaphysical beliefs are usually regarded as ultimate beliefs about the abstract existence or non-existence of entities (for example, God, the soul, ultimate matter, causation, time), even when these are not or cannot be experienced. These beliefs form dualistic pairs that conflict with each other, because all alternatives are interpreted in terms of that dualism (if you're not with us, you're against us), and cannot be modified in the light of new evidence, because any challenge is taken to undermine an indivisible truth on which our basic identity is staked.

As such it seems that any kind of metaphysical belief is incompatible with the Middle Way, and thus there can only be a 'Middle Way in metaphysics' in the sense of a critical metaphysics, pointing out the unacceptability of either the acceptance or denial of metaphysical claims. Sangharakshita seems to implicitly affirm this point when he writes:

> *Following the Middle Path in metaphysics consists in understanding that reality is not to be expressed in terms of existence and non-existence and in recognising that positive and negative indications of Nirvana...possess not absolute but only relative validity.*[11]

In practice, then, that Middle Path cannot be successfully characterised through metaphysical claims, which are bound to suck us back into the absolute affirmations and negations that we were trying to avoid. We can only find the Middle Path in practice through the other aspects of Sangharakshita's practical approach that have already been discussed in this section – creativity, provisionality, integration, and individuality – and through the practical application of the Middle Way in finding a way between absolute extremes. The assumption that metaphysical statements can take the place of

---

10 *Majjhima Nikaya* 63, Ñanamoli and Bodhi (1995) pp. 533–6.
11 Sangharakshita (1987a) p.161.

the transformation of mental states must always be questioned, even when Sangharakshita himself appears to be doing it.

Against this perspective lies that of the many philosophers who insist that metaphysical beliefs are in some sense inevitable. They are likely to argue that we cannot interact with an object without assuming it 'exists', and we cannot move through a world of space, time, and causality without assuming necessary 'truths' about their consistency. However, if I were to experience the conditions that I normally rely on becoming inconsistent (for example, if some rivers suddenly started to flow uphill), there is no reason at all why I should not be able to reconsider my beliefs – there is nothing inevitable about them, only a consistency in my experience so far. If these claims about whether things 'exist' make no difference to my experience, I can't be said to have any functioning beliefs about them, at least beyond the social benefits of conforming to a group that believes in them.

Sangharakshita's concept of provisional belief, as discussed in the earlier chapter (2.c), thus implies that metaphysical beliefs are not inevitable. We can always question any belief that seems inevitable or inescapable, as the passage already mentioned from Sangharakshita's lecture on non-duality suggests:

> We have to find the entry into Nonduality within the situation. How are we to do this? We have to question the very terms of the situation. That is to say we have to question their absoluteness.[12]

If metaphysical belief is not inevitable, and provisional belief that encourages and allows such questioning is possible, that also implies that the Middle Way should not be referred to as a metaphysical belief. This is inconsistent not only with the account of the Middle Way in his *Survey of Buddhism* discussed above, but also with his treatment of enlightenment as a source of knowledge of 'Reality' (see 4.a below) and his top-down approaches, appealing to that knowledge, to many other issues discussed in this book.

The other problematic aspect of Sangharakshita's account of the Middle Way is his claim that 'All extreme or one-sided views and practices are manifestations of either eternalism or nihilism.' This implies that all metaphysical views fall into consistent clusters that are either eternalist or nihilist. Sangharakshita also states that the

---

12 Lecture 148.

ethical attitudes of eternalism and nihilism are 'absolute' in their dependence on associated psychological views and in turn on metaphysical views.[13]

It is easy to see that this may have in practice been the case in the Buddha's time and context. Then, for example, the affirmation of a fixed self was always accompanied by belief in karma and thus an absolute standard of natural morality that had to be fulfilled to get positive karma. If this cluster of absolute beliefs always went together, so would its 'nihilistic' or 'annihilationist' opposite, where the denial of a fixed self also implied a lack of moral standards applied to conduct.

However, there seems to be no reason to believe that any such clustering of metaphysical beliefs necessarily applies today. It is easy to think of counter-examples. For example, one could be a 'nihilistic' scientist who denies the fixed self or soul, but who is highly ascetic and hard-working, dedicated to science. Or one could be a Catholic having a sincere belief in the immortal soul, but somewhat self-indulgent. These people's one-sided views appear to be *both* eternalistic and nihilistic, or involving a mixture that cuts across the clustering of the Buddha's context.

When I questioned Sangharakshita on this point, he agreed that eternalism and nihilism did not necessarily imply fixed clusters of ideological beliefs, but nevertheless claimed that they could be identified from their motive. Eternalism, he said, was associated with *bhava-tanha* (craving for existence) and nihilism with *vibhava-tanha* (craving for non-existence). He admitted that these motives could be mixed up and appear relatively. However, this just seems to add yet more dubious elements to the theory. Is he really claiming that all 'nihilistic' materialists and hedonists are at bottom suicidal, having a craving for non-existence? Or, if there is only a complex and unpredictable relationship between these types of craving and these types of absolute belief, why make the claim at all?

Once again, the problems here are problems in the traditional Buddhist account of 'eternalism' and 'nihilism', and Sangharakshita seems determined to stick by them and make sense of them on the grounds that they must be right, even though he has been prepared to abandon other traditional beliefs. Given the practical and universal basis on which his approach must now be judged, though, the

---

13 Sangharakshita (1987a) p. 162.

appeal to Buddhist tradition is no longer enough to justify acceptance of these contradictory elements in his account of the Middle Way.

Fortunately there is an alternative possible interpretation that seems to be entirely compatible with all the helpful ideas discussed so far – creative mind, provisionality, integration, and individuality – as well as the examples he discusses in 'Twenty Years on the Middle Way'. That is simply to regard the Middle Way as a navigation between any two pairs of absolutes, positive or negative. These absolutes will cluster with each other in complex ways, but there is no reason to expect today's clustering to be consistent with what the Buddha observed in his context.

That the concepts of 'eternalism' and 'nihilism' serve no particular practical purpose, even though the Middle Way itself obviously serves a very important purpose, can be readily seen if we return to Sangharakshita's examples of the Middle Way as it has actually been employed in Triratna. Let's take his example of the Middle Way between obedience to one's parents and rejection of one's parents. Is obedience to one's parents 'eternalism' and rejection 'nihilism'? Not if one's parents are materialists or hedonists, and they command us to join their drug-fuelled orgies. Rejection of one's parents may then be motivated by ascetic impulses of self-control. All we can say in general about this Middle Way is that it involves the avoidance of positive absolutes opposed to negative ones.

It might be possible to construct a further complex theory about what 'eternalism' and 'nihilism' 'really mean' so as to make them consistent – a line of thinking that I have tried out myself in some detail, though I ultimately concluded that I had failed.[14] However, if the motive for doing so is defence of tradition, the reasoning is likely to consist in *ad hoc* rationalisation rather than helpful theory of practical value. There is no particular practical value in maintaining 'eternalism' and 'nihilism', just as there is no practical value in describing the Middle Way as a metaphysical position – but there is a great deal of practical value, as Sangharakshita has amply demonstrated, in employing the Middle Way as a basis of practical judgement. The extent to which he has employed the Middle Way and recognised its value is one of the things that marks him out from other thinkers, including Buddhist ones, but his theoretical basis for

14 See Ellis (2001).

it needs considerable revision to provide a helpful support for the practical use of the Middle Way.

There is a great deal of inconsistency, not only in the way Sangharakshita has presented the Middle Way, but in the way Triratna has treated it. On the one hand, Subhuti has been quoted as saying that Buddhism should re-evaluate its teaching 'to see the Dhamma in terms of the Middle Way',[15] but on the other, it gets very little explicit emphasis in Triratna teaching. There are no books devoted explicitly to the Middle Way, nor does it feature prominently in the basic training given to mitras[16] and ordinands. It is very rarely the subject of talks or retreats. Perhaps this is because, at some level, it is recognised that a more rigorous exploration of the subject would lead to questioning of many of the traditional claims that Sangharakshita has staked his authority on.

---

15 Quoted by Nissoka (undated) p. 96.
16 I.e. people who have entered into a formal committed relationship with the Triratna Order, but prior to ordination.

3. Practice

3.a. The Eightfold Path

In this section of the book I am going to discuss the distinctive emphases in Sangharakshita's approach to what is often called 'Buddhist practice' or 'spiritual practice'. These terms may mask the more general application of what he has to offer beyond committed Buddhists, or even beyond those who are happy to use the term 'spiritual' (though to me, as to many Western Buddhists, 'spiritual' does not necessarily imply 'supernatural' in any sense). 'Practice' in this broad sense is the application of awareness to modify one's habitual actions, develop one's character, overcome delusion, and improve one's effect on the world. It can incorporate individual disciplines such as meditation or yoga, moral observance, expressive or artistic practice, and shared ways of acting and living at the social level. All of these can be undertaken for their own obvious experiential value by those without Buddhist commitments, and are shared to some extent with many other traditions.

Practice in this sense is the central point of Triratna Buddhism as Sangharakshita developed it. The emphasis on practice, and the wealth of techniques of practice available, is one of the things that sets Buddhism in general apart from other traditions, even though Christianity, Islam, Judaism, and Hinduism all have their own mystical traditions with some of the same practical emphases. Sangharakshita has also reacted negatively to what he regarded as the lack of genuine practice in some of the other Buddhist organisations he worked with earlier in his life, such as the Buddhist Society in London and the Maha Bodhi Society in India. Other Buddhist groups, particularly those of Theravada and Tibetan origin, do maintain the Buddhist emphasis on practice, but can also undermine it with too much emphasis on practices that are more the expression of a particular Asian culture than of the universal values to be found in Buddhism: for example, the performance of the traditional alms round by Theravada monks in Chithurst,[1] or the concealment of expensive jewels in Tibetan stupas.[2]

Though I will be considering Sangharakshita's interpretation of the more traditional Buddhist doctrinal structure in the following section, the practical approaches discussed in this section could well be approached only on the basis of the universal ideas from his work that I have discussed so far, without the need to worry about the vexed interpretation of concepts like enlightenment, conditionality, or karma. Although many of Sangharakshita's followers do indeed use these concepts and would assume them to lie at the foundation of their practice, Sangharakshita's strength is that he found a variety of ways for people to access the process of practice. People can, for example, engage in meditation, and indeed in all the other practices I will discuss in this section, in order to develop their creativity, provisionality, integration, and individuality. The Middle Way can also provide a broader justificatory concept drawing these kinds of qualities together and showing how they relate to each other. By becoming more integrated, we can avoid the rigid or absolute assumptions represented by either 'extreme' of the Middle Way, making possible a more creative response to the world around us because we are open to new options or ways of thinking.

Sangharakshita has talked about practice as a whole particularly through discussion of the Buddhist Eightfold Path. Sangharakshita's account of the Noble Eightfold Path is offered in his book *Vision and Transformation*, which is compiled from a series of lectures given in 1968. Here he frames the whole of Buddhist practice (as suggested in that title) as the process by which an initial vision of spiritual development is realised. He is at pains to point out that this 'vision' is not just an intellectual belief about the nature of the way, but 'something direct and immediate, and more of the nature of a spiritual experience than an intellectual understanding.'[3] The vision that inspires the way obviously involves a simultaneous recognition of relationships within oneself and between oneself and the world, so needs to take the form of a *gestalt*, an intuitive grasp of a whole, not an analysis reaching a conclusion. However, at the same time, Sangharakshita accepts that there can be intellectual *expressions* of that vision.

1 Batchelor (1994).
2 http://www.stupa.org/stupas.htm (accessed 2018).
3 Sangharakshita (1990b) p. 22.

However, Sangharakshita's choice of language in discussing this vision is unfortunate. The Eightfold Path consists of eight 'limbs', each of which is preceded, in the original Sanskrit or Pali, by the term '*samyak*' or '*samyag*' (Sanskrit), or '*samma*' (Pali): a term meaning 'proper', 'whole', 'thorough', 'integral', 'complete', or 'perfect'. In his presentation of all of these limbs, Sangharakshita selects 'perfect' out of these options as being the most appropriate translation, without giving any further reasons for doing so.[4] He is obviously at pains to avoid both a merely analytic and a merely moralistic interpretation of the Eightfold Path, but in the process he chooses, instead, a word with all kinds of absolutist and Platonic associations that seems to fit his own leanings in that direction.

As the term is most often used, 'perfect' means absolute, and thus excludes all the messy, imperfect experiences and motivations that humans actually have. Perfection is normally also purely conceptual in a way that Sangharakshita is expressly trying to avoid here. We cannot even imagine perfection, let alone create it, so how much less should it be associated with the Eightfold Path! From the list of possible translations it seems likely that Sangharakshita did not intend this kind of exclusiveness or pure conceptuality, but rather the idea of moving towards the fulfilment of an integral vision by overcoming conflicts in experience. He would thus have probably done much better to have selected a term like 'integral' rather than 'perfect' to convey this point. Given the prominence of the term 'perfect' in his whole exposition of the Eightfold Path, there might be a huge difference of tone (and perhaps derived argument) if the term 'integral' was used instead.

In this selection of language there is perhaps a test of the Middle Way at stake. Sangharakshita seems to have perceived his audiences as tending towards relativism and conventionality, and thus wanted to challenge them by stressing transcendence as the alternative. He thus rejected the description of the limbs of the Eightfold Path as 'right', because for him this represented conventional moralism. However, by substituting 'perfect' he introduced the opposite extreme – a term highly redolent of abstract philosophy and theology stressing the transcendent. We do not need to question his judgement in the short term in addressing a particular audience in a particular context (where this over-balancing might possibly have

4 Ibid. p. 17.

been appropriate – who knows?) to question the adoption of the products of this particular occasion to the whole subsequent exposition of the Eightfold Path (a very basic and important teaching) in the context of Triratna. Generations of Triratna Buddhists may have since thought of themselves in unnecessarily idealistic terms as practising 'perfect speech', 'perfect mindfulness', etc., rather than the level of ethical speech or mindfulness that it is practically sustainable for them.

The first 'limb' of the Eightfold Path is *samyag-dristi* or *sammaditthi*, often translated as 'Right Understanding', but Sangharakshita translates it as 'Perfect Vision'. This vision is then followed by 'transformation' through the practice of the other seven limbs. The first limb of transformation, which Sangharakshita translates as 'Perfect Emotion', also raises issues that are due to the language used and the framing it suggests. His account of it utilises a common false dichotomy between reason and emotion to emphasise that 'reason' is not enough:

> *We find it easy simply to* understand. *We can understand the Abhidharma; we can understand the Madhyamika…we can understand everything. But to put into practice even a little of this knowledge and make it operative in our lives, this we find very difficult indeed.*[5]

This does, indeed, describe a common enough problem, which the emphasis on practice in Triratna has always attempted to address. Our 'understanding' can be alienated from our practical motivation for a variety of reasons. Perhaps the 'knowledge' remains abstract and insufficiently meaningful. Perhaps we lack the practical energy or resources to put it into practice. Perhaps group norms do not encourage us to do so. Perhaps we are still insufficiently aware of how it can be put into practice. However, Sangharakshita claims that

> *For most of us the central problem of the spiritual life is to find emotional equivalents for our intellectual understanding.*[6]

This frames the problem entirely in terms of a contrast between 'intellectual understanding' (or 'reason') and 'emotion' which seems to be the result either of unjustified assumption or unwise oversimplification. Although this is a traditional division in Western

5 Ibid. p. 34.
6 Ibid. p. 36.

thinking, it is a false dichotomy. Emotional states require understanding and belief about the things we have emotional responses to, and understanding and belief, in turn, would not be motivated without emotional states. This interdependence is well established in psychology and neuroscience.[7]

When we have an intellectual understanding of a Buddhist teaching, then, we *already* have an 'emotional equivalent' for it. Our inability to act on the insight that we have gained, to the extent that (in our most insightful states) we would like, is a result of conflict between *different* emotional states, each of which has attendant beliefs. The model that Sangharakshita already draws on (that of integration) assumes the possibility of bringing together emotional states (with associated beliefs) that are previously divided from each other. The idea of an 'emotional equivalent', on the other hand, maintains the popular dichotomy of reason and emotion, which may have unhelpful effects. Anti-intellectualism is one easy misinterpretation for those who take this concept out of its wider context, especially for those who find intellectual practice challenging – and seek easy ways to avoid it by seeing Buddhist practice as solely 'emotional'. A failure to appreciate the relative spiritual benefits of a typical Western education, even if it has indeed been one-sidedly cognitive, may be another effect of this approach. But every limb of the Eightfold Path requires us to work with our assumed beliefs inextricably from our emotional states.

Sangharakshita's attitude to 'emotional equivalence' also seems to feed through in his attitude to 'emotional' practice, such as the traditional Buddhist practices of *dana* or generosity, the *brahmaviharas* or states of positive emotion cultivated in meditation, and *shraddha* or faith cultivated through puja or devotional ritual.[8] On the one hand, these practices can all be highly beneficial to people, but on the other, they depend on certain cognitive conditions to be so. That's hardly surprising given the constant interplay between cognition and emotion, and the way in which both need to work together to address any specific set of conditions in an individual or in society. But Sangharakshita's approach to these rarely seems to go beyond a counter-balancing emphasis on what he assumes to be a neglect of emotional cultivation in Western audiences.

7 Storbeck & Clore (2007).
8 Sangharakshita (1990b) pp. 43–59.

When asked about this, Sangharakshita agreed that 'reason' and 'emotion' are interdependent, and effectively seemed to regard 'emotional equivalence' as a more integrated position to correct perceived over-intellectualism in his audience. As often, however, the fact that he can offer a more balanced view of the issue when challenged does not do much to mitigate the long-term effects of a one-sided approach in his earlier presentations.

On the theme of generosity, for instance, in *Vision and Transformation* Sangharakshita stresses that giving could be of time, energy, thought, knowledge, or fearlessness, as well as material things. He also argues that even if giving has become somewhat socially formalised in many situations, it still has a beneficial effect in encouraging people to think 'a little bit about others'.[9] Nowhere in this exposition, however, does he include any mention of the many complex cognitive judgements that actually surround giving in practice. We all have limited resources, so how far should we prioritise giving these rather than using them for ourselves? Is it not irresponsible to give too much? Is there not an equally big issue of over-giving, especially with the socially-sanctioned giving of time and energy to others by women to the neglect of their own cultivation? How should we respond to requests for giving that may be more or less manipulative?

If you consider giving *only* in an isolated 'emotional' context without an accompanying cognitive one, the danger is that your view of it becomes simplistic and naïve. In some cases, at least, this kind of simplistic approach to it does seem to have influenced Triratna practice. For example, the *Future Dharma Fund* website offers the following under the heading 'Transforming yourself through giving more':

> *Our attachment to money is one of our strongest experiences of self-clinging. We identify ourselves through our possessions. Being so malleable, money is an alluring symbol of abstract happiness, security, love or whatever our wanting mind yearns for. Yet like all phenomena, money is ungraspable and when we let it flow freely into and out of our lives we experience the bliss of that great open-handed Buddha, Ratnasambhava.*[10]

In exchange for our emotional loosening we are offered an emotional reward – the bliss of Ratnasambhava – in a way that can easily

---

9 Ibid. pp. 43–6.
10 https://futuredharma.org/transform-self (accessed 2018).

be interpreted as manipulative because of the whole cognitive context that it fails to acknowledge. When someone has an 'emotional' access of generosity they do not cease to have cognitive states and make cognitive assumptions (e.g. that being generous will lead to bliss), but they fail to reflect on them. If the Middle Way was being practised here, fund-raising would not only emphasise the emotional value of giving, but also prompt reflection on the wider practical effects of a particular gift. If the giver gets carried away by this but cannot afford to pay the rent next month, some measure of responsibility lands on those who presented giving in such a one-sided way.

Similar points can be made about the cultivation of emotional states in meditation (which relates to the next chapter) and in the context of devotional practices. These 'emotional' practices are not free of cognitive context, and it can hardly be good integrative practice to present them as such (any more than it is good practice to tackle 'intellectual' issues with false neutrality, as though they had no emotional context). A meditation practice that cultivates loving-kindness towards others is unlikely to change our behaviour towards them unless we also challenge our beliefs about others. Devotional practices, too, depend for any positive effect on the cognitive as well as the emotional states of the individual performing them, and thus are unlikely to have any positive effect if they are just developed on the basis of a traditional or institutional prescription rather than an approach that takes into account those cognitive assumptions and individual emotional states (see 3.g below).

In the rest of this section we will see a variety of Sangharakshita's approaches to practice in ways that continue to reflect other limbs of the Eightfold Path. Meditation, ethics, friendship, and the arts, for instance, are all approached in ways that reflect some of the distinctive strengths of Sangharakshita's interpretation of Buddhism discussed in section 2. These are integrative practices that can be followed in a provisional and individual spirit, following the Middle Way. However, at times we will also see the further negative effects of the two problematic aspects of Sangharakshita's approach to the Eightfold Path mentioned above: idealisation and decontextualised treatment of emotion. In each of these it is also possible to trace a failure to apply the Middle Way.

3.b. A System of Meditation

At the time Sangharakshita first started teaching meditation in England, it was an almost unknown, exotic practice. By contrast, fifty years later, basic mindfulness practices are becoming increasingly widely used beyond the sphere of Buddhism. Sangharakshita made an appreciable contribution to this process by starting a movement in which, firstly, meditation practice was emphasised and, secondly, a wide variety of meditation practices from the Buddhist tradition were drawn on. Though meditation doesn't seem to have been his most central interest, he nevertheless appreciated its importance and maintained a strong personal practice. He also inspired a generation of remarkable meditation teachers working within Triratna – people like Kamalashila, Vajradaka, and Vessantara.

The distinctive emphasis of Sangharakshita's approach to meditation is encapsulated in a lecture he gave in 1978 entitled 'A System of Meditation'.[1] This has already been discussed in 2.d above. The four stages of this 'system' correspond to different types of meditation practice: the mindfulness of breathing providing a basis of integration; the *metta-bhavana* (cultivation of loving-kindness), the second stage, of the development of positive emotion; the six element practice and other vipassana practices providing the third stage of spiritual death; and the visualisation or *sadhana* practices providing an element of spiritual rebirth. As already mentioned in 2.d, these stages can easily be seen in terms of one another, and all of them can be seen as consistent with 'integration' as a model for spiritual development in general, even though Sangharakshita only uses the term for the first stage of meditation.

This 'system' provides the conceptual underpinning that has motivated much meditation teaching in Triratna. With beginners, Triratna meditation classes teach the mindfulness of breathing and *metta-bhavana* practices, confining themselves to the first two stages of the system. Positive emotion practice is seen as an important counterpart to the mindfulness focus of the 'integration' stage, because of the danger of alienation that Sangharakshita stressed as lying in mindfulness practice alone.[2] The third and fourth stages, however, are generally reserved for ordination training. During the

---

1 Lecture 135.
2 Lectures 84 and 135.

period leading up to ordination, ordinands typically do the six element practice, in which there is a systematic reflection on the interdependence between the body and mind and the six elements. This involves a symbolic dissolution, or 'spiritual death'. On ordination, the ordinand also then receives a sadhana practice from his or her preceptor: a visualisation practice of a Buddha or bodhisattva figure representing the ordinand's positive rebirth in the symbolic world of enlightenment.

This system has obviously offered great practical benefits for generations of Buddhist practitioners. However, a number of assumptions inform this system of meditation practice. Perhaps the most basic of these is the separability of the four stages, and thus the need for distinct practices to address each of them. There is also the question of the relative status and relationship between *samatha* and *vipassana* types of meditation (an issue on which there are varied views within the Buddhist tradition). There are also cultural questions about the origins of the forms of meditation that Sangharakshita adopts in the final two stages.

If positive emotion is, as I've already discussed, just as much an aspect of integration as mindfulness is, then one would expect any practices that cultivate mindfulness to also cultivate positive emotion. My own experience is that the less distinction is made between these two types of practice, the more effective each can be. When mindfulness practices are rooted in bodily awareness, and the meditator seeks experiences of contentment so as to allow them to develop further within that bodily awareness, a more concentrated and sustainable mental state emerges in which positive emotion provides the continuing motive. Why, after all, would anyone want to practise mindfulness unless there were positive emotions embedded in it? Similarly, positive emotion can only be cultivated in a rather stretched, unsustainable fashion if it is not based fully on body awareness and the mindfulness that is dependent on it.

The need for Sangharakshita's degree of rigour in this regard can thus be questioned. It was well-motivated by a desire to help people develop more integrated states, but apparently founded on an over-strong distinction between two meditative qualities that can only ever be genuinely cultivated in relation to each other. His concern about people practising mindfulness in an alienated way seems to have arisen from his experience on returning to the UK in the 1960s, when meditation may often have been badly taught in the

West – particularly by Asian teachers with little understanding of typical Western psychological states. However, fifty years later, the ground for this concern is much weaker, with a much greater number of mindfulness teachers and a wider sharing of strategies. There may still be people who develop alienated awareness in meditation, but to do so is so far from the perceived goals of mindfulness practice that any competent teacher should be able to challenge the approach that creates it.

It is also questionable whether the *metta-bhavana* (cultivation of loving-kindness) is always the best way of avoiding 'alienated' approaches to mindfulness practice. Taking up two different practices from the beginning makes an already challenging meditation practice more difficult for beginners. Some may take to the practice readily when they already feel positive emotion, and others struggle with it because they don't. It is very easy to merely reflect conceptually on the 'love' one would like to feel for everyone, or go through the motions of imagining such a love, without actually cultivating positive emotion very effectively. In some ways, then, the danger of alienation may be greater, or at least as great, in *metta-bhavana* practice as in mindfulness practice. As discussed in the previous chapter, the cultivation of an emotion without an acknowledged cognitive element to it may simply mean that other unacknowledged cognitive assumptions take their place. To change one's emotions in the longer term, one needs to change one's attitudes, beliefs, and sense of meaning.

Thus, although there may still be a good case for the effectiveness of the *metta-bhavana* practice as a supplement to the mindfulness of breathing for some people, that case can hardly justify the universality which Sangharakshita's system has given it in Triratna Buddhism. Since the first and second stages of the system are scarcely distinct, they do not necessarily need distinct practices to go with them, but rather the rich development of meditation practice itself through the incorporation of greater awareness of emotion in the mindfulness of breathing (or whatever other practice one begins with).

When we get to the third and fourth stages, though, the further question looms of the relationship between samatha and vipassana types of meditation. Although the term 'vipassana' has been used more broadly in some contexts, in the context of Sangharakshita's thought it means meditation practice that is intended to produce insights into the nature of conditions – particularly their impermanence, insubstantiality, and unsatisfactoriness. This is contrasted with 'samatha', meaning calming and integrating meditation working more directly with mental states.

Some Buddhist schools though, particularly Zen, have denied the validity of this distinction, claiming that insight comes simply from the development of awareness that samatha practices may help us to cultivate. For example, the Sutra of Hui Neng argues that *samadhi* and *prajña*, which are respectively the goals of samatha and vipassana meditation, are 'inseparably united and not two entities.'[3] However, wanting to maintain a strong distinction between them, whilst also seeing Zen teachings as essentially in harmony with mainstream Buddhist ones, Sangharakshita adopts an uncharacteristically scholastic solution – claiming that the sense of 'samadhi' in the context of Zen is completely different from that in the rest of Buddhism, and thus that Zen is only focused on vipassana.

> Confusion has been created in the minds of western students of Zen because they wrongly assumed that the Samadhi that Hui Neng spoke of was Samadhi in the sense of mental concentration, thus making nonsense of the entire scheme of Buddhist self-development. In the Mahayana Suttas, Samadhi corresponds to the chetovimutti *or state of spiritual emancipation of the Theravada texts rather than to Samadhi in the sense of concentration.*[4]

Whether or not this claim is correct from a scholarly point of view is something we do not need to pursue, because from a practical point of view it misses the point, and shows every sign of being an *ad hoc* defence of Sangharakshita's strong distinction between samatha and vipassana. Sangharakshita himself seems happy to acknowledge the interdependence that Hui Neng was pointing to, but also seems to be carried away by an absolute use of terms in this context. Why, indeed, should he be so worried about 'making nonsense of the entire scheme of Buddhist self-development', given that he would presumably also accept that this scheme is entirely provisional? Maybe it needs, in some sense, to have nonsense made of it.

Samatha and vipassana are both based on awareness as a common factor, applied to prevent closed feedback loops of reactivity. In the case of samatha, it tries to soften and integrate the reactivity of anxiety and obsession producing closed loops of *prapanca* or

---

3   Price & Mou-Lam (1969) ch. 4 (p. 42).
4   Sangharakshita (1985) p. 11.

proliferating thought. In the case of vipassana, we try to integrate our beliefs (explicit or implicit) with the wider tendencies in conditions that those beliefs are inclined to deny because of closed feedback loops. Samatha soothes the disturbing processes coming from our limbic area, such as the flow of dopamine or cortisol which can hijack our awareness, whilst vipassana addresses the beliefs in the linguistic areas of the pre-frontal cortex more directly, but this merely means a focus on different stages in the same loop. Without the kind of temporarily integrated awareness produced by samatha, it is much harder to change our beliefs in a sustainable way, because the proliferating loops will drag us right back to our old assumptions in practice. Without the long-term work implied by vipassana, however, the effects of samatha are likely to be limited and temporary, for our habitual beliefs will tend to drag us back to habitual mental states.

Sangharakshita's emphasis on 'spiritual death' and 'spiritual rebirth' as the third and fourth stages in his system of meditation, then, do not offer a process that is completely distinct from the integration process discussed in 2.d. 'Spiritual death' involves letting go of our attachments to deluded beliefs, and 'spiritual rebirth' adopting better, less deluded ones. Clearly, Sangharakshita has identified a process of progression that can be, and has been, helpful for the development of a number of individuals. The question remains, however, as to whether it should have the universality he attributes to it. Should everyone move on to these vipassana practices after gaining a grounding in the samatha ones? Are the vipassana practices he recommends universally appropriate?

In the case of samatha practice, though there are some other practices that may have *partially* similar effects (such as yoga), there seems to be no other one that works quite so directly to reduce closed feedback loops and thus promote our creativity, provisionality, integration, and individuality. In the case of vipassana, however, the advantages of using the context of meditation to transform our beliefs seem to be more marginal, since the process involved is one of systematic and imaginative reflection, sometimes accompanied by visualisation. Systematic reflection can also form a practice in its own right (coupled with solitary walking, for instance), or take the interactive form of 'direct pointing' (the practice developed by the 'Liberation Unleashed' movement in recent years). A strong imaginative dimension can be given to such reflection through the arts. This doesn't imply that vipassana practice cannot be beneficial, but that those benefits can also be accessed in other ways.

In addition to this, we can also ask questions about the *cultural* appropriacy of the practices recommended by Sangharakshita. Whilst samatha practices are shared by the entire Buddhist tradition, vipassana reflections are confined to the non-Zen schools, and the *sadhana* visualisation practices given to every new Triratna Order member on ordination are overwhelmingly the product of the Indo-Tibetan branch of Buddhism, taught in forms derived from Sangharakshita's Tibetan teachers. It seems odd that a movement that prides itself on drawing on the whole of Buddhist tradition for development of a kind recognised throughout Buddhism should thus put so much emphasis on culturally specific practice as being definitive of a whole stage of spiritual development.

Sadhana practices generally involve the visualisation of a specific Buddha or bodhisattva (such as Tara, Padmasambhava, or Amitabha), following the features, colours, and dispositions prescribed by the tradition of Tibetan Buddhism. They are also often accompanied by the recitation of a mantra specific to that figure. The exact details of how to perform the *sadhana* are technically a secret only communicated to the initiated.

By the time a new Order member reaches this stage of the track of spiritual practice laid down by Sangharakshita, he or she has moved quite a long way from the distinctive and universal approaches to Buddhism that form the strengths of Sangharakshita's approach, discussed in section 2. From the adaptation of Buddhism to wider contexts through the adoption of Western strengths, we have moved to a position where certain quite culturally specific (Tibetan) practices are generally taken to be the price of acceptance into the group. All practices will, of course, take a culturally specific form, but it is not at all clear why the form adopted in Triratna has to be a *Tibetan* culturally specific form, for people who are not Tibetans.

In my experience many Order members fail to maintain their sadhana practice (and when I was an Order member, I was one of them). The reasons for its difficulties are not hard to find – it is at one and the same time quite a demanding practice, one with cultural roots that are alien to many, and one that is far from necessary for spiritual progression, even if for some people it may be beneficial. Thus it is not their practice but their institutionalisation that is problematic, and this institutionalisation can be readily traced back to the influence of Sangharakshita's 'system of meditation'.

In response to this, Sangharakshita pointed out that sadhanas have been adapted from their Tibetan forms, and that there is some flexibility as to whether or not Order members do a sadhana practice. Some do not. However, at the same time he affirmed that every ordination includes instruction in a sadhana practice. The adaptations of sadhana practices are also relatively minor, and their overall form is still as prescribed by Tibetan tradition. It thus seems clear that there is still a general expectation that Order members will do a culturally specific practice that has descended from Indian origins through substantial Tibetan influence. The tolerant response to their failure to do so seems to be a way of maintaining this expectation rather than re-considering it.

Even more controversial material can be found in these further reaches of the Triratna practice of 'spiritual rebirth' through meditation. Whilst preparing for ordination, many people engage in the practice of visualising, chanting, and prostrating to a 'Refuge Tree' containing the image of Sangharakshita, together with his teachers and many other past Buddhist teachers going back to the Buddha himself. Sangharakshita himself also appears in the 'Guru Yoga', which involves the visualisation of one's teacher together with further teachers in a lineage stretching back into the past. In Sangharakshita's thinking, this involves an *archetypal* use of his image which he says needs to be separated from him as a real person. This is discussed in more detail in 5.b below.

That our inspirations towards integration should take an archetypal form is not surprising. The archetype represented by the Buddha figure is a symbolisation of our own potential integration, and is thus a potentially appropriate image for visualisation to inspire us towards 'spiritual rebirth'. But the value of archetypes lies in their universality: they represent functions for human beings in general that are then symbolised in various ways in different cultural circumstances. There are thus no grounds to criticise the fact that archetypes take one particular form rather than another in particular cultural circumstances. However, there *are* grounds for criticising any assumption that one particular symbolic expression of an archetypal function is uniquely superior to others, so that it becomes the basis of prescription for all regardless of background. The successful starting point of Sangharakshita's presentation of Buddhism is its universality, but this universality then becomes lost in increasing degrees of cultural prescription as the practitioner progresses. Some, of course, may accept and adapt to this cultural prescription, but others do not. In a successful universal Buddhist movement, nobody should have to face such unnecessary stumbling-blocks in a path of transformation that is far from easy in any circumstances.

3.c. The Ten Precepts

Sangharakshita's emphasis on ethics is one of the most important aspects of his presentation of Buddhism in the West. The context in which he broached the subject was (and remains) one of confusion and turbulence, in which ethical concepts continue to be widely used and invoked, but there are basic disagreements fracturing society about what they mean and how they are justified. As Alasdair MacIntyre writes, contemporary moral disagreement is characterised by its 'interminable character', because there is 'no rational way of securing moral agreement in our culture'.[1]

An ever-declining section of the population maintains the unquestioning belief in an absolute ethics, in which the rules of society are backed up by belief in an absolute source such as God's command. The increasing number of us who have freed ourselves of this dogma, however, are left with the problem of how we can justify the moral assumptions that suffuse all our talk about individual and social responsibility, law, politics, and professionalism. To just appeal to the social conventions or methods of one context or tradition is never enough when they can conflict with another – creating the problem of relativism.

Sangharakshita's contribution to ethical thinking in this situation is distinctive and practical. It consists in an insistence on ethics being part of a wider path that has the potential to defuse the assumptions behind the clash between absolutism and relativism.

> *The term ethics can be used in two senses, a broader and a narrower. Ethics in the broad sense is the art or science of human character and conduct as possessing value in relation to a standard or an ideal.... As such, ethics is more or less identical with religion in its most practical aspect. Ethics in the narrow sense is concerned with external, bodily or vocal behaviour....*[2]

It is the separation of ethics from this wider sense that creates many of the problems people have with understanding it. When ethical questions are asked in a narrow linear form, requiring answers to questions like 'Should I pay this bribe to save an Indian business deal?', they only invite answers that are either absolutist ('Bribery is always wrong') or relativist ('Bribery is OK in India – it's how they do things there'), rather than ones that are specific but take

---

1 MacIntyre (1981) p. 6.
2 Sangharakshita (1989) p. 48.

the full context into account. Our values arise from our position in life and the ways in which we take responsibility for that position and its development, so they are part of a wider path. In relation to that path, there are better and worse choices, but in the abstract and beyond that path, ethical arguments founder in dualistic conflict. Sangharakshita's most important ethical text, *The Ten Pillars of Buddhism*, is important precisely because it puts ethics clearly in the context of that path.

This contextualisation of ethics in a wider path might be thought of as a basic teaching of Buddhism. After all, morality is one of the three elements of the Threefold Path of morality, meditation, and wisdom, and (as right action, speech, and livelihood) it also offers three limbs of the Eightfold Path. However, Sangharakshita has offered a new emphasis in a Buddhist tradition that has tended to neglect this relationship. One of the main reasons for that neglect is the monastic-lay divide in traditional Buddhism, which leaves monks struggling to keep 227 specific rules of conduct intended to create the conditions for the attainment of nirvana, whilst laypeople are only expected to keep the five basic precepts avoiding harm, theft, sexual misconduct, lying, and intoxication. Sangharakshita's abandonment of this division in Buddhism demanded the development of a morality that would require more than the five precepts but be more flexible and less formalistic than the monastic rules. Sangharakshita found the answer to this in a rediscovery of the Ten Precepts, which are to be found in the Pali Canon,[3] and an emphasis on the relationship between these general moral principles and the whole of the Buddhist path.

Sangharakshita discusses these Ten Precepts both in general and individually. In general, he stresses that they are principles rather than rules. There is no legalistic expectation that they will be obeyed according to (some unambiguous interpretation of) their meaning. Rather they offer an indication of the sorts of approach that are likely to support progress on the path. They are 'rules' only in the sense of 'rules of training', voluntarily undertaken as an aspect of one's practice rather than in obedience to a power that requires them. Their relationship to the path as a whole can be seen from the ways in which they are concerned with body, speech, and mind. The body precepts involve abstention from killing, taking the not-given,

3 Ibid. pp. 19–30.

and sexual misconduct; the speech precepts the avoidance of false, harsh, frivolous, and slanderous speech; and the mind precepts abstention from covetousness, hatred, and false views. Obviously the mind precepts here involve not just ethics in the narrow sense, but take us into the practices of meditation and wisdom.

Another aspect of Sangharakshita's approach that gives a bigger context to the Ten Precepts is his use of positive equivalents.[4] Whilst the Ten Precepts are all negative in form, consisting in abstentions, he gives each of them a positive equivalent, which he argues can also be rooted in the same canonical sources that provide the negative versions.[5] For example, whilst the first precept is the training principle of abstention from killing living beings, its positive correlate is the practice of loving-kindness. Whilst a negative emphasis in ethics can create an association with moralistic repression, more emphasis on positive qualities helps to link ethical cultivation with motives for pursuing the rest of the path.

However, despite this helpful context given to the Ten Precepts, the question remains of why we should follow moral instructions of this kind at all, and if we do so, why we should follow this particular set rather than another. It is possible to give justifications for each of the Ten Precepts in terms of the avoidance of absolutes in the Middle Way and the cultivation of integration. If we kill, steal, or commit sexual misconduct, for instance, we treat another exclusively as an object that is absolutely separated from our own identification. If we lie, we make it impossible to integrate our beliefs with those of others. Positively, the qualities of generosity, love, and wisdom, and indeed all those mentioned in the positive precepts, help us to develop by broadening our emotional identification beyond the narrow range and the absolute boundaries that we may often confine it to. However, it is still possible that another set of precepts might fulfil these values as well or better, so their authority in the Buddhist tradition apparently remains an unavoidable part of the justification Sangharakshita gives for them.

Being very general, these precepts also require much interpretation to be of any use as guides to action. For example, what does it mean to abstain from killing living beings? Do we give equal weight to all living beings, or is killing a fly less important than murdering

4   Listed in the preliminary pages of Sangharakshita (1989).
5   Ibid. pp. 19–30.

a person? Should we be concerned about indirectly contributing to killing through eating meat or other animal products? What about paying taxes to the state that might be used to support killing people in defence, or indeed serving in the army or the police force? Once we get into the specifics of moral actions in specific situations, things rarely look as simple as the precepts make them appear. Of course, Sangharakshita or other teachers may give us further moral advice, but this advice cannot be purely justified by the precept itself, only by a relationship with the wider path.

As we saw in Sangharakshita's talk on 'Twenty Years on the Middle Way', he has sometimes discussed in some detail the way in which the Middle Way can be used as a guide to ethical issues (such as how to relate to one's parents), and when I questioned him on this point, he agreed that it was important. However, there is no mention of the Middle Way at all in *The Ten Pillars of Buddhism*, nor in any other of Sangharakshita's writings on ethics, and he was unable to account for this when I asked him about it. Given the ways in which the Middle Way could clarify the interpretation of the precepts, or even to what extent we should follow the precepts, this is unfortunate.

For example, if we take the First Precept, on abstaining from killing living beings, the Middle Way as a general principle of avoiding positive or negative absolutes would imply that we cannot interpret this simply as an absolute rule against any killing whatsoever. Some killing and harm is unintentional or unforeseen, some the indirect partial effect of actions that are on balance justified. In a context of great causal complexity, we cannot always isolate actions that cause killing or harm and avoid them, whether that involves eating crops where killing of small creatures was incidental to harvesting, or buying poisons that may either take life or save it (when used in small quantities). To take this precept seriously is an important part of the path, because of the conflicts (both internal and external) that we create through killing or any other kind of harm, and the way those conflicts will interfere with integration. But at the same time this does not imply that we can, or even should, always avoid killing.

The Middle Way is implicitly suggested in Sangharakshita's discussion of the power mode:

> *The love mode comes into operation only in the case of exceptional individuals, and even they may not always find it possible, or even desirable, to act in accordance with the love mode.... Whenever one has to operate in accordance with the power mode, the power mode must always be subordinated to the love mode. A simple, everyday example of such subordination is when the parent, out of love for the child, forcibly restrains him from doing something that will harm him.*[6]

We cannot absolutise the belief that we should never use power – or even the expressions of power in violence and killing. This provides a strong argument against absolute beliefs in pacifism or anarchism. However, in avoiding that absolute view we are freed up to adopt the more adequate overriding attitude that Sangharakshita here describes as 'the love mode': an attitude that is overwhelmingly concerned with reducing conflict, and appreciates each person and their welfare as we may be led to do by more mindful and open mental states.

In other parts of Sangharakshita's exposition of the Ten Precepts, however, this kind of use of the Middle Way is more marked by its absence. Take the example of the speech precepts, which he discusses both in *The Ten Pillars* and in *Vision and Transformation*. Here he gives an inspiring account of how the qualities of speech urged by the four speech precepts – truthfulness, affectionateness, helpfulness, and harmony – are interdependent and build on each other. We can only be fully truthful in attitude to another person, he suggests, by being fully aware of them, truthfulness being so much a property of our representation of the world as a relational quality of being communicative in ways that are affectionate and helpful towards them, rather than projecting our ideas of what they ought to know.[7] However, there is no allowance made in his presentation for the actual confused, deluded position in which most of us have to work out what to say or not say in practice. In that situation, the unification of the four speech precepts may just seem like an ideal, and we may only see conflicts between truthfulness, affectionateness, helpfulness, and harmony. To decide whether someone is ready to listen to an uncomfortable truth, for instance, we have in practice to decide between truthfulness and harmony as priorities in that particular situation. That's where we need the Middle Way

---

6 Ibid. p. 62.
7 Sangharakshita (1990b) pp. 65–77.

most, as a general moral principle reminding us of the limitations of the absolute ideas we might develop about each, even when we might not be able to see how to fully unify them in this particular situation.

Apart from the absence of the Middle Way limiting the practical helpfulness of Sangharakshita's account of ethics, another limitation arises from his tendency to hierarchise ethical practice. Ethical practice is for humans, consisting in a series of decisions made under unavoidable uncertainty as we go through our lives, but Sangharakshita feels obliged to take up the elements in traditional Buddhism that idealise this process and thus undermine the value of ordinary practice. This is most fully expressed in his early essay, 'Aspects of Buddhist Morality'. Here he presents the path as divided into the 'mundane' and 'transcendental' phases, with the mundane still subject to craving and delusion and the transcendental free of it. This is another application of the unnecessary discontinuity between the 'Arya Sangha' and ordinary practice, already discussed in 2.e. Morality, he says, is similarly divided: 'mundane morality brings about an improvement in one's future conditioned existence' and 'requires for its maintenance a constant deliberate effort', whilst transcendental morality 'requires for its maintenance no effort at all'.[8] This is said to be because the *klesas* or defilements of craving, hatred, and delusion have gone, but we have no way of knowing in any practical situation whether or not this is the case.

The effect of this approach on Sangharakshita's overall view of ethics is, as often, to idealise, and it is also to decontextualise. A Buddhist approach to ethics that is generally distinguished by its practicality is thereby undermined, as we are told that the ethics we practise in ordinary human life is somehow an inferior or not true ethics. On the contrary, ethics as part of the process of the path can only get its value by stretching our habitual ways of judging. If we focus on ethics as a practical process rather than in terms of specific types of actions producing specific results, it becomes clearer that any 'ethics' that does not involve effort of some kind at some point, at least slightly stretching our habitual egoistic assumptions, is not worthy of the name, because it is not a practice. This absolutised 'ethics' supposedly practised by Buddhas is so remote from our experience that it can hardly even form an inspiration, for a moral

---

8   Sangharakshita (1993b) pp. 24–5.

inspiration would consist in people exerting moral effort. It is, in short, irrelevant to the actual complexity and uncertainty of human life.

Within the 'mundane' path of ethics Sangharakshita also distinguishes three different patterns according to one's level of spiritual development. The lowest of these consists of the basic lay ethics of the Buddhist tradition; the middle, of the creation of a more rigorous context of practice to enable the transformation of mental states; and the highest, of the avoidance of over-attachment to (or misinterpretation of) religious beliefs and observances.[9] This distinction in levels of ethical observance also relates to the monk-lay division in traditional Buddhism.[10] Despite Sangharakshita's abandonment of that division in Triratna, a distinction in levels of ethical observance persists in the fact that Order members recite the Ten Precepts, whilst Buddhists who are not Order members only recite the Five Precepts (to abstain from killing, taking the not-given, sexual misconduct, false speech, and taking intoxicants).

There is, of course, an argument that people will indeed have different moral priorities at different points on their individual path, and also in accordance with their personal circumstances. However, the attempt to formalise these different priorities into two grades of people with distinct moral practices is just a minor reproduction of the same mistakes made in the monk-lay division. As discussed earlier (in 2.d), integration is subject to many asymmetries, so is not a smooth or uniform path. Any benefits that arise from the extremely approximate matching of moral needs to people in this moral split are surely far outweighed, in modern society at least, by the negative impact of creating such a distinction. From one standpoint, there are as many ethical paths as there are people to tread them, and from another, there is only one such path, the universality of which arises from our shared human needs, structure, and functions. The Middle Way needs to be judged by each in the tension between these two considerations of the universal and the individual – it does not in any sense imply only two ethical paths, or even only three or four.

---

9 Ibid. pp. 26–7.
10 Ibid. pp. 27–8.

3.d. Friendship

Sangharakshita's emphasis on friendship is distinctive both as an interpretation of Buddhism and as an engagement with Western conditions. Friendship is often taken for granted as an aspect of human life, even when the social conditions tend to undermine it: but by putting emphasis on friendship as a *practice*, Sangharakshita has encouraged his followers to take much more conscious notice of it, and to cultivate it deliberately. As a result, Triratna is now noted for the depth and strength of its community.

The Buddhist term that Sangharakshita translates as 'spiritual friendship' is *'kalyana mitrata'*. As a concept this is highly interdependent with the concepts of individuality and integration, because one can only develop spiritual friendship with another on the basis of individuality. For this reason, Sangharakshita gives much emphasis to the separation of friendship either from power relationships or from dependency relationships, which interfere with the integration of our responses to others and tend to trigger obsession and anxiety in our relationships with them.

> *Friendship is a relationship that can exist only between two, or more, free people, that is to say people who are equals. The ancient Greeks realised this, and the ancient Greeks maintained that there could be no friendship between a free man and a slave. We can take this metaphorically as well as literally. And this brings us to another very important point – the relation between master and slave is based upon power. It's an expression of what we sometimes call in the FWBO 'the power mode'. But friendship is based upon love. It's an expression of what we've come to call 'the love mode'.*[1]

The love concerned here is metta or loving-kindness, the disinterested positive emotion cultivated in the metta-bhavana meditation (discussed in 3.b). Sangharakshita takes great care to distinguish this from Romantic love for a sexual partner, which he believes to be over-emphasised in Western culture, and to often be a context of dependency relationships rather than the friendship between equals. This raises many issues that we will need to return to.

As his reference to the Greeks may suggest, in his emphasis on the value of equality in relationships here, Sangharakshita also engages with Western values of liberal democracy in ways that he often seems unwilling to acknowledge. He stresses the psychological and

---

1 Lecture 177.

spiritual value of such relationships, but they also have an epistemological value (people's beliefs are not distorted by the need to placate someone with power over them) and a political value (they enable participatory decisions in which everyone has a stake).

In his lecture on fidelity, Sangharakshita also stresses the value of maintaining loyalty in one's relationships with friends. This loyalty to friends is an expression of individuality rather than merely of dependency. We are consistent because we have developed more consistent standards of awareness both of ourselves and others.

> *Fidelity involves consistency. Whether in the case of fidelity to self, fidelity to ideals, or fidelity to other people. It involves consistently behaving in a certain way. Now consistency implies continuity in time. It means behaving in the same way over – or if you like through – a longer, or shorter, period of time. Indeed it means more than this. It means consciously and deliberately behaving in the same way over or through a period of time. But in order to be able to do this, we must have an idea of ourselves as continuing to exist in time. We must have an idea of ourselves as existing in the past and in the future as well as in the present. In other words we must have self-consciousness. We must be individuals.*[2]

The awareness of ourselves existing over time (and thus as having responsibilities over time) is a basic aspect of integration, also consistent with the Buddhist quality of *sampajana* as a constituent of mindfulness.

The cultivation of fidelity in this sense, together with other aspects of mature awareness, is a psychologically realistic emphasis for many of us. However, it's also not difficult to conceive of situations where even the most autonomous fidelity to a person may need to be overruled by fidelity to ideals. For example, a person that we have a loyal relationship to may start to act immorally against us, or to exploit that loyalty. For Robert Kegan, drawing in turn on previous researchers into psychological development, the transition from Stage 3 (interpersonal values) to Stage 4 (institutional values) is a recognisable one that is gone through by many young adults when they reach university or begin a demanding profession.[3] In this kind of transition, personal loyalties may need to be overruled by loyalties to wider ideals. Sangharakshita shows a recognition of the need for fidelity to ideals as well as fidelity to persons. His awareness of

---

2   Lecture 155.
3   Kegan (1982) ch. 7.

the wider limitations of our views would doubtless also lead him to agree that fidelity to ideals, in turn, may need to be overridden (a transition that Kegan finds made by a small minority of mature adults, from the institutional stage 4 to the inter-individual stage 5).[4]

Friendship, then, is a particular loyalty based in our embodied situation, but nevertheless one that is especially suited to help us develop spiritually. It stretches our sympathies towards others with whom we may initially feel a limited amount in common. It offers the Middle Way between the assumption that our affections are necessarily limited, on the one hand, and the idealisation that we should love everyone, on the other. As embodied beings we unavoidably do have limited sympathies and capacities, but friendship nevertheless helps us to develop those.

For Sangharakshita, friendship involves 'persons treating each other as persons'. He says that there are two aspects to this: communication and 'taking delight'. Communication involves the 'vital mutual responsiveness' of self-disclosure to another: sharing inspiration, understanding, and even the mistakes we can learn from. 'Taking delight' means enjoying 'the spiritual beauty of our friend', appreciating their virtues and celebrating them.[5] Both of these are obviously basic functions of common social interaction, but stretched in the direction of a conscious practice. They imply, for example, that we may deliberately cultivate friendship with a spiritual friend by creating opportunities to spend time alone together, and communicating in more depth about things that matter. Everyday practice in Triratna takes this for granted. The pairs of men or pairs of women going for walks together to deepen their communication are a feature of the countryside immediately around Triratna retreat centres that has become well-known to local residents.

Sangharakshita distinguishes between 'vertical' and 'horizontal' types of friendship. 'Vertical' friendship is friendship with someone who is much more, or much less, spiritually advanced than you, and it forms the basis of his reinterpretation of the traditional Buddhist guru-disciple relationship. 'Horizontal' friendship, on the other hand, is friendship between people who are roughly at the same spiritual level, but who can share their differing strengths and inspirations as well as supporting each other on the path. The underlying

---

4 Ibid. ch. 8.
5 Sangharakshita (1990c) pp. 108–9.

metaphor here is that spiritual development is verticality – a metaphor that is used to justify a belief in spiritual hierarchy. However, an over-reliance on this metaphor may obscure the complexity of the conditions that underlie these relationships. As I have already noted in 2.d, integration has both asymmetries and temporary effects. Whilst Sangharakshita recognises that 'horizontal' friends may in fact have different strengths that may help them support each other on the path, once a specific relationship has been identified as 'vertical', similar differences in strength and weakness may well be obscured by the projection of spiritual strength on the 'higher' person by the 'lower' one (or indeed vice-versa).

Triratna is far less hierarchical and far less formalistic in its 'vertical' relationships than most traditional Buddhism, with teacher-disciple relationships being interpreted as ones of *kalyana mitrata*: simply human friendships rather than power relationships. Nevertheless, difficult questions remain about the use of the idea of 'verticality' and spiritual hierarchy within it, following Sangharakshita's teachings. When integration is in fact asymmetrical, and people who appear to be 'spiritually advanced' may in fact have big unrecognised weaknesses, the whole idea of verticality *of persons*, as opposed to a recognition of strengths and weaknesses in more particular respects, becomes a potentially dangerous over-simplification. A mere theoretical recognition that 'vertical' relationships are more complex than their 'verticality' might otherwise initially suggest is not enough, given the ways in which humans are prone to exploit every kind of hierarchy and turn it into a power-hierarchy.

There is also a basic incongruity between the statement we saw earlier from Sangharakshita, that friendship can only occur between equals, and this concept of verticality in friendship. If there is equality, there are no grounds for identifying a hierarchy in friendship, and the presence of a hierarchy undermines functional equality. One can assert this without falling into relativist or what Sangharakshita refers to as 'pseudo-liberal' ideas, because one is not concerned with denying differing strengths and weaknesses between people, but rather judging how they should relate.

Sangharakshita perhaps intended the 'equality' to be that of individuality, but since he also regards true individuality as dependent on enlightenment, it seems that his view of friendship as 'between equals' is actually very idealised. His account of friendship is not 'equal' between two messy, imperfect people, but, like his view of individuality, dependent on the concept of the Arya Sangha.

> To be a really dependable friend, a friend in whom someone can take refuge in this way, he has to be really a member of the Arya Sangha. Then he can be technically a refuge. Do you see what I mean? So you might even go so far as to say that true friendship implies Insight, a degree of Insight. How can you give your friend the refuge that he may need unless you have something very deep and very solid within you – some kind of spiritual attainment? Otherwise you will just be at the mercy of your own emotional states, your own psychological limitations.[6]

It turns out that the equality between spiritual friends is seen by Sangharakshita as dependent on this discontinuous guarantee of 'true' friendship, rather than being genuinely present but as a matter of degree at each stage. On the one hand this undermines the genuine equality of friendship of people who have only developed a degree of integrated individuality, and on the other sets up impossible expectations of perfect reliability for anyone who may be supposed to have actually reached the exalted position of stream entry. As though stream entrants, if they exist, could possibly be exempted from psychological limitations, or non-stream entrants lack 'some kind of spiritual attainment'!

When questioned on this point, Sangharakshita just said that 'If you're a Buddhist you believe in the possibility of Arahantship.' But this statement falls back on an implicit appeal to the Buddhist tradition (which he has been willing to override in other respects) rather than engaging with the potential practical problems created with this discontinuous idealisation of spiritual status.

When Sangharakshita acknowledges that friendship needs to be between equals, he has an insight that needs to be followed through, with an openness to learning from Western tradition as well as from Buddhism. Equality as it has developed politically in modern Western democracies depends not on one's level of individuality, but merely on one's political status as citizen. It is a formal, social relationship governing the way in which people seek to interact, not a complete description of a quality shared by two people. Levels of individuality, however spiritually desirable they may be, do not give a justification for power, because of all the delusions and uncertainties that attend our beliefs about ourselves and

---

6 Seminar 118 p. 223.

others in practice. Only the State, or other bodies that represent citizens collectively, can justifiably exert power and thus be 'above' an individual.

There are good reasons why we have largely abandoned formal hierarchy between individuals in this way. Even if theoretically not power-based, it tends to *become* power-based, and to enable social elites to perpetuate their worldly advantages. The history of democracy also tells us a good deal about the tendency of elites to perpetuate their power whilst formally denying it and making a pretence of equality. There are multiple examples of this, from the institution of slavery in the US to the social and political position of women in recent history. It was Thomas Jefferson the slave owner, for instance, who wrote the line in the US Declaration of Independence including the statement that 'All men are created equal.' In most cases, well-intentioned patriarchs are simply not aware of the degree of power over others that they are wielding and its degree of contradiction with their theoretical ideals.

The idea of genuine friendship between different levels of a hierarchy is thus one, at least, that is heavily prone to self-deception, with the outward appearance of a depth of personal relationship often masking complex projections. If it is argued that such self-deception can be overcome with enough spiritual practice, it can be responded that there is really no need to take the risk that it will not be. Friendship of a kind that offers inspiration and support in spiritual practice is dependent only on recognising that another person has *specific* strengths and virtues that we lack ourselves, not that they are in any sense wholly superior as persons.

When questioned on this, Sangharakshita agreed that there is much scope for self-deception in friendship, but not that this offered any case for not formalising vertical friendship. He thought that self-deception needed to be dealt with by Order members through the trusting and intimate discussions that are intended to take place in a chapter. Again, this is idealistic. Many chapters do not in fact function in this way, or do not do so sufficiently well. Those involved in vertical friendships in Triratna are also not all Order members.

The theory of vertical friendship informs the practice of Triratna, which takes a hierarchical form in terms of the formal differentiation between Order members, *mitras*, and 'friends'. There is also a hierarchy within the Order, in the relationship between preceptors who perform ordinations and those who are ordained by them, as well as between a prospective Order member and his or her two 'kalyana mitras' – more experienced friends who have entered into a formal commitment in which they are expected to have a more or less 'vertical' style of relationship with him or her. None of these 'vertical' relationships are generally treated with the amount of rigidity that accompanies the guru-disciple relationship in more traditional forms of Buddhism, but they can nevertheless have a negative effect on friendships between those placed at different levels by this structure, precisely because they introduce an expectation of 'verticality'. By doing this, they can distract from the complexity and uncertainty that attends the appreciation of someone else's strengths and weaknesses, and encourage the projection of authority or its absence.

I have experienced these disruptive effects of the doctrine of 'verticality' myself within my friendships in Triratna, particularly in finding that my critical arguments about Sangharakshita's teachings, however carefully considered, were seldom taken seriously as long as I had 'junior' status. Instead, they were likely to be interpreted as indicative of my own lack of integration. In the introduction I have also already mentioned my earlier experience of finding Sangharakshita's views on language most unsatisfactory, but feeling unable to challenge them (even though by temperament I am probably more likely to challenge authority figures than most other people).

The idealisation of friendship in Sangharakshita's work can lead to an underestimation of the basic human conditions on which friendship depends. The most basic starting point for feeling connected to somebody else is commonality of some kind, which makes it much more likely that we will make friends with those with whom we have 'something in common': whether that is a profession, an interest, a gender, an age, a nationality, or whatever else. We also maintain friendly social relationships with people who are, whether directly or indirectly, explicitly or implicitly, of use to us: perhaps in relationships of buying and selling, learning or teaching, sex, comfort or support. Sangharakshita insists, however, that we should be constantly generous and kind to our friends, keeping our word to them 'come what may', looking after their welfare, and treating them as ourselves.[7] In theory, spiritual friendship in

---

7 Lecture 177.

Triratna enters a universality that goes beyond these baser motives, but in practice, it occurs because people have a Buddhist group in common and are useful to each other in the context of Buddhist practice. It is very easy to underestimate how important these ordinary human motives continue to be when under the influence of Sangharakshita's rhetoric of idealised friendship.

My personal experience of 'vertical' friendship in Triratna can also illustrate this idealisation of friendship in general. When preparing for ordination I formally entered a committed friendship with two *kalyana mitras*. Such was the idealisation of this relationship in the ceremony, that it was stated explicitly that this was a lifelong relationship that would even continue to apply if I left the Order: a point I took very seriously at the time. When I did actually leave, however, this was unexpectedly put to the test. With one of my *kalyana mitras*, friendship had already been established on the basis of a long-shared experience, but with the other, it was much more imposed by a sense of duty to each other in a particular institutional situation. For the latter, the relationship was a product of the Order, and no longer applied after I left.

For an embodied human being, most of what Sangharakshita demands of a friend is actually impossible. We have one body with limited time, attention, and resources, and our prime responsibility in the use of that body is to ourselves and our own welfare and development. Even the most intimate relationships in human practice – in marriage or between parents and children – seldom come near Sangharakshita's idealised account of friendship, not because of a lack of motive but merely because of our inherent limitations. That we should be able to get anywhere near it with a particular friend, even if we limit our friendships to dozens rather than hundreds, is simply impracticable in most cases. Given that the great strength of Sangharakshita's stress on friendship (as opposed to mere universal love) is its degree of psychological practicality, it is a shame that Sangharakshita should then undermine that strength through idealisation. This is one more instance of him marring the exposition of potentially important practical ideas through impractical and inconsistent exposition, and forgetting the actual importance of the Middle Way to reconciling ideals to practical conditions.

3.e. Institutions and Power

The practical effectiveness of much of what we do together with others depends very much on the kinds of institutions we set up. Institutions can support other practices, and can thus help to foster integration and individuality, or they can hinder such development by supporting relationships of power. Sangharakshita's thinking has had a big effect on the development of the institutions of Triratna and the extent to which they are practically supportive or otherwise. His thinking in this respect was not laid down in advance in a blueprint, but is more evident from the interventions he made during his career in leadership of Triratna, either to encourage or discourage certain developments. They have only occasionally been discussed more theoretically in talks about the 'distinctive emphases' of Triratna.

Perhaps the central institutional judgement that Sangharakshita started with was that he should found a new Buddhist movement at all, and that that movement should be centred on an order as well as being non-monastic. I have already discussed his judgement on monasticism above in 2.c. However, Sangharakshita was also determined to avoid another social model, the drawbacks of which had become clear to him in his contacts with the Buddhist Society and with the Maha Bodhi Society – the membership organisation. He had 'trod on the toes' of people in those organisations.

> Now some of the people on whose toes I happened to tread were not Buddhists, and in some cases they didn't even profess to be Buddhists, but they were members of Buddhist organisations. Now how was this? This seems rather odd – not Buddhists but members of Buddhist organisations! How had they become members? Well, they'd become members in a very simple way – simply by paying the subscription. So, having paid the subscription, they became a member; having become a member they could be elected as an office-bearer; and being an office-bearer they could determine policy – even though, perhaps, they knew little or nothing about Buddhism or even had no real sympathy with it! ... So the lesson was therefore clear; we needed a new kind of Buddhist organization; an organization that one could not join simply by paying a subscription. We needed an organization that one could join – if that is the right word – only by actually committing oneself to the ideals for which it stood. In other words, we needed an Order; we needed a Sangha.[1]

---

1 Lecture 133.

The underlying issue here is that of power. How should power be bestowed and used in ways that is subordinated to the love mode, and that helps to create conditions that aid spiritual development? Sangharakshita assumes that the reason these membership organisations that he had encountered were not very effective in supporting spiritual development was because they were not sufficiently controlled by committed Buddhists. However, that can hardly be the whole explanation, given that another institutional arrangement that he rejected on the other side – monasticism – was very clearly controlled by very committed Buddhists.

The 'non-Buddhist' members that Sangharakshita complains about might also not agree with his definition of who counts as a Buddhist and who doesn't. 'Buddhism' is a highly contestable concept. That raises the question of Sangharakshita's views on the unity and essentiality of Buddhism, which will be discussed in 4.e, but for the moment we only have to note that identification with Buddhism by itself is no guarantee of the ability to use power effectively to support spiritual development.

A much more significant indicator of the appropriate use of power, in a world of uncertainty, is the presence of checks and balances to ensure creative and provisional rather than reactive decision-making, which means that there must be openness to correction rather than the maintenance of the same patterns of corporate judgement. This is a constitutional requirement of a kind that the framers of the US constitution understood very well, when they created many checks and balances between the three parts of government (executive, legislature, and judiciary) so that they could correct each other.

In practice, however, it is not actually just being identified as a Buddhist that is the basis of decision-making in Triratna. Instead of a membership organisation, Sangharakshita created an order, where one of the main criteria for admission, as we have already seen, is a 'degree of integration'. That degree of integration, approximate and asymmetrical as it may be, is probably a much better indication of the ability to use power wisely in an organisation than mere allegiance to Buddhism, which by itself is not much of an advance on having merely paid a subscription. That 'degree of integration' has at least been certified by a preceptor, in consultation with other Order members, so that the judgement has a degree of credibility. Someone with a degree of integration should be relatively more likely to effectively correct their own mistakes, or to respond to the feedback from others. However, given the uncertainty and asymmetry of their integration, they still require socio-political checks and balances to make sure that they do not persist in error.

Within Triratna, the institutions are usually set up so that only those Order members appointed as trustees, working together in consensus, have the power to determine their policies. Each local Triratna centre or group is legally and financially independent, and is governed by its trustees. These trustees will normally make their decisions by consensus, although a vote is held when this is legally required. This system maintains a number of balances that tend to avoid the abuse of power. There has been no formal power over the centres from Sangharakshita when he was head of the Order, nor subsequently from the college of preceptors that has succeeded him. Nor, on the other hand, is it particularly easy for a localised group with extreme views (whether 'Buddhist' or not) to hijack a centre, as only those who have been through the ordination process will normally be trustees, and there is continuing influence from the centre even in the absence of formal power.

However, there has still been one instance of a centre being 'hijacked', in the process revealing the limitations of this system. The Triratna Centre in Croydon, a town on the southern edge of the London conurbation, developed a number of cult-like features during the 1980s, under the leadership of an Order member called Padmaraja. There was exploitation and bullying, protected by the over-certainty of a closed group mentality.[2] After gathering pace during the 1980s, however, it was critical influence from the rest of the movement, including from Sangharakshita himself, that led this situation to implode in 1988. The cult atmosphere then ceased and Padmaraja resigned. In response, Sangharakshita proposed that each centre should have a president – an influential senior Order member from elsewhere who could maintain contact with that centre's trustees and keep an eye on its situation. If anything, Triratna's response to the Croydon episode seemed to indicate a wider provisionality and responsiveness in the institutional system, together with the effectiveness of moral authority in the Order of a kind that does not require legal power.

2 Vajragupta (2010) pp. 25–7.

However, it can also be argued that if Order trusteeship had really been sufficiently responsive, the situation in Croydon would not have arisen in that way in the first place. This point can also be illustrated by some of the other abuses of power that have been reported in Triratna, usually connected with the controversies that will be explored in the final section of this book. One example of these is that reported at Padmaloka Retreat Centre: the allocation of attractive young male retreatants to be accommodated in Sangharakshita's bedroom – for what have been assumed to be purposes of tacit sexual convenience.[3] Anyone raising questions about this at the time would probably have met a stone wall of rationalisations, because the Order members in charge of the allocation were not accountable to anyone outside their circle and its group assumptions.

In Western society, democracy is the evolved system to avoid such abuses. Liberal democracy is part of the root social system in which Triratna has grown up, and in which (as discussed in 2.e) individuality has been valued and cultivated. Liberal democracy normally extends to voluntary organisations in the sense that their office-holders are subject to election by members and out of the ranks of members. As Sangharakshita noted, this does not always result in the wisest people becoming office-holders, just as it doesn't in the democratic state. In the democratic state, as Churchill observed, democracy is 'the worst system – apart from all the others'.[4] However, its relative advantage is the way in which it encourages participation and informed judgement, making members into stakeholders in the voluntary organisation. Democracy, for all its many faults, ensures that critical voices are heard, and prevents conflict by keeping people on board.

In the case of Triratna, the institution of Order trustees without democratic forms of accountability may indeed result in better decisions in the short or medium term, but it may also have contributed to conflict and alienation in the longer term. Many of Sangharakshita's critics are frustrated by the fact that they have to rely on the judgement of those in central Triratna organisations like the Preceptors' College, and there is no way of pursuing their

---

3 A response to this issue from the Triratna safeguarding team is given at https://thebuddhistcentre.com/node/14140#id.668jwjih5jx (accessed 2019).

4 Winston Churchill, House of Commons, 11 November 1947.

complaints with such bodies (apart from legal action) when they feel that they are not being satisfactorily responded to. The fact that such organisations have influence but not power over local Triratna centres is also double-edged, as it can mean that central bodies can disavow forms of responsibility that in many respects they still have. By analogy, parents have no formal power but usually much influence over their adult children, and a parent who prevented the recognition and addressing of complaints about the behaviour of their adult children would still reasonably be considered irresponsible.

This problem is related to that of discontinuity, that has already been mentioned. Becoming an Order member means that an indeterminate and asymmetrical degree of integration is formalised into a single social status all at once in one step. Politically speaking, some degree of discontinuity between those who have power and responsibility and those who do not is unavoidable, so it can also be argued that this is the least worst system to have in Triratna. But politically, that discontinuity is somewhat mitigated through democracy. Those elected as MPs, for instance, are subject to the discontinuity of a sudden social status that they did not have before, but they are also obliged to listen to critical voices because of the danger that they may be removed.

I can see no reason why the same should not apply to institutional power in Triratna. The principle of only Order members (or those who, by some means, have been credibly judged to be reasonably integrated) being appointed as trustees could be maintained, but those Order members could nevertheless be subject to the democratic control of a wider membership, who could bring issues to their attention, and remove the trustees if necessary. The trustees of any body, after all, need to be appropriately qualified, and the level of integration required to become an Order member can just be seen as a necessary qualification. There also seems to be no reason why the leading Order members in institutions like the Preceptors' College could not be similarly subject to election and removal, even if there were also spiritual requirements for membership that were judged by consensus among Order members. In many cases, there would only be a limited number of people available to do the job, and thus no real contest; nevertheless, the very possibility of electoral accountability could only have a positive effect on institutional awareness.

When I suggested to Sangharakshita that there should be some degree of democratic scrutiny and accountability in Triratna organisations along these lines, he responded that he did not believe that people outside the Order should have any such scrutinising role, because they did not share the values of the Order. When I suggested that the value of this would be openness to new perspectives to support provisionality, he questioned the value of 'openness' – in contradiction to his recognition of the value of provisionality in other contexts of discussion.

Triratna's response to new organisational issues is often just to set up a new committee of Order members, with the organisational structure of the movement thus becoming ever more complex and the pressures on Order members continually increasing. This puts far too much emphasis on the discontinuity of ordination as the basis for trust, and tends to create a siege mentality in which other voices from beyond the Order have no satisfactory input.

These issues of governance apply, not just to local centres, but to the other institutions of Triratna that Sangharakshita has promoted as part of their distinctive approach: the 'Three C's' (centres, communities, and co-ops) that formed the basis of a 'New Society' that is 'the achievement of the creative mind'.[5] Communities and Right Livelihood businesses ('co-ops') have contributed to wider creativity, integration, and individuality by providing social support and a context of spiritual friendship in both housing and livelihood. Though they were primarily a feature of the earlier days of the movement, they exist to some extent to this day. Though these were not generally the result of planning on the part of Sangharakshita, they have generally received his blessing and been regarded as outcomes of his overall vision. He defined the purpose of a residential spiritual community as 'to provide a situation in which spiritually like-minded people can live together in a way that is expressive of Buddhist values', and of a Right Livelihood business as 'to help people develop spiritually through the experience of work, especially through the experience of working together'.[6] However, for them to fulfil these functions sustainably, the way they are set up becomes vital.

5 Lecture 133.
6 Lecture 174.

Like centres, communities and businesses are independent and responsible for their own governance. However, my personal experience of both during the late 1980s was that they followed the same patterns. The business I worked for, Windhorse Trading, was wholly owned by the Windhorse Trust, which followed the standard Order trusteeship model, and the business in turn owned and controlled the communities. Though I learnt a great deal during the year I spent living in a men's residential community (for part of which I also worked in the business), there was little doubt that the structure was patriarchal. The older, experienced Order members made all the decisions. They were, indeed, far better placed to do so successfully than the less experienced, but the absence of any limitations on their power meant that that there was no constraint on any mistakes they might make.

In all Triratna institutions, there has been a tendency for the structure that Sangharakshita initially created to be continued unchanged rather than for constitutional evolution. Often an appeal to the independence of local centres together with the relative integration of Order members is assumed to be sufficient for effective and responsive decision-making. However, for the practice of provisionality in institutional politics, it is the possibility of open feedback loops, correcting mistaken policies, that is far more significant than the formal means by which this is achieved. The main check and balance in the system consists of influence from above in the form of the Preceptors' College and the presidential system, an arrangement that reflects Sangharakshita's belief in vertical friendship. However, the complete lack of formal power from above can be a weakness as well as a strength, and the lack of any checks from below also limits the potential for correction in a way that often creates too much conservatism of judgement.

The objections to any proposal for greater democracy in Triratna are likely to appeal to Buddhist tradition, where such democracy is unknown, and there is a strong belief in the insights of the spiritually advanced. The weaknesses of the social organisation in Buddhist tradition, however, can be readily recognised without any need to idealise Western democracy by contrast. As Sangharakshita himself has identified, Asian Buddhism is often characterised by over-formal relationships between guru and disciples,[7] rather than

---

7 Lecture 90.

relationships of friendship based on equality. One of the key features of that equality (as discussed in the previous chapter) is the free exchange of critical perspectives, and the ability to respond creatively to criticism without reaction. Individual Buddhist practice can make a big positive difference to people's ability to engage in such friendship, and thus to manage social organisations in a creative and responsive way. However, if one imports hierarchical relationships from the Asian model into Western Buddhist practice, this is likely to undermine that responsiveness, with the social model creating a repression that is in conflict with the integration of the psychological model.

All of this relates to the insight that Sangharakshita seems to have had, at least partially and sporadically, that the Middle Way is not a monopoly of the Buddhist tradition, and that Western advances may in some respects provide better models of integrative practice. The high degree of success of liberal democracy in the West is not something that should be lightly dismissed, either by cherry-picking its failings or by idealising the traditional Buddhist alternative in contrast. Instead its successes in supporting relatively creative decision-making need to analysed and learned from, and its failures avoided. Liberal democracy is not simply a constitutional arrangement that operates at the highest level of state power, but something that permeates the whole of society. One ignores its power at one's peril.

3.f. The Arts

Sangharakshita's response to the arts, as mentioned in 1.b, is profound and goes back to his youth. He annoyed his family by listening to loud classical music, composed Persian-style quatrains on the parade ground in the army, and, soon after his return to the West, undertook a tour of artistic sights in Greece and Italy with profound enjoyment. Sangharakshita has written poetry all his life, much of which has been published, and has also written a number of essays reflecting on Western artistic inspirations such as William Blake's poetry and El Greco's painting.

This unapologetic devotion to the high arts has had a major impact on the practice of Triratna. Many of his disciples have been stimulated by Sangharakshita's influence to engage with the arts themselves, and indeed a number of artists, poets, and musicians are involved in the Order and see the arts as a core aspect of their Buddhist practice. For my own part, I first met Triratna as an undergraduate studying English Literature at Cambridge, and I can testify that the way in which appreciation of the arts was integrated into Triratna practice provided a major part of my initial attraction to the movement.

Sangharakshita's thinking about the relationship between the arts and spiritual practice is also distinctive. I have not come across any other Buddhist, or indeed religious, teacher with the same emphasis. Rather than rejecting the arts entirely, as some traditional Buddhists do, or seeing the arts as in some way an optional embellishment to Buddhist practice, he argues for a full integration of the arts with spiritual life. The core of his argument for this is contained in his book *The Religion of Art*.

One of the key arguments in that book is a parallel between the type of development that occurs in Buddhism and that in art (whether in its creation or its appreciation). That shared development consists of an expansion of awareness:

> *Expansion takes place in two planes, the vertical and the horizontal. By an upward or downward movement of expansion in consciousness is meant a heightening or deepening...of experience, an increase of insight, an augmentation of understanding; by a movement of expansion outwards is meant a constant multiplication of our points of contact with the external world, a ceaseless enlargement and elaboration of that delicate network of sympathy*

*and affection by which we are connected in a thousand ways not only with all human beings, but with every other form of life.*¹

This is obviously the process of integration as we have previously discussed it, linked to creativity, individuality, and provisionality. The 'enlargement and elaboration of that delicate network' is at root the enlargement of a neural network, increasing our potential ways of interpreting our experience so that we can respond in different ways, and synthesise our experience in increasingly powerful ways.

The relationship between this integration process and works of art is illuminated through Sangharakshita's analysis of a work of art as made up of 'substance' and 'form':

> *By the substance of a work of art we mean the degree of sensitiveness or sensibility, the state of consciousness, the kind of experience or realisation, which it expresses or communicates. Form, on the other hand, is the pleasurable pattern of sensations into which the rarified thoughts and emotions of the artist condense and crystallise themselves and through which they find embodiment and expression.*²

Sangharakshita's use of the term 'substance' here is odd, but he seems to be talking about the overall experience that inspires or motivates a work of art, and which then finds expression in the 'form'. He explains further:

> *These pleasurable patterns of sensations, which comprise the form of a work of art, are in turn arranged in such a way as to express the artist's feelings and sense of values, which make up what we have termed its substance.*³

He thus sees the arts as part of the practise of Buddhism because they are integrative. The arts have value because they enable integrated experience to be expressed and communicated through form – whether that 'form' is visual, musical, or verbal.

Sangharakshita here assumes a definition of art of a kind that he describes as 'normative', because his purpose is to communicate the spiritual value of art rather than to describe everything that people might see as art.⁴ That definition states:

---

1 Sangharakshita (1988a) pp. 30–1.
2 Ibid. p. 32.
3 Ibid. p. 33.
4 Seminar 129 p. 51.

> *Art is the organisation of sensuous impressions into pleasurable formal relations that express the artist's sensibility and communicate to his audience a sense of values that can transform their lives.*[5]

The sensuous impressions of the person experiencing the work of art (visually or aurally) have been organised by the artist through the form of their art, in a way that is pleasant in some senses, but also potentially challenging because it is transformational.

Sangharakshita's attitude to art may be seen by many as over-idealising, because he sees art in an intensively normative way as a spiritual practice, and in the process neglects a lot of what actually goes under the heading of 'art'. Much art, for instance, is simply produced to fulfil commercial requirements or social needs. Art can be 'applied' as well as 'fine', popular as well as classical, and thus more often than not unconcerned with the refinement of sensibility or the expression of more integrated states. Even the creation of art, for many people, may be undertaken with far less elevated motives in mind.

However, there seems no reason why Sangharakshita's account of the value of art cannot be extended to apply in some measure to all manifestations of art, as indeed to all areas of action. Even a commercial graphic designer following a client's specification, or the designer of ceramics produced in a factory, can apply their consciousness to the task so as to produce 'pleasurable formal relations', and in the process either take the opportunity to express helpful values, or fail to do so. Much depends on the level of awareness applied even to the most mundane tasks, so even sweeping a floor could be seen as 'art' if approached in a way that shapes and expresses awareness.

The wider application of Sangharakshita's approach to art could in my view be supported by looking more closely at its relationship with meaning. Art can have an integrative effect because it adds to our resources of meaning[6] – namely, the range of symbolic expressions we can appreciate and/or use to express and interpret our experience. Those symbols can be words, music, visual impressions, or objects – all that is important is that they have meaning for us. The more adequate our range of symbols, the better we are generally able to understand and respond both to the world and to our

---

5 Sangharakshita (1988a) pp. 84–5.
6 Ellis (2013b) 5.b.

inner experience, with greater flexibility and complexity. The idea that meaning is a resource is consistent with the recognition that it *also* (not only) consists of neural links in the brain and body: as these links increase in complexity, so do our meaning resources. 'Meaning' in this sense is not dependent either on beliefs about the world, nor upon communication with others, though both of these interact with meaning and depend on it. In the embodied meaning thesis of George Lakoff and Mark Johnson, it consists in association between active experience and basic categories and schemas found in that experience, laid down in early infancy and then increasingly elaborated through metaphor.[7]

If I develop with one stock of meaning, dependent on my experience and culture, and you have another, we may not understand each other if we do not sufficiently share similar meanings for the symbols we use, even when these are used to form sophisticated language. The barriers may be cognitive or emotive, but very likely both in varying proportions: I may simply not be able to make a neural connection to associate anything with your symbol that resembles what you associate with it, or I may not sufficiently care about it to give your symbol enough attention. Either way, a condition for social integration will be missing. In the same way, I may not even understand myself in a past time, when I favoured different symbols. The integration of meaning, as I prefer to call it, is dependent on the symbols that we use being compatible, and the chances of that happening are increased by having a greater range of symbols with which to express and interpret. This doesn't only consist in the 'learning' of symbols (though that is part of it), but also the development of new forms of compassionate awareness.

Thus, although art may not always be accompanied by an elevation of mental states, it will always at least have Sangharakshita's 'movement of expansion' and 'constant multiplication of our points of contact' in the sense that it provides us with more meaning. It will always be integrative, if not directly by uniting previously opposed energies, then at least indirectly, by providing us with better conditions for doing so. Not only the arts, but much education, learning languages, or simply talking to new people from different groups can also integrate meaning in this way. Of course, the most powerful works of art can also more directly integrate our beliefs by not

---

7   Ibid. 1.d and e; Johnson (2007).

only helping us appreciate other points of view but also inspiring us to change our beliefs into more adequate ones.

However, there is no denying that Sangharakshita himself is so taken up with the value of fine art that he gives little indication of the potential wider application of his ideas. His emphasis throughout is on the refined levels of consciousness and sensibility that can be applied to the most uplifting and inspiring art. However, not all creative actions are necessarily undertaken in highly refined states of mind, and it is the movement towards awareness from the point where we begin that is more universally significant to the integrative value of art.

Another issue with Sangharakshita's view of art concerns its relationship with morality. The claim that art in itself is valuable in a sense that is not merely personal or relative traditionally clashes with morality, because art and ethics do not necessarily accompany each other. Artists can behave in highly unethical ways even when they are producing highly refined art. A striking example of this is given in the film *Schindler's List*, where a Nazi officer pauses briefly in the midst of the mass slaughter of Jews in the Warsaw Ghetto, and sits down at a piano he has encountered to play a beautiful piece of Mozart. He then gets up and returns to his butchery. If we can credit both ethical and aesthetic development to integration, we have to admit that this integration can also be asymmetrical, sometimes in strikingly inconsistent ways.

Sangharakshita, however, insists that the true artist is 'egoless'. Those artists who seem immoral may not be true artists, he says, or their aesthetic integration may be less conscious than that of the developed Buddhist (which presumably implies it is inferior), or they may indeed have a 'finer morality' of their own, implying that we are mistaken about their immorality.[8] This is a quite transparent idealisation and results in a circular argument: a true artist is moral, so thus we must necessarily be mistaken when we think we find an immoral artist. Sangharakshita simply cannot face up to the evidence of experience that artists very often are immoral and refined at the same time. In order to square this circle, he does not have to cease to appreciate the integration that is potentially produced by their art, but he does have to appreciate its asymmetry and uncertainty.

8 Sangharakshita (1988a) pp. 100–1.

Practice

Sangharakshita's account of the value of art as a *practice* is nevertheless relatively clear, and compatible with ethics. We should train our emotions through the creation of works of art, and also stretch ourselves in the contemplation of the beauty of art:

> *The mind, even after being stretched by art beyond the limits of the rational, does not relapse into quite the degree of rigidity as it was habituated to formerly…. The impression produced by looking at a painting, listening to a symphony, or reading a poem, does not disappear…even when the memory of the delight they gave us has vanished, but remains a permanent part of our character modifying, in however slight a degree, the whole course of our life and conduct.*[9]

Here he makes it clear how art *can* have a positive influence on ethics, and his understanding of that process remains compelling, as long as he does not over-state the certainty of the results – for our whole life and conduct are also slightly modified by many other conditions apart from those of art.

The practice of creating art, or more commonly of appreciating it, has become part of the culture of Triratna under Sangharakshita's influence. It is primarily so, in my experience, in the sense that one expects to find aesthetically refined minds within Triratna, and friendships are often cultivated in which appreciation of the arts forms an important part. It is less often a habitual part of Triratna practice in classes or on retreats, but artistic creativity may be applied in the preparations for ritual, and there are some retreats devoted to the visual arts or to creative writing.

More broadly, artistic practice consists in a practical appreciation of the role of the imagination:

> *Imagination is a Pillar of the FWBO…. You should look for…imagination in the realm of myth, especially in the myth of the Order, the myth of the Movement; should look for it in archetypes and ideals. Should look for it in poetry, in the broadest sense of the term. More concretely, should look for it in ritual and ceremony; should look for it in meditation. Should look for it in the scriptures, especially in some of the great Mahayana sutras. Should look for it in the fine arts. Should look for it in all these places, and in many others.*[10]

The impact and justification of these words depends very much on whether we are merely being directed to places we might look for

---

9 Ibid. pp. 113–14.
10 Lecture 174.

imaginative inspiration, or to places where we necessarily expect to find it. Imaginative inspiration always offers us some helpful input if we interpret it on that level alone, as it adds to our resources of meaning. However, some of these places where we might go looking for imaginative inspiration are also subject to many other accompanying expectations, whether of a doctrinal or a social kind. A good example of this is ritual, which I turn to next.

3.g. Ritual

Sangharakshita has placed much emphasis on ritual as a way of working with the imagination and the emotions, and has challenged what he sees as a common but unnecessary Western disparagement of ritual. He rejects two extremes of response: either to regard ritual as an optional extra to a religion that is seen as essentially intellectual, or to regard ritual as necessarily primitive. In his view, ritual is a key part of religion, and it is usually only the most advanced practitioners who might be able to dispense with it.[1]

Sangharakshita quotes Erich Fromm's definition of ritual as 'shared action, expressive of common strivings, rooted in common values'. It involves the whole of us in practice in an embodied way.

> *Only too often in the West our approach to Buddhism is too one-sided. We pick and choose what we feel suits us, and the result is that part of us is simply never engaged in our practice. We may meditate and study, but if we miss out devotion and ritual, part of us is not involved. We need a Buddhist tradition in the West which provides not only for the head, not only for the heart, but even for the body and speech.*[2]

Ritual, he says, creates human solidarity around common striving. It involves effort, attention and mindfulness, and should be meaningful and aesthetically appealing.

> *Ritual is like acting out of symbol or myth. By expressing what is deep within our being, we externalise it, see it, make it something we can know.... Not only do we externalise and make conscious our deep spiritual feelings; we also strengthen and intensify them.*[3]

It is clear, then, that Sangharakshita sees ritual as an integrative practice. However, ritual is integrative primarily through finding 'emotional equivalents' as discussed already in 3.a. As in Sangharakshita's other applications of the idea of emotional equivalence, the assumption is that we have an 'intellectual' theory about our spiritual development that is separated from our 'emotional' energies. The emotional and imaginative aspects of Buddhist ritual are intended to correct the balance. However, this way of framing the matter is a simplistic reduction of the nature of the conflicts we

---

1 Sangharakshita (1995) pp. 25–6.
2 Ibid. p. 29.
3 Ibid. p. 32.

often encounter in spiritual practice, where there are always both 'intellectual' and 'emotional' aspects on both sides of any conflict. It is unlikely, then, that simply focusing on 'emotional' practices as such will necessarily help us with an integration process, unless the 'emotions' concerned are exactly the right ones (and accompanied by appropriate beliefs or ideas) so as to help us resolve our conflict.

Sangharakshita's account of ritual is thus a particularly poignant example of his tendency to idealise. Its defenders may well give accounts of ways that they have personally found communal rituals moving, and where they have indeed encountered the sense of communal solidarity in spiritual practice, aesthetic delight, full attention, and meaningfulness that Sangharakshita urges as the goal of ritual. In many years of doing *pujas* (devotional rituals) in Triratna, I also experienced these things on a few isolated occasions. However, the great contingency, indeed rarity, of those occasions should be an indication that Sangharakshita's theory of ritual is often not adequately realised in actual rituals in Triratna.

Generally these actual rituals consist in the Sevenfold Puja (which is adapted from a Mahayana text, the *Bodhicaryavatara*), the simpler Threefold Puja, or sometimes adapted pujas following a similar format to these but adapted from other Mahayana scriptures. The bulk of these rituals consist in call and response, with a leader reading out the words and the rest repeating them, but there is also chanting of mantras and of the refuges and precepts, and making of offerings.

The test of a helpful practice needs to be whether it generally helps us to move transformatively in an integrative direction, rather than whether it occasionally leads to enjoyable experiences when the conditions are propitious. In the case of devotional ritual as it was actually designed and supported by Sangharakshita in Triratna, there are a good many conditions working against it having a helpful transformative effect – none of which Sangharakshita seems to give much thought to.

The first and most basic of these conditions is the *group effect*. When a group of people that he or she wants to be part of starts to engage in a ritual, the individual will feel pressure to join in so as to conform to the group. All the group biases mentioned in 2.e may come into play here, but particularly groupthink. A communal ritual in Triratna is generally an organised group event with a set order and procedure, which removes any acceptable individual expression apart from (possibly) leaving the ritual. Far from cultivating individuality, it places the individual in a situation where they are forced to either conform to a fairly rigid group expectation, or risk what they may feel to be the group's potential displeasure. Though to some extent that may be the case in any group activity, it is far greater in a highly structured group ritual than in, for instance, a group discussion where individual ideas can be expressed.

The second of these conditions is *traditionality*. The forms of the pujas are prescribed by tradition: actually a combination of Triratna tradition and earlier Mahayana Buddhist tradition. That means that there is very little flexibility in the way the puja is conducted. Sangharakshita, indeed, discourages even modest modifications of the puja like including more music, because that might turn it into an individual 'performance' and prevent the puja being 'the act of the spiritual community as a whole'.[4] That traditional authority is in conflict with provisionality as discussed in 2.c. It discourages puja leaders from even considering much by way of changes, and makes it unlikely that the puja will be adapted very much to the emotional states or needs of the participants. In my past experience, many puja leaders in Triratna seem to think that a creative approach to the puja means different decorations on the shrine, or using a different scriptural liturgy (though in a similar format), or changing round the mantras. Occasionally, indeed, there are reports of more creative re-writing of pujas, and of new elements such as dance or soap bubbles being introduced. However, these are often superficial modifications of the traditional base, and the Sevenfold Puja remains the default, to be returned to in the most important rituals such as rites of passage. If the format and words of the puja itself are not adapted to help individuals engage with the particular emotional challenges that they need to engage with, it becomes far more likely to be an alienating experience, and less likely to be integrating.

The third of these conditions is the *Asian culture* of the puja. Although most of it is generally done in English (or the native language of the participants in non-English-speaking countries), the style of language, the symbols used, and the general approach to ritual is still that typical of Asian rather than Western culture. 'With mandarava, blue lotus, and jasmine…'[5] the puja begins, starting with two flowers that only grow in tropical and sub-tropical regions, and

4 Ibid. p. 48.
5 Dhammadinna & Suvajra (1999) p. 9.

that, due to the primacy effect that emphasises beginnings in our memories, will thereafter create a strong impression that the puja is alien to temperate zones. If the path is genuinely universal, there is no reason at all why it needs to prescribe such cultural specificity. The cultural strangeness of the puja for Westerners creates an immediate barrier, again making it far less likely to actually be emotionally or imaginatively engaging in the way that Sangharakshita idealistically envisages.

If we put together the group effect, the traditionality and the Asian culture, the result is a behemoth of an institution that seems to rumble on implacably from decade to decade, unreconsidered and unreconstructed. It is in direct conflict with many of the other values that have been so distinctive and helpful in Triratna. The influence of Sangharakshita's approach discourages creativity or provisionality in the way ritual is planned and executed, meaning that it is often in conflict with the development of individuality, and thus often not integrative in its effects. It is often certainly not expressive of the Middle Way, but rather of an absolute adherence to tradition. This is not because Sangharakshita was wrong about the potential value of ritual, which can indeed be very powerful, but because of a huge gap between his theory of ritual and his prescriptions for the institutional practice that is supposed to put it into operation.

In part that gap can be understood as one between linear and systemic ways of thinking. A ritual, if it is to be a genuine source of inspiration, needs to be respected as a living system: one formed of the relationships between (and within) the participants, and between them and their cultural and spiritual context. Living systems adapt themselves gradually to a set of conditions rather than being discontinuously engineered. One cannot design and manufacture meaningful ritual, nor can one import it in a discontinuous way without it losing its rootedness. In a context where most of the participants are not Asian, much more effort to develop new ritual forms rooted in the context is necessary. But instead, Sangharakshita has tended to proceed by prescription, being sure that he knew what was good for people so that they could develop: an inappropriately linear approach for the purposes that he believes ritual ought to have.

When questioned on this point, Sangharakshita said he was 'open to experimentation' in matters of ritual. I have had similar responses from other Order members on this point. The problem seems to be that what they consider 'experimentation' actually consists only of minor tinkering with the institution of puja, not with a genuine reconsideration of the ways that it operates so as to address the three major conditions listed above that undermine its effectiveness in fulfilling its function. Commonly, Order members respond that nobody is obliged to do puja, and some people get used to it after initial resistance. This tends to underestimate the actual psychological power of group pressure, which often operates at an unconscious level, and where theoretical ideas of voluntariness often mask the deeper operations of power. The fact that one can get used to an institutional feature and go along with it also does not make it effective.

If the aim of ritual is indeed to 'externalise and make conscious our deep spiritual feelings', then to be effective it needs to start with those feelings, not with unquestioned forms justified by implicit traditionality, groupishness, and Asian culture. I would argue that each ritual should be created from scratch by the participants, reflecting each time on what symbols would actually externalise their deep spiritual feelings. Ritual leaders should start not with a preconceived framework or liturgy, but at most with a menu of possible types of ritual activity that could be shared by the participants. Consultation is indispensable to any ritual that is going to be reliably, rather than accidentally, meaningful to all the participants. If what the participants want is to feel a connection with tradition because that is meaningful to them, they can then choose traditional forms of ritual; but there is a big difference between an imposed traditionality and a chosen one. If consultative ritual takes longer, that is still worthwhile, because it is potentially so much more meaningful.

Of course, the boundaries between 'ritual' and 'art' would then be much less clear, but that is very much in harmony with Sangharakshita's understanding of the role of imagination as a 'Pillar of the FWBO' (see 3.f). 'Imagination' is not a thing that can be generally prescribed as taking specific forms. Rather it consists in the exercise and expression of each individual's imagination. Where group ritual is created, this should be an expression of Sangharakshita's ideal of a group of individuals, working together on the basis of consensus and inspired by each other's creativity. A ritual of this kind is as relatively unknown beforehand as, say, a dramatic performance. An overall creative purpose takes shape in a dedicated place and time, with some planning and structure but also a good deal of contingency. In some cases the actors may choose to replay an old classic: but the very fact that they have chosen to do so invests it with a creativity and life that would have been wholly absent if it had merely been expected from the beginning that that is what they would do.

There are some areas of Triratna where such a creative approach to ritual is sometimes already found habitually – notably Buddhafield: a group organising camping retreats that are often open to a wide variety of people, including non-Buddhists and children. Here creative experimentation with forms of ritual has become the norm, in response to a variety of influences (particularly paganism and New Age) brought into contact with Buddhism, and an audience that is not limited to committed Buddhists. This very much illustrates the creative advantages of opening the doors, and shows what could be done. Yet Buddhafield is not a direct project of Sangharakshita, and owes much more to the creativity of others.

This brings me to the end of the section on practice. Throughout this section, whether I was discussing the Eightfold Path in general, meditation, ethics, friendship, institutions, the arts, or ritual, there has been a fairly clear pattern emerging. Sangharakshita has inspired people to do all of these practices by highlighting them and showing their role in the path. Yet he has proven very much weaker in applying the Middle Way so as to support people adequately in finding ways to pursue these practices. An idealisation does not make an adequate practical instruction, and too often his ways of articulating these practices have not enabled people to start where they are or really take the conditions into account. In theory he is in favour of a practical and balanced path, but in practice that is not always what is communicated or supported.

All of this helps to show more than anything why Sangharakshita's ideas are so important and potentially creative at the same time as having serious limitations. So in many ways this has been the most important section. However, to do justice to Sangharakshita's ideas it is also necessary to consider more deeply the ways that his approach is rooted in an interpretation of the Buddhist tradition. This will help to explain both his successes and his failures, and is the subject of the next section.

4. Interpreting Buddhist Tradition

4.a. Enlightenment and 'Reality'

I can now no longer avoid engaging with what Sangharakshita would regard as the intellectual starting points and underpinnings of his work in the key doctrines of the Buddhist tradition. These begin with his traditional Buddhist concern with nirvana as the goal of the Buddhist tradition.

Like virtually everything considered in this book, this area of Sangharakshita's work seems shot through with contradictory approaches. On the one hand there is a highly nuanced intellectual and practical approach to nirvana based on the Middle Way, and entirely compatible with the approaches I discussed in section 2. On the other, there is a sense of certainty that often seems to lead Sangharakshita into rhetorical excess, into a state where he is, at least momentarily, dogmatically convinced of an absolutist position. The principle of charity would lead me to interpret Sangharakshita's more basic position as the balanced, reflective, and practical one, but critical responsibility also requires that I try to raise awareness of the inconsistent and less justifiable aspects of Sangharakshita's philosophy.

The subtlety and balance with which Sangharakshita can approach enlightenment is perhaps best expressed in his lecture on 'Nirvana'. Here he begins by briefly outlining the conventional Buddhist approach to explaining nirvana that he is *not* going to take:

> One usually begins by discussing the etymology of the word Nirvana, whether it means a blowing out or whether it means a cooling down, and so on and so forth. And one usually goes on then to explain that Nirvana, at least according to the Pali texts, consists in the extinction of all lobha, or greed or craving or desire; all dvesa, anger or antagonism or hatred; and all moha, mental confusion or bewilderment. Nirvana is the extinction of all these three unwholesome roots.

> *Then one usually goes on to say that Nirvana is a state of supreme, of incomparable bliss, to which the bliss of this world cannot be compared. Also, if one wants to go into the subject a little in detail, one describes the two kinds of nirvana: the klesa nirvana, nirvana consisting in the extinction of all passions and defilements; and skandha nirvana, that is to say, nirvana as consisting in the extinction, or the waning, of the skandhas, the five aggregates or heaps of psychophysical existence, which takes place upon the death, as we call it, of the person who has already gained klesa nirvana during his lifetime.[1]*

This is an example of the rhetorical device of apophasis, in which a point is discussed in the process of pretending that you are not discussing it, and shows how these traditional conceptions of nirvana are actually still important for Sangharakshita. However, he then goes on to examine the role of nirvana in people's experience in a much more practically relevant way. First he remarks that 'A goal is something that we want to be', and that 'we can want to be only that which we are not', so that identification of nirvana as a goal unavoidably involves a projection of our current frustrations and our longing for a vague happiness beyond them.

> *The setting up of goals is really a substitute for awareness, for self-knowledge. As I said, if we find ourselves bad-tempered, we don't try to understand, to be aware of why we are bad-tempered, we simply, almost automatically, set up the goal of being good-tempered. If, taking the more general view, we feel unhappy, miserable, instead of trying to understand why very deeply, we automatically, almost instinctively, set up a goal of being happy in order to get away from the unhappiness and the misery. But it's all automatic – there's no real awareness, no real self-knowledge in it at all at all....*

> *One just latched onto Nirvana, labelled as the supreme bliss, because it happened to fit in with one's subjective needs and feelings at that particular time. But this is what is happening constantly. We try to use...Nirvana, in a quite unaware, unconscious, almost automatic way, for the solution...of problems which can only be resolved through awareness.[2]*

This way of understanding nirvana is very much an application of the Middle Way, showing Sangharakshita's acute awareness of the dangers of turning it into a mere concept that is then made part of an absolute belief. Awareness of the actual conditions in which we practise is then undermined by the idealisation of nirvana, the path being distorted by the conception of its goal.

---

1 Lecture 26.
2 Ibid.

Sangharakshita has also warned elsewhere of the dangers of putting too much emphasis on the idea of nirvana at the expense of the path when approaching Buddhism:

> We know the end to which we are going, that is to say Nirvana, as we should know as Buddhists, but we shouldn't take it for granted that it's all that evident to other people. So we should start rather with their problems and their difficulties, analyse them, going into them deeply, try to throw light on them, and eventually if the light does seem to be the light of Nirvana or perhaps the faint shadow or reflection of that, well so much the better – let us follow it up, but we shouldn't be in too much of a hurry to bring in ultimate things. Let them come in naturally, let them emerge.[3]

At times, including in conversation with me, Sangharakshita has also emphasised that he perceives enlightenment from one possible point of view as 'transcendental', and that this implies that it occurs outside time. In this respect he adopts the universal Mahayana view of enlightenment. Our perceptions of enlightenment from within time are thus highly likely to be distorted and the result of our limited awareness.

Sangharakshita discusses four kinds of accounts of nirvana: the negative, positive, paradoxical, and symbolic.[4] Negative descriptions, such as that of nirvana being signless, unconditioned, and empty, he sees as accurate but bloodless. Positive descriptions may present enlightenment in terms of ultimate freedom, knowledge, or positive emotion, or as the person of a Buddha. Paradoxical accounts place the negative and positive descriptions together, whereas symbolic ones use metaphor to evoke aspects of enlightenment.

What this account seems to neglect is that in terms of the negative description, all other descriptions of nirvana must be metaphorical or symbolic. If we don't have an experience of nirvana, and cannot even be reasonably sure if someone else has that experience, a term like 'nirvana' cannot be associated with an experience for us. It is thus a misleading absolutisation and a distraction from awareness (of the kind Sangharakshita has discussed) in every case, except the possible case in which we are experiencing it ourselves and thus experience directly what it means, or the case in which we are aware that we are talking symbolically.

3 Lecture 7.
4 Sangharakshita (1967) ch. 14.

It is perhaps Sangharakshita's Platonic assumptions about language that lead him to believe that there can be any non-metaphorical ways of talking about nirvana at all. In a framework of Platonic assumptions, our words gain their meaning from a hypothetical relationship with an essential reality that they describe. He thus assumes that we can distinguish between, for instance, discussing nirvana as knowledge (which Sangharakshita sees as a 'positive' description) and symbolising it as the Pure Land of Amitabha, because nirvana as knowledge can be taken to gain its meaning from a relationship to actual knowledge. In practice, however, there is no such knowledge in our experience on which to base such talk, but rather an analogy between everyday knowledge and that of nirvana, so that we only understand nirvanic knowledge as an extension of the kind of knowledge we believe we experience now. Even the 'knowledge' we think we have now, in its turn, can be seen as a metaphorical extension of the experience of seeing or of having ideas that we take to be essences,[5] which would even make samsaric 'knowledge' metaphorical in form, and 'nirvanic' knowledge thus a further extension of that metaphor.

If all positive ways of talking about nirvana are symbolic, then paradoxical ways of talking about it are also dependent on the contrast between symbolic and negative, which does not create a literal contradiction of any kind. Symbolic ways of talking about nirvana can also be understood as archetypal: in other words as gaining their meaning from our experience of basic and universal human needs and functions. We can have an experience of growth and development, and we can have a glimpse of a potential level of integration that is awe-inspiring because it is so much bigger than the more limited states we experience now: something like a vast plain before us momentarily illuminated by a flash of lightning. That seems to be a universal type of human experience, found not only in Buddhism but also in the context of other cultures and religions,[6] and is thus consistent with the universal Mahayana framework being used by Sangharakshita. He also uses the concept of archetypes himself, a discussion that I will return to later.

Sangharakshita's cautions about people's approach to nirvana can be understood as cautions about the dangers of projecting an

---

5   Lakoff & Johnson (1999) pp. 53–4 and 365–6.
6   See Ellis (2018) 2.b and c.

archetype: reducing something that is a potential within their experience to an object external to it. An archetype, however, can't be legitimately turned into a Platonic abstraction or a source of certainty in the way that Sangharakshita often seems to do. To see some of the inconsistency with which he treats it, then, we need to look at some of his contrasting uses of it.

For the most part, his accounts of the path seem to be conditioned by his early experience of 'utter certainty' when confronted with the paradoxes of the *Diamond Sutra* at the age of sixteen. That sense of certainty remains even when much modified by intellectual awareness of the limitations of human understanding. In this sense, his personal experience is much removed from that of a typical Westerner first approaching Buddhism, who will do so with great uncertainty. Rather than being primarily focused on the uncertain judgements that are the basis of the human condition, then, he tends to make frequent references to the 'transcendental' standpoint of 'Reality', which for him is justified by the theoretical relationship between the Middle Way and conditionality.

This key passage from the *Survey of Buddhism* simultaneously illustrates both the great strengths and the weaknesses of Sangharakshita's account of nirvana:

> *Reality being ineffable, positive and negative definitions are equally out of place. By following a Middle Path between affirmation and negation the Buddha's insight may, however, be formulated as the principle of universal conditionality,* **pratitya samutpada,** *or Conditioned Co-production. This doctrine is an all-inclusive Reality, or formulation of Reality, within which are included two trends or orders of things, one cyclic between opposites, the other progressive between factors which mutually complement and augment each other. The second trend is not merely the negative counterpart of the first, but possesses a positive character of its own. Upon this second trend the spiritual life is based. In relation to the first trend Nirvana may be described only negatively, in terms of cessation; from the viewpoint of the world it will inevitably appear as a purely transcendental and, as it were, 'static' state. In relation to the second trend, Nirvana may be described as the farthest discernible point of the increasingly positive and progressive series of reactions away from the Samsara; here it appears as 'dynamic' rather than static, the archetype of time rather than of space.*[7]

We have here references to two helpful aspects of Sangharakshita's approach that have already been discussed: the use of open and

---

7   Sangharakshita (1987a) p. 141.

closed feedback loops (mind creative and reactive), and the relationship between this and the Middle Way. The Middle Way is understood as leading us into open feedback loops that will help us to use our awareness to gradually refine and improve our responses to conditions. Within a closed feedback loop, however, we cannot yet understand the value of the new discoveries we have not yet made, and may either interpret them negatively or idealise them. With the experience of development characterised by open feedback loops, however, an open amount of progress seems possible, but its precise extent can't be judged because we haven't experienced it yet.

On the other hand, Sangharakshita apparently sees no contradiction in referring to the standpoint of nirvana as 'Reality' throughout. In doing this he turns the emergent experiential material of feedback loops, that can be experienced by anyone at any time, into an absolute metaphysical claim. 'Reality' is a static concept characteristic of the 'cyclic order of conditionality' rebounding between opposites, which take the form of beliefs about absolute truth and falsehood. Above all, if one claims to know about 'Reality' in the way he evidently claims to in his writing, one is taking insufficient account of the limitations of one's own standpoint as a human being. One is apparently completely ignoring the epistemological standpoint necessitated by finite human experience and assuming the ontological standpoint of God.

His favoured language in this regard betrays the early influence of idealist Western philosophers such as Hegel and Schopenhauer, both of whom he mentions as key influences in discussion. Both of these thinkers are concerned with overcoming human delusion, but nevertheless do so in a way that is shaped by strong assumptions about a final destination for human endeavour beyond those delusions. For them, there is a strong contrast between the deluded or 'mundane' human realm and the transcendental realm of enlightenment. This contrast between the 'mundane' and the 'transcendental', together with the tendency to treat the 'mundane' as inferior, and the belief that he personally has access to the 'true' 'transcendental' perspective, is frequently found in Sangharakshita's work. This especially features in some of the rhetorical excesses of the *Survey*:

> Others go so far as to maintain that the various expositions of the principle of pratitya samutpada found in Buddhist literature are 'contradictory'. Any absurdity rather than admit their own incomprehension! Such people genuinely think it more likely that the Buddha did not understand his own

Doctrine than that they should have failed to understand it. Profane impertinence could hardly go further than this.[8]

Although Sangharakshita wrote this for the first edition of the *Survey* in 1957, he also states clearly in his introduction to the sixth edition (dated 1984) that he sees no reason to revise it even in matters of detail.[9] It seems fair to conclude, then, that this approach was a fair expression at least of one stream of Sangharakshita's thinking. It does not merely reveal a personal weakness for getting carried away by rhetoric, but more importantly an epistemological incoherence. In appropriating the Buddha's position to his own Sangharakshita apparently completely fails to recall all the limitations of our knowledge of the Buddha that he freely acknowledges elsewhere:

Even if it is possible to isolate the most ancient texts, the problem of the relation of these to the oral tradition which preceded them and of this to the Buddha's own utterances remains insoluble. It is doubtful whether any known Buddhist text contains a line that preserves the Dharma in the same language or dialect in which it was originally expounded by the Buddha.[10]

At one and the same time, he is prepared to acknowledge that we cannot assume that we understand the Buddha's teachings correctly, but also to castigate those who find inconsistencies in the records of the Buddha's teachings – inconsistencies that, being noted, presumably could help us to construct a more sustainable and consistent account of those teachings. In addition to an obvious identification of his own position with that of the tradition and in turn to that of the Buddha, there is a clear appeal to authority here of a kind that we also often find in Sangharakshita's work. We are assumed to have a hotline to 'Reality' because of the mere association of a source with the Buddha.

If Sangharakshita had been influenced by a more balanced selection of Western philosophers in his youth, it seems likely that this would have been less of a problem. He shows a devotion to rationalistic philosophy (including a lifelong interest in Neo-Platonism), but no interest at all in the empiricist philosophy that has positively shaped the liberal, democratic, scientifically-influenced England

---

8 Ibid. p. 114.
9 Ibid. p. xii.
10 Sangharakshita (1967) p. 49.

he arrived at in the 1960s. Empiricist philosophy has many weaknesses,[11] but his approach is not to critically appraise it: rather it is generally to ignore it, together with the standpoint of ordinary human experience that it begins with.

However, if we are to take Sangharakshita's account of nirvana most charitably, his account of it as 'the farthest discernible point of the increasingly positive and progressive series of reactions away from Samsara' is well worth taking seriously. This offers a radical interpretation that is incompatible with the historical view of it as an event in time. The Buddha, if he was to reach a point that he called 'Nirvana', would presumably still be able to discern the possibility of further progress before him. It is also incompatible with Sangharakshita's view of faith (saddha) in Buddhism as 'the act…or state…of acknowledging unquestioningly that the man Gautama, or what appears as the man Gautama, is in possession of Full Enlightenment'.[12]

Sangharakshita would evidently like us to hold both these approaches in mind at the same time, not to 'take them literally', but to accept them as different aspects of the paradoxical nature of nirvana from our limited perspective. But if we are to judge by practical standards, the result of attempting to do this is simply inconsistency, together with an inexhaustible source of *ad hoc* argument against objections: if we adopt one of these views and conclude that it leads us to different conclusions from Sangharakshita's, the other can always be appealed to as convenient by those who wish to defend him.

We have already seen multiple examples of the implications of this inconsistency in Sangharakshita's approach to practice, in the form of incompatible appeals to the practical Middle Way on the one hand (in which nirvana recedes incrementally and is thus an archetype) and to tradition on the other (in which it is a historical event providing a revelatory source of knowledge). In the issue of 'vertical' friendship, for instance, the asymmetrical integration of the 'higher' friend tends to be discontinuously absolutised, just as nirvana is in traditional Buddhism. An archetype can be valued as such without being projected onto a specific individual or their achievements at a particular time. In the issue of ritual, too,

---

11 See Ellis (2012) 2.e.
12 Sangharakshita (1987a) p. 312. See 4.f below for more discussion of faith.

Sangharakshita's ideas of how ritual can help people with spiritual progression in a way that can be archetypally represented by enlightenment are insufficiently distinguished from actual ritual practice. That actual practice is mainly concerned with following a traditional norm that constantly appeals to the authority of the supposedly enlightened.

We will also see the same fault-line running through all the other aspects of Buddhist teaching interpreted by Sangharakshita that are discussed in the remainder of this section. Whatever the aspect of Buddhist teaching, his followers have found much of practical value in his interpretation of it, but at the same time that they are asked to hold in mind traditional absolutist views that contradict and undermine that practical value. For instance, these traditional absolutist views include the belief that spiritual practice depends on believing that the Buddha was enlightened, or the idea that Buddhists should make rebirth 'part of their mental furniture' (see 4.c). Perhaps, due to their personal confidence in him, disciples have tended to interpret these contradictory elements as part of a higher teaching that they have yet to understand – but they are probably better understood simply as the effects of Sangharakshita's own limitations. Specifically these limitations seem to involve a difficulty in applying his insights consistently and even-handedly across all areas of his thinking.

4.b. Conditionality

Sangharakshita gives constant emphasis to conditionality (*pratitya samutpada*) as the core insight of enlightenment, and is able to provide plenty of supporting material from the Pali Canon to maintain that emphasis:

> *This being, that becomes; from the arising of this, that arises; this not becoming, that does not become; from the ceasing of this, that ceases.*[1]

Every 'thing' we experience, including ourselves, is not independent, but dependent on other 'things' – so our deluded reliance on their substantiality, permanence, and satisfactoriness is what Buddhist practice requires us to cast off.

It is the centrality of conditionality that creates the context for Sangharakshita's account of mind reactive and creative (see 2.b) with its closed and open feedback loops. For him, reactive mind is in the 'cyclic order of conditionality' and creative mind in the 'creative order of conditionality'. The difference between them consists in a basic response to each new stimulus at each moment.

The moment of judgement that makes the difference between reactive and creative responses is traditionally analysed in terms of the twelve *nidanas* or links of cyclic conditionality visualised on the Wheel of Samsara. The key point in those twelve links is that between feeling (that is, experience of something pleasant, unpleasant, or neutral) and craving (our response of wanting more of the pleasant and avoiding the unpleasant).

> *Now, as these feelings arise, how do we react? To pleasant sensations we react most of the time with craving. We want them to continue, we don't want to lose them, so we try to cling on to them. Our natural tendency is to try to repeat pleasant experiences. This is the fatal mistake we are only too apt to make. We are not content to let the experience come and go; we want to perpetuate it, and so we react with craving. If, on the other hand, the sensation is unpleasant, painful, or at least unsatisfactory, we instinctively, even compulsively, try to thrust it away from us. We don't want it.*[2]

To be able to avoid that compulsion we need a wider awareness and a basis of contentment. That awareness involves recognising

---

1 *Majjhima Nikaya* 79.7: Ñanamoli & Bodhi (1995) p. 655. Quoted in Sangharakshita (1987a) p. 109.
2 Lecture 10.

experiences just as experiences, and avoiding the construction of further assumptions about them. To represent this, Sangharakshita quotes the teaching of the Buddha to Bahiya of the Bark Garment:

> *In the seen, only the seen. In the heard, only the heard. In the touched, only the touched. In the tasted, only the tasted. In the smelt, only the smelt. In the thought, only the thought.*[3]

Sangharakshita describes this as the 'sudden path', though there seems to be no reason why it should not be applied gradually. As an alternative approach that it seems could also complement this one, he also discusses the first two links of the positive nidanas – the spiral path to enlightenment that receives a distinctive emphasis in his teachings:

> *The first and second links leading up and away from the cyclical mode of action and reaction are duhkha, suffering or unsatisfactoriness, and sraddha, faith or confidence. In the twelve links of the Wheel of Life, suffering corresponds to feeling, the last link in the effect process of the present life, and faith corresponds to craving, the first link in the cause process of the present life. What this means is that when sensations and experiences impinge upon us we do not have to react with craving and thus perpetuate the cyclical movement of existence. We can react instead in a positive way. As we experience pleasant, unpleasant, and neutral feelings, we can begin to see, to feel, that none of them are really very satisfactory, not even the pleasant ones. Even they are not enough. Even if we could perpetuate pleasant experiences and eliminate painful ones, there would still be some hidden lack, something unsatisfied and frustrated. So…we begin to realize, that this whole conditioned existence – our life, our ordinary experience – is not enough. It cannot give us permanent, true satisfaction or happiness. If we analyse it deeply, in the long run it is unsatisfactory.*[4]

At one and the same time, this account of the way to avoid reactivity and seek creativity offers a vital practical strategy – the avoidance of craving through mindful awareness based in our embodied experience – but also presents that strategy as a way out of our 'whole conditioned existence'. That totalising view is far from necessary to the experiential insight telling us how to respond at each moment, but Sangharakshita, despite the practical emphasis of his teachings on mind reactive and creative, also chooses to take that totalising view from traditional Buddhism.

3   *Udana* 1.10: Ireland (1990) p. 20. Quoted in Lecture 10.
4   Lecture 10.

Sangharakshita's assumptions in relation to the Bahiya episode are probably related to those he makes about the possibility of dissatisfaction with our whole experience. In each case it's assumed that a complete alternative of some kind is possible, when a more realistic partial alternative would be sufficient to provide a context for practice. However, the teaching to Bahiya can be most helpfully interpreted as a call to avoid unnecessary *assumptions* about our experience, although it is also often taken to be asserting the possibility of pure experience free of all conceptions. Psychological research suggests that pure experience free of all conceptualisations or expectations is impossible, because our attention is limited, and the very direction of our attention is framed by expectations.[5] Even in meditation that attains the deepest samadhi, there is still a subtle direction of our thoughts in accordance with our overall objectives. However, there are also substantial avoidable biases in our experience that provide an experiential basis for the belief that we can *limit* our prior expectations. We can be open to alternatives to the frames we have been using. In the same way, we cannot avoid conditioning *in general*, but there are specific conditions that we can avoid through mindful responses to pleasant or painful stimuli. To be an organism is to be conditioned, but not necessarily to be *reactively* conditioned in every case.

The totalising view adopted by Sangharakshita as an interpretation of traditional Buddhism involves a contrast between the 'compounded' and the 'uncompounded' (*asankhata* – also translated variously as 'unconditioned', 'unfabricated' and 'not-formed'). This can be derived from a famous verse found in the *Udana* and *Itivuttaka*:

> *There is, monks, an unborn, an unbecome, an unmade, and uncompounded; if, monks, there were not here this unborn, unbecome, unmade, uncompounded, there would not here be an escape from the born, the become, the made, the compounded.*[6]

Sangharakshita's interpretation of this passage is that it

> *...constitutes the very basis of the possibility of emancipation from phenomenal existence...being the very goal of the religious life.*[7]

---

5   Chabris & Simons (2011).
6   *Udana* 1.3, quoted in Sangharakshita (1987a) p. 88 from Thomas's 1935 translation.
7   Ibid. p. 88.

The value of disentangling some kinds of conditioning, it seems, has to be certified by the possibility of exiting phenomenal existence entirely. Stephen Batchelor, on the other hand, points out that the 'unconditioned' or 'uncompounded' has been quite unnecessarily reified as well as totalised.

> Gotama takes a noun, 'the unconditioned', and treats it as a verb: 'not to be conditioned' by something. He seems acutely aware of the relational nature of language. There is no such thing, for example, as freedom per se. There is only freedom from constraints, or freedom to act in ways that were not possible because of those constraints. Nor is there any awakening per se, but only awakening from the 'sleep' of delusion, or awakening to the presence of others who suffer. And there is no such thing as the unconditioned, only the possibility of not being conditioned by something.[8]

The avoidance of conditioning *by something* is the path that Sangharakshita points out in his treatment of mind reactive and creative. That specific way of avoiding conditioning operates at each moment for each person, and thus has a universality that is not available to those who insist that the motivation for following the path has to be a final and discontinuous goal that is *totally* unconditioned by craving, hatred, and delusion. Whilst he has provided access to the *process* of 'unconditioning' for many, his continuing attachment to an absolute formulation of the goal also undermines and distracts from that process by providing new and unnecessary belief-attachments for Buddhists.

This belief in total unconditioning also supports his account of stream entry, which I have previously mentioned as a source of his idealisation in relation to such issues as individuality and 'vertical' friendship. Stream entry is believed to be the point of spiritual development after which it is impossible to fall back. Sangharakshita represents this as the point at which one can 'see' Reality.

> Knowledge and vision of things as they really are arises when, in the state of samadhi, we get our first glimpse of Reality itself, free from all veils and obscurations. It's like the moment when you get up to the top of a high mountain and the clouds roll aside to reveal the vast expanse of the horizon. Samadhi represents getting to the peak, the vantage point from which you can see Reality itself.[9]

---

8   Batchelor (2015) pp. 144–5.
9   Lecture 10.

He also explains the irrevocability of stream entry in terms of a metaphor of gravitation:

> ...we may say that one's progress is rather like that of a space probe launched from the Earth. After a certain distance – so many thousand miles – it is no longer so affected by the Earth's field of gravity and begins to be influenced instead by the gravitational pull of the Moon, Mars, or whichever body it is heading for. So at a certain point the gravitational pull of the Wheel of Life ceases to have an influence, and one begins to feel more and more powerfully and decisively the gravitational pull of the Unconditioned, of nirvana. This is the moment of conversion within Buddhist practice, the beginning of the transformation from a conditioned to an Unconditioned mode of being. According to Buddhist tradition, if we reach up this far, if we undergo conversion in this sense, we are assured of Enlightenment within no more than seven further rebirths in the wheel of conditioned existence.[10]

Both of these metaphors reify something that is encountered in experience as a process in lots of individual cases, turning it into a single thing that transforms one's whole view of everything. This seems to stem, in turn, from treating 'the unconditioned' as a distinct thing. But insight, as an experience relevant to human life, does not work like this. Not only have we no way of ascertaining whether anyone ever goes through such a totalising change as this (making it irrelevant to all practical judgements), but the emphasis Sangharakshita puts on it tends to distract from the way people do commonly experience it – namely as an avoidance of conditioning *by something*.

We have insights into our lack of a fixed identity that we thought we had – not a lack of identity in general. We can come to recognise that some specific relationship or possession whose permanence we unconsciously assumed is impermanent – not impermanence in general. Over time, we may build our experiences of insight together into a general appreciation of insubstantiality or impermanence. But we don't suddenly see the 'Reality' of insubstantiality or impermanence or even enter its orbit. Our integration remains asymmetrical and unpredictable. If we remember our humanity, rather than being swept away by implicitly metaphysical rhetoric, we will maintain awareness of those limitations in our understanding, and avoid claims to have seen 'Reality' regardless of how extraordinary our spiritual experiences may seem.

10 Ibid.

One crucial theoretical understanding that can help to underpin this point is that of embodied meaning theory. If we recognise that meaning arises in our experience from an associative relationship between words or symbols and *our bodies*, and that the basic meaning we get from those associations is then elaborated by metaphor, it becomes clear that taking metaphorical structures 'literally' and assuming that they represent 'reality' must be mistaken. Over-literalness is something that Sangharakshita constantly warns us against, but this perspective has evidently not extended to recognising general talk of 'conditionality' and 'the unconditioned' as a metaphorical extension of the more basic experience of being impacted upon by specific conditions. The most basic experience that we metaphorically extend to concepts of causality or conditionality seems to be that of force,[11] as Sangharakshita's gravity metaphor suggests. But the forces we actually experience are not those of 'the unconditioned' drawing us towards it. Rather we experience the *absence* of craving or hatred that previously 'pushed' us into particular judgements.

Another theoretical perspective that can illuminate this point is that of systems theory. As individuals, we are part of a complex psychological system that in turn is embedded in organic, social, ecological and other systems. The 'forces' of samsara are disruptions creating conflict in that system, and inducing closed feedback loops when it is open feedback loops allowing new information that are required to help us to adapt to our environment. However, Sangharakshita tends to confine these relational systems to a linear narrative in which we make progress along a single path and pass certain fixed waymarks. Though individuals may often need to think in this way, it can hardly provide an adequate total model for the spiritual life. It takes into account neither the inter-relationships of a complex system, nor the uncertainty that arises from that complexity. Instead, it assumes an implicit God's-eye view of spiritual development even whilst formally denying it.

---

11 Lakoff & Johnson (1999) pp. 184 ff.

4.c. Karma and Rebirth

Sangharakshita's continuing reliance on a 'top-down' model of spiritual progress, uncritically adopted from the Buddhist tradition, is also evident in his attitude to karma and rebirth. Karma can be seen as the moral dimension of conditionality, consisting of beliefs about the kinds of effects that result from either reactive or creative responses to feeling at the point of intersection between feeling and craving.[1] As with conditionality, we can interpret karma in 'top-down' terms as a universal and absolute causal law, or we can approach it from the 'bottom-up' in ways that concentrate on the probable causal relationships between specific creative responses and beneficial effects from those responses (or specific reactive responses followed by negative effects). Sangharakshita's approach to this, as often, is inconsistent and ambiguous.

Sangharakshita's account of karma does challenge the more established traditional Buddhist one in several respects, particularly by making use of the teaching of the five *niyamas* or levels of conditionality. He challenges the retrospective view of karma that enables current states to be necessarily blamed on past actions, and at least superficially challenges the assumption that karma is an 'iron law'.

The teaching of the five niyamas is presented by Sangharakshita as a traditional Buddhist categorisation of different levels of conditionality: inorganic, organic, psychological, karmic, and dharmic. These are taken to provide evidence that Buddhist tradition is compatible with the scientific explanation of physical processes as operating independently from human judgement and its effects.[2] Thus, contrary to a popular Buddhist account of karma still found widely both in the Theravada and in Tibetan Buddhism, everything that happens is not due to it. Planets proceed in their orbits (the inorganic level), vegetation grows (the organic level), and illness affects the mind (psychological level) – all independently of karma.

---

1 There is a potential further argument that could be entered into here as to whether the gap between feeling and craving is always the point at which creative responses may arise. I discuss this in Ellis (2019) 6.a, but here I have decided not to explore it, so as to avoid introducing a new element of complexity that might distract from the central practical issues.

2 Sangharakshita (1967) p. 69; (1994) pp. 105-7.

Dhivan Thomas Jones, however, traces this interpretation of the niyamas to the early translator of Pali texts, Mrs Rhys Davids, who misinterpreted the sources of it found in Pali commentaries and in the *Abhidhamma*. Although, for both Rhys Davids and Sangharakshita, this analysis is used to try to prove that Buddhism is compatible with scientific explanation, in textual terms it does not do so. According to Jones, the niyamas in their original contexts referred to five different types of natural regularity (cyclical, repetitive, inevitable, sequential, and uniform) rather than five different orders of conditionality.[3] Nevertheless, at points in the Pali Canon the Buddha is depicted as pointing out that not all phenomena are necessarily due to karma,[4] and it can also be argued that (however much he may prefer it) Sangharakshita does not need this sanction of Buddhist tradition, but only obvious observation, to argue that the revolution of the planets or the growth of an oak tree are not results of human action. Sangharakshita's interpretation of the fifth or 'dharma' niyama as equivalent to the spiral type of conditionality is also evidently a misreading of the traditional Buddhist sources, but similarly only needs the justification of spiritual progress in experience.

Initially, too, Sangharakshita is keen to avoid the interpretation of karma as any kind of 'reward' or 'punishment':

> *Our unskilful mental states are those dominated by craving..., by aversion..., and by ignorance. We are not punished for them – they simply make us miserable, inasmuch as unskilful states of mind involve a contraction of our being and consciousness which we experience as misery. Skilful mental states, by contrast are characterised by contentment, love, understanding, and clarity of mind. And again, there are no prizes handed out to reward us for these. Skilful actions...result by themselves in a sense of expanded being and consciousness which we experience as happiness. In a sense, skilful action is happiness.*[5]

This seems clear enough, but it implies, indeed, that good judgement is its own reward and bad judgement is its own punishment, without any need for a causal or conditioning process at all. So why associate this with the doctrine of karma?

---

3   Jones (2012).
4   E.g. *Samyutta Nikaya* 36.21: Bodhi (2000) pp. 1278–9.
5   Sangharakshita (1994) p. 108.

Sangharakshita also argues that karma is not an 'iron law':

> According to Buddhism, some karmas, whether skilful or unskilful, are just cancelled out in the course of time. They may be counterbalanced by opposite karmas, or simply lose their force. Lacking an opportunity for expression, they may just fade away. So there is no 'iron law' of karma: some karmas do not produce any effect at all.[6]

This, however, is in direct contradiction to Sangharakshita's account of what he elsewhere describes as 'the most important ethical findings of Buddhism':

> A man will reap the consequences, not only of what he has intentionally said and done, but also of what he has deliberately thought, or allowed himself to think.... A mind-volition of the degree of intensity that normally results in word or deed or both will, even if denied overt vocal or bodily expression, undoubtedly bring about the same pleasant or painful experiences that the actual performance of the deed would have done.[7]

This much more closely fits the standard Buddhist view of karma, which, even if it cannot be used retrospectively, requires a moral equivalence working forwards in time. What we do now, whether mentally or physically, will have, not just some possible effects, but *morally equivalent* effects in future. If Sangharakshita was effectively saying in his 'not an iron law' comment that there is such a 'natural law' operating, but then that it didn't always operate, he would no longer be advocating a natural law: he has effectively falsified it by allowing for even a single exception. However, when asked about this, Sangharakshita said that the reason some karmas 'just fade away' is because they were too weak to make any difference in the first place. Thus he seems to remain dogmatically certain about the reality of morally equivalent effects above the level where they will become significant.

What seems likely is that Sangharakshita, as on other occasions, finds his breadth of experience contradicting the limitations of assumption in Buddhist doctrine. The insights on which the doctrines are based, which are 'bottom-up', are expressed by the tradition in a 'top-down' form that can't be justified. However, despite his willingness to reinterpret Buddhist doctrine in some respects, such is his rootedness in Buddhist tradition that he is unwilling to

---

6   Ibid. p. 113.
7   Sangharakshita (1967) p. 7a.

fundamentally question it in others. Instead of thinking through the implications of aspects of Buddhist theory being wrong, he hangs onto it and insists inconsistently that it is essentially right. In the case of karma, Sangharakshita accounts for discrepancies between theory and experience only by reference to the complexity of karmic operation (a point that became clear in discussion as well as in his writings). No such discrepancies will ever allow him to question his belief that karma does operate as a necessary top-down moral equivalence of effects, or to compare it to alternative forms of theory that might explain the same phenomena better.

Sangharakshita's account above of the ways in which skilful and unskilful judgement are their own reward through the expansion or contraction of experience that accompanies them, does provide one kind of 'bottom-up' basis for karma at one time (rather than causally extended over time). The effects of neural entrenchment in the brain also provide a basic piece of scientific evidence for the *general tendency* of past actions to dictate the conditions of future ones. William James, writing more than a century ago, expresses this memorably:

> *We are spinning our own fates, good or evil, and never to be undone. Every smallest stroke of virtue or vice leaves its never so little scar.... Down among his nerve-cells and fibres the molecules are counting it, registering and storing it up to be used against him when the next temptation comes. Nothing we ever do is, in strict scientific literalness, wiped out. Of course this has its good side as well as its bad one. As we become permanent drunkards by so many separate drinks, so we become saints in the moral, and authorities and experts in the practical and scientific spheres, by so many separate acts and hours of work.*[8]

This insight has important moral implications, in the general sense that we need to beware the habits we slip into because of their long-term effects on our whole way of thinking. However, these 'bottom-up' versions of karma make no specific claims either about the inevitable effects of particular judgements, or about the moral equivalence of those effects with the judgements that created them.

Not only does Sangharakshita's view of karma appear to be 'top-down' as described in the *Three Jewels*, but many of his other approaches are inconsistent with anything else. His belief in stream entry, for instance, requires a definite point where new karmic

---

8 James (1905) vol.1, p. 127.

effects cease to be created so as to allow the practitioner to then cruise effortlessly towards enlightenment. As I have already mentioned, this takes no account of asymmetry of integration or of uncertainty. It also takes no account of the ways in which our spiritual development may not produce necessary and predictable results of the kind envisaged by the theory of karma.

Sangharakshita's approach to unresolved questions about karma and rebirth is to assume that the traditional framework of explanation is correct, but also to say that it needs 'a thorough reformulation'. He expects that scientific investigation will 'eventually convince all open-minded people of the truth of karma and rebirth'.[9] This puts him in the position, scientifically, of the last few scientists hanging onto a discredited paradigm, desperately clinging to 'evidence' that supports that paradigm and unable to look seriously at alternative explanations of the same evidence. Putting the theory first and then looking for 'evidence' that one is already convinced must fit it is the basis of the top-down approach, and it leads to *ad hoc* theorising and dogmatic thinking. This is entirely in conflict with the spirit of provisionality that I discussed in 2.c, where spiritual development is understood as demanding the capacity to consider alternatives to current assumptions. If there are massive holes in the theory, at the very least you need to weigh it up against possible alternatives that could account both for the strengths of the original theory and the holes.

Sangharakshita's approach to rebirth also shows this continuing top-down approach. The weight of evidence on rebirth is very clear. The overwhelming bulk of human experience is that habitual judgements of any kind are associated with specific brains in specific bodies. We have no way of explaining how a set of neural habits could transfer itself into a new body that does not yet have any neural habits. Against this, we can set a few unexplained phenomena such as certain experiences under regressive hypnosis, child prodigies or child memories, nearly all of which bear possible alternative explanations – but which at worst could be simply recognised as unexplained. It is the height of a top-down approach loaded with confirmation bias to assume that these unexplained phenomena offer 'evidence' for rebirth sufficient to outweigh everything on the other side of the scale.

9 Sangharakshita (1994) p. 118.

Sangharakshita, however, appears to at least be confident that this 'evidence' will eventually show rebirth to be true, even if he admits its weakness for the moment.[10] He also maintains the traditional reason for *wanting* to believe in rebirth, which is that it allows karma to operate consistently over lives.

Sangharakshita goes on:

> *Do you have to believe in karma and rebirth to be a Buddhist? ... No, but on one condition. You need not believe in karma and rebirth provided that you are willing to go all out for enlightenment in this life.... The teaching of karma and rebirth does provide an answer – perhaps the answer – to certain questions. It helps to solve the mystery of death, which is also the mystery of life – and very few people can follow the path to enlightenment without bothering, at least sometimes, about such questions. A few may be happy to get on with their meditation and not worry about philosophy, but most people require some answers.*[11]

The rhetorical deceptions here are multiple. He reinforces a certain framework of assumptions by asking a rhetorical question and answering it solely within that framework of assumptions – often an effective way to make people feel that they have gone through a critical process when in fact they haven't considered any alternatives to that framework at all. In this case, also, the reasoning is thoroughly circular. There is only potentially any alternative to spiritual progress in this life if you believe in rebirth to begin with, so if the question is a genuine one in the first place its answer has already been assumed. 'Going all out for enlightenment in this life' is only potentially even relevant if you have an absolutised view of enlightenment as a specific point in time – which Sangharakshita himself has questioned. There is also a conflation of the idea of asking questions about the meaning of life and death with the acceptance of a particular set of answers.

I asked Sangharakshita, in discussion, how he reconciled a view of nirvana as not necessarily a single point in time with the need to 'go all out for enlightenment in this life' in the absence of belief in rebirth. He said that he thought that even if we give up the idea of individual attainment in enlightenment in order to achieve it, we still have to proceed 'as if' we were making individual attainments – against a background of karma and rebirth that would calibrate

10 Ibid.
11 Ibid. p. 119.

those attainments. He also said that different people 'need different degrees of detail', so that some might need to believe in rebirth, and others not. So he was at least accepting a pragmatic frame for the question of whether we should believe in rebirth here – but not for the wider questions of whether belief in rebirth is either justified or helpful.

I find Sangharakshita's attitude to karma and rebirth ironic, because he has already also provided so many experiential ways forward. It is hard not to think that at some level he remains aware that all of this material could simply be dispensed with. We are not going to make spiritual progress by adopting top-down linear beliefs in any case, but rather by building up appropriate, meaningful, and justifiable general beliefs in relation to our experience. Everything Sangharakshita has said about provisionality, individuality, and integration suggests this. Yet when it comes to issues like this he apparently still wants us to abandon our individual judgement in favour of traditional authority. Here is how Sangharakshita himself puts this at one point in the *Survey* – if only he could follow his own injunctions!

> *Living as he already does in the midst of phenomena that are ultimately wrong mental constructions, the true disciple does not set up fresh barriers by seeking to elicit from them by means of a process of progressive abstraction a concept which, merely because it possesses the highest possible degree of generality, he regards as being ultimately real, nor does he tighten his bonds by endeavouring to 'realize' or to attain union with that concept.*[12]

---

12 Sangharakshita (1987a) p. 108.

4.d. The Buddha

Throughout Sangharakshita's teachings, the theme of the Buddha regularly emerges and provides a unifying focus. From his view that enlightenment is outside time, one might expect a lack of emphasis on the historical Buddha and more emphasis on the symbolic Buddhas of the Mahayana. But, instead, Sangharakshita sees the historical Buddha as the lynchpin around which a wider synthetic understanding of Buddhism can be reached. Where the Theravada focuses on a historical revelation and the Mahayana turns this into a universal principle, Sangharakshita is determined to have both. He does this by emphasising the universality of Pali Canon teachings from the historical Buddha, which do not necessarily have to be interpreted as the Theravada has traditionally done, and also bringing the fantastic Mahayana sutras (featuring a symbolic Buddha Shakyamuni) down to earth through a careful process of interpretation.

The reconciliation seems to lie, once more, in his ideas about enlightenment being both in time and timeless when viewed from different points of view:

> *Enlightenment – the Buddha's or anybody else's – represents 'the intersection of the timeless moment'.... It's rather like...the flowing of a river into the ocean, where the river is time and the ocean is eternity.... Suppose we imagine that the ocean into which our river is flowing is just over the horizon. From where we are, we can see the river flowing to the horizon, but we can't see the ocean into which the river is flowing, so it seems as though the river is flowing into nothingness.*[1]

The only problem with such images is that they presuppose a God's-eye view in which we *can* actually see the ocean as well as the river. If we really can't see the ocean, we don't know *whether or not* the river is flowing into an ocean. However, if we ask what sorts of experiences relate to the timelessness or the ocean, they are ones that involve glimpses of unrealised greater potential. It is this that can be helpfully symbolised by the Buddha as archetype: what the Buddha effectively *means* in terms of embodied experience. Sangharakshita argues both that the historical Buddha can represent that archetype, and that the symbolic Mahayana Buddha can inspire us with glimpses of what seems like the ocean.

1 Sangharakshita (1994) p. 151.

Sangharakshita's discussion of the symbolism of the life of the Buddha[2] is amongst his most distinctive and important. In the past I have given it to seventeen-year-old Religious Studies students to read, and they have sometimes come back with their assumptions about religion transformed as a result. He is determined to challenge the all-too-common literalistic and dualistic treatment of religion in general as necessarily lacking relevance because lacking empirical 'truth'.

> *Consciousness is just like a light froth playing and sparkling on the surface, whilst the unconscious is like the vast ocean depths,* dark and unfathomed, lying far beneath. *In order to appeal to the whole person, it isn't enough just to appeal to the conscious, rational intelligence that floats upon the surface. We have to appeal to something more, and this means we have to speak an entirely different language from the language of concepts, of abstract thought; we have to speak the language of images, of concrete form.*[3]

Sangharakshita then interprets a whole set of images found in the Pali Canon as well as Mahayana scriptures. The bizarre 'twin miracle' in which the Buddha is depicted as emitting fire from his top half and water from his bottom half (then the reverse) is explained in terms of the universal symbolism of fire and water for conscious and unconscious, masculine and feminine, etc. The Buddha's staircase to the heavens (resembling Jacob's Ladder) is shown as symbolically uniting the opposites of heaven and earth. The tree beneath which the Buddha gained enlightenment is likened to the World Tree found in many other mythologies. Incidents from the time of the Buddha's enlightenment are also explained in archetypal terms: the attack of Mara, the evil one, representing the resistance to enlightenment found in the unconscious. The Earth Goddess who is called upon to bear witness to the Buddha's enlightenment is understood as symbolising the helpful earthy energies in the Buddha's (or our) own experience. Mucalinda, the serpent king who shelters the Buddha from the rain, represents the energies of wisdom from the unconscious.[4]

In conversation on these matters, Sangharakshita said that he had not read Jung very extensively, but that many of his ideas about integration as well as archetypes had arisen in his own experience.

---

2 Sangharakshita (1990c) pp. 33 ff.
3 Ibid. p. 33.
4 Ibid. pp. 35–42.

This would help to explain the ways in which he has customised Jungian ideas in what seem to be helpful ways. Chief amongst these is his focus on the four principal archetypes: Hero, Anima/Animus, Shadow, and Wise Old Man/Great Mother (which in Jungian terms is also Self or God). These are the focus in the opening section of Jung's book *Aion*,[5] but are not emphasised much elsewhere in his works. They may well have been adopted instead from an introduction to Jung's psychology written by Frieda Fordham, who does present them in this way.[6] I have made considerable use of this way of presenting and understanding the archetypes myself in other writings,[7] because it seems to offer a key to the differing underlying ways that they function, beyond the mere categorisation of different forms of appearance.

Archetypes are, after all, most basically universal human functions gaining a variety of expressions in different cultural contexts, so that the Hero can be understood as representing the ego function, the Self an integrated psyche, and the Shadow and Anima/Animus the respective energies of fear and desire that can either support or disrupt the integration of the psyche. If we project any of these archetypes, assuming that they lie beyond us, we thereby subject ourselves to delusions that hinder us on the path, but if we recognise them as aspects of our wider potential selves then we can engage with them positively.

Sangharakshita makes these points only in conjunction with a comparison with Christianity that I find simplistic. He unnecessarily essentialises 'Christianity' (a complex tradition) by identifying it with a projected interpretation of archetypes that could be found in the context of any tradition, including Buddhism. However, the more important point here is that he distinguishes projected archetypes from integrated ones.

> In Buddhism these archetypes, these forms, these figures are regarded...as projections, as really alienated parts and fragments of ourselves, so that we can reclaim what is our own property, and integrate them all into our conscious mind.... So in as much as in Christianity these archetypes are regarded not as archetypes but as objectively existent beings, therefore the possibility of their full integration, and therefore the possibility of the individuation process taking place, therefore the possibility of gaining full Enlightenment

5   Jung (1959).
6   Fordham (1953) ch. 3.
7   Ellis (2013b) ch. 4.

> *doesn't occur, these archetypes are left unresolved out there, and the process of integration is not completed. In other words there's no Buddha. You see in the Buddhist myth you've got Mara, the earth goddess, Brahma, and Mucalinda, and you've also got the Buddha, the integrated consciousness which emerges out of the resolution of these archetypes.*[8]

Sangharakshita points out the key symbolic role of these archetypes in the life of the Buddha: Brahma as the Wise Old Man (Self or God archetype), the Earth Goddess as the Anima, Mara as the Shadow, and Mucalinda as the Hero (though the Buddha himself is also the Hero – and the Self). He also parallels these forms to God the Father, the Virgin Mary, Satan, and Christ respectively.[9] Whatever view one may have of these specific symbolic interpretations, the more important point is that he is productively applying Jungian thinking to the interpretation of the myths of the Buddhist tradition, and interpreting it in a way that reveals the spiritual or integrative value of those myths without any requirement for historical-revelatory claims to be made.

This archetypal account is one that can apply just as much to the many symbolic forms of the Buddha found in the Mahayana. That would include the symbolic Buddha preaching in a fantastic world such as we find, for instance, in the *White Lotus Sutra*. It would include the five symbolic coloured Buddhas of the Five Buddha Mandala, each of which represents aspects of enlightenment, just as white light is broken up into a spectrum. It would also include the various bodhisattva figures found in the Mahayana. All of these are, in a sense, elaborations of the archetypal meaning of the Buddha, and Sangharakshita explores them in depth in a whole series of lectures on texts such as the *White Lotus Sutra, The Sutra of Golden Light,* and the *Vimalakirti-Nirdesha*.

The richness of the world that Sangharakshita has thus opened out for many people is breathtaking: another aspect of 'imagination' as a 'Pillar of the FWBO' (see 3.f). For much of his audience, after all, these Mahayana texts were not only culturally alien but incomprehensibly obtuse in their symbolic outlook. Sangharakshita constantly urges them to treat them as they would poetry. For those in the Order, the symbolic power of Buddhas and bodhisattvas also interacts constantly with their use in meditational visualisation. This use of the Buddha as a source of archetypal inspiration has formed

8   Lecture 37.
9   Sangharakshita (1990c) pp. 43–4.

an important part of the cultural stimulus of the Triratna Order, resulting, for instance, in the Western Buddha images of the sculptor Chintamani, and the new creative development of the tradition of Buddhist iconographic painting by a number of Order members, of whom the best-known is probably Aloka.

The critical questions that can be asked about archetypes in general are often based on misunderstandings of their functional role. Doubts about their status become irrelevant when an archetype is experienced as meaning, prior to any beliefs about what archetypes 'really are'. On the one hand are those who insist on seeing them in terms of supernatural 'belief', and on the other those who require them to be based on a scientific account of their cross-cultural genetic (or epigenetic) basis. In both cases there can be no certainty, and the quest for such certainty is a distraction from their functional role. Sangharakshita did not even attempt to define the meaning of 'archetype' too closely,[10] but for the most part appeared to simply recognise the archetype as the best available formulation to describe a pattern of meaningful experiences shared both by traditional Buddhists and Westerners. By using the concept of archetype, he potentially freed the Buddha-figure from the tyranny of religious 'belief', whether in the Asian or Western context.

It is also an appropriate expression of the Middle Way, together with the distinctive aspects of Sangharakshita's presentation of Buddhism in the West discussed in section 2 – creativity, integration, individuality, and provisional belief. Absolutised views of the Buddha as ultimately 'Real' or ultimately 'material' are equally incompatible with the path of developing practical awareness. Within the terms of that path, the Buddha needs to be understood as part of *our* system rather than something linear and separate from it: but nevertheless an element of that system that challenges and inspires from beyond the current identifications of the ego. In this way the Buddha is an embodiment of creativity.

The story of the historical Buddha's own development can also offer a symbolic model for integration and the development of individuality through the exercise of provisionality as well as commitment to the path. Sangharakshita comments on the way that the Four Sights, which bring an awareness of suffering into Gautama's life, are the basis of a move from reactive to creative thinking.[11] He

10 Ibid. pp. 33–4.
11 Sangharakshita (1994) pp. 39–41.

brings out the ways in which leaving the initial group to which he belonged, and then later dealing with the desertion of his ascetic friends, required a development of individuality.[12] Most importantly, he explains how the abandonment of the austerities through which the Buddha was unsuccessfully trying to force himself into spiritual progress shows a recognition of integration:

> *The effort that we put into our development needs to be directed towards the growth of the whole psyche, not just a part of it. We need to unify our energies, and this means enlisting the co-operation of our unconscious energies.*[13]

Sangharakshita very much pointed the way in helping us recognise that the story of the Buddha's life is not helpfully related to as a historical event to be argued over as true or false, but is nevertheless hugely significant as a symbolic story illustrating the development of insight into the Middle Way. This is however, a line of thinking that can be taken much further, as I have attempted to do in other recent writing.[14] There, I suggest that the Buddha is not only a model of integrative development, a heroic archetype (as Sangharakshita explores particularly),[15] and a Self or Wise Old Man archetype for us at different times, but that he also represents an archetype of the Middle Way itself.

Despite the helpfulness of these archetypal approaches to the Buddha, I have already discussed some of the aspects of Sangharakshita's approach that are incompatible with it, because they involve at least an implicit imposition of conceptual beliefs on the archetype. These involve the insistence, on the one hand, that Buddhism requires a version of faith that is based on belief in a historical enlightenment, and on the other, that the universal Buddha of the Mahayana represents the 'Reality' of enlightenment. Like most absolute beliefs, these two different beliefs are not compatible with each other – but their mutual incompatibility is in turn symptomatic of the way in which both neglect the Middle Way. The interpretation of the Buddha as an archetype is an important and effective application of the Middle Way, but this continues to conflict with those aspects of Sangharakshita's thinking that are inconsistent with it.

12 Ibid. pp. 41–4, 46–7.
13 Ibid. p. 46.
14 Ellis (2019).
15 Sangharakshita (1994) ch. 4.

4.e. The Unity of Buddhism

The unity of Buddhism consists in the fact that, through differences and divergencies of doctrine innumerable, all schools of Buddhism aim at Enlightenment, at reproducing the spiritual experience of the Buddha.[1]

Thus Sangharakshita opens his most definitive discussion of one of the most problematic areas of his thinking. If 'enlightenment' was indeed an identifiable discontinuous state reached through a linear path, then it would be easy to agree that an identity of goal in different Buddhist schools at least gives them something in common. But we have already seen that Sangharakshita's most insightful discussions of nirvana do not take this view. This is the same person, remember, whom I quoted in 4.a as saying 'The setting up of goals is really a substitute for awareness, for self-knowledge.' A substitute does not necessarily have the same function or scope as what it replaces.

So, what does it mean for all schools of Buddhism to 'aim at enlightenment'? It seems to mean that they all support development of awareness, integration, creativity, individuality, and provisionality. But such aims are neither necessary nor sufficient to Buddhism: some Buddhists schools appear to rather neglect such qualities, using devotion to the mere abstract idea of 'nirvana' as a substitute for them. A great many non-Buddhists also advance such qualities without needing to 'aim at enlightenment'.

To 'aim' at something also means to have some commitment to achieving it, which shows the relationship to going for refuge in Sangharakshita's view of the unity of Buddhism. I will be looking at going for refuge in the next chapter, but for the moment it just needs to be noted that for different people to share a commitment to something expressed in certain words tells us almost nothing about how similar their commitments are and what they mean to each person. By way of analogy, how many people, including seasoned warmongers, would claim to be committed to world peace? 'World peace', like 'enlightenment' just becomes an abstraction of such manipulable vagueness that it can stand equally as the shared goal for approaches that are in practice completely opposed.

In order to adapt Buddhism to the West, it is of course necessary to justify a view about what Buddhism is in the first place. Empirically, however, Buddhism is an extremely complex tradition,

1 Sangharakshita (1987a) p. 228.

comprising not only many schools and national versions, but also a number of past schools only preserved now in texts. Any empirical statements about it will need to incorporate a wide spread of approaches: Theravada monks of a kind who spend their lives memorising texts; Pure Land or Nichiren lay people whose 'Buddhism' consists almost solely in devotional chanting; and American Zen practitioners who find that meditation helps them to run a software company. To cap this, Buddhism is not a religion that empirically is defined by distinct doctrinal beliefs in the same way as Christianity tends to be, and in practice has a tendency to merge seamlessly with other traditions: Hinduism in India and Nepal, Confucianism and Daoism in China, Shinto in Japan, and New Ageism in the West.

In order to bring Buddhism to the West in what he regarded as the correct form, Sangharakshita asserted both that Buddhism was distinct and that it was unified. This can only possibly be done by prescription rather than by description. Not only does it seem that no single definition could satisfactorily encompass the empirical diversity of the whole Buddhist tradition, but any attempt to generalise it would need to be based on systematic, if not scientific, evidence of a kind that Sangharakshita does not offer. Without this, we can only make claims about what Buddhism *ought* to be or how it *ought* to be interpreted. This 'ought' does carry implications of certain kinds of factual assumption, but these are factual assumptions about how humans develop, not about the essential unity of a diverse religious tradition.

Practically speaking, Sangharakshita does largely proceed by prescription, but unfortunately in his writings and lectures there is never any acknowledgement that this is what he is doing. In discussion he did agree that his definition of Buddhism is prescriptive, and that the implication of this is that some people who are formally 'Buddhist' in the empirical sense are not Buddhist in the prescriptive sense. As an example of this he offered Burmese Buddhist monks who urge violence against the Rohingya Muslim minority.

However, that admission does not create a clear separation between empirical and prescriptive senses of 'Buddhism', since although he recognises that empirical Buddhism is not *sufficient* for prescriptive Buddhism, he does not accept that it is not *necessary* either – that is that a person could be 'aiming at enlightenment' without being formally Buddhist or even formulating the goal in a Buddhist way.

Sangharakshita's prescriptive account of the unity of Buddhism also suffers from the same inconsistency that I have been noting in previous chapters, between bottom-up and top-down approaches. Is the Buddhism that we should be following one that we can incrementally discover according to its practical value in our experience, or is it one that can be deduced from Buddhist formulae passed down by tradition? Is it provisional or fixed? Sangharakshita gives us both kinds of answer, and apparently assumes that they can always be made compatible.

This can be illustrated by two quotations within a page of each other in the *Survey*. Firstly, there is the apparently bottom-up, open approach:

> *From the fact that Dharma is, as the Buddha explicitly declares [in the parable of the raft], essentially that which conduces to the attainment of Enlightenment, it necessarily follows that whatever conduces to the attainment of Enlightenment is the Dharma.*[2]

But this is rapidly followed up with a clampdown:

> *Our spiritual experience must be in accordance with the spirit of the Scriptures, and, what is more necessary still, its authenticity must be attested by one whose own enlightenment has been the object of similar attestation. Ultimately, this chain of pupillary succession is stapled onto the rock of the Buddha's own Enlightenment, which is at once the support and the criterion of all succeeding attainments.*[3]

We begin with a pragmatic criterion of what is 'Buddhist', but this criterion is immediately undermined by a total epistemological reliance on Buddhist tradition as the absolute arbiter of what is Buddhist. Such a reliance in practice completely cancels out the supposed pragmatism, reducing it to a completely theoretical, or indeed formalistic, claim.

Pragmatism in human experience depends on human beings being able to judge an alternative belief as preferable to the accepted one, on the grounds that it seems highly likely to produce more helpful results. We need that freedom to be able to judge on increasingly integrated grounds as our judgement develops. But such options are closed off by the approval of scriptural precedence and guru that Sangharakshita requires here. The appeal to authorities to

2 Sangharakshita (1987a) p. 229.
3 Ibid. p. 230.

approve spiritual experience as genuine is, indeed, reminiscent of the tests required by the Roman Catholic Church, which will only accept religious experience as genuine if it is compatible with the church's teaching. It results in a circularity according to which no new inspirations can be accepted.

The anxiety behind Sangharakshita's appeals to tradition seems to be one about relativism. Between the two passages quoted above he writes 'This does not mean the setting up of mere subjective feeling as our criterion.' He seems concerned that if people really take pragmatism seriously as their guide to Buddhism, they will assume that their current feelings or intuitions are necessarily correct, without accepting that there are any better values to refer to than those current feelings or intuitions, and without going through a process of reflection or testing them in the light of any wider awareness. This is indeed a danger, but that danger doesn't make the appeal to tradition any more appropriate in the modern context. People who haven't yet understood that Buddhism is a path involving a gradual process of development, rather than a set of 'truths' instantaneously grasped, will not necessarily benefit more from accepting traditional dogmas than they will from merely following their individual intuitions of the moment.

This is a crucial point where the values discussed in section 2 (most centrally the Middle Way, but also integration, creativity, individuality, and provisionality) become incompatible with those that will result from tradition being taken as primary. The Middle Way involves a navigation between two kinds of absolute extreme, with these being treated even-handedly as both to be avoided. Yet Buddhist tradition, based on commentarial literature,[4] favours eternalism over nihilism, treating eternalism as the second-best path, to be undertaken by lay people, whilst nihilism is more thoroughly rejected as less preferable than eternalism. That favouring of eternalism may also be taken to require absolute sources of authority rather than putting the emphasis on experience. Sangharakshita has abandoned the monastic-lay distinction in the path that provides the major motivation for favouring eternalism, but he continues to favour eternalism over nihilism, as he affirmed directly when I questioned him on this point.

4 *Saratthapakasini*: Buddhaghosa's commentary on *Samyutta Nikaya* 22.1 (not translated into English).

There is an argument about skilful means to be had here, as to whether it is practically preferable to offer an absolutised moral framework as a stage of progression that is all that people can cope with psychologically before they move onto a more open one. This is an argument that I discuss in more detail elsewhere.[5] However, there is a great difference between maintaining a skilful means because one can justify doing so in entirely pragmatic terms (as one can, for instance, in limiting the information one gives to children), and maintaining it as an absolute claim on absolute grounds that directly conflict with your other grounds – which is what Sangharakshita appears to do. Such a vast general claim as one about the essential unity of Buddhism cannot be maintained merely as a skilful means intended to meet the needs of a specific audience, and a religion that still maintains the Middle Way as one of its chief teachings can hardly enforce its unity on the grounds of a spurious authority that is justified only by ignoring that teaching.

Much of the confusion that Buddhists may feel over the unity of Buddhism arises from the complex treatment of the yanas, or three different 'vehicles' of Buddhism taught by Mahayana Buddhist schools. Whilst Theravada Buddhism claims to be the only true school of Buddhism as taught by the historical Buddha, Mahayana sees itself as an improved version of Buddhism, built upon and incorporating the earlier version, and based on the rediscovery of key insights of the Buddha that had been forgotten. The schools of pre-Mahayana early Buddhism, including but not limited to the Theravada, are referred to by Mahayanists as 'Hinayana' or 'lesser vehicle' (a term that Sangharakshita continues to use), but a third yana is also said to have emerged from the Mahayana – the Vajrayana.

Sangharakshita offers helpful conceptual clarification of this picture by analysing the 'yanas' in three different senses: as historical classifications, as polemical terms, and as stages of individual development.[6] The yanas as historical classifications are ways of analysing the development of Buddhism in successive stages from the basic or early form that probably reflects the teachings of the historical Buddha. As polemical terms, they are the basis of chauvinistic claims by the Mahayana schools as to their superiority over

5   Ellis (2019) 4.e.
6   Subhuti (1994) pp. 37–53.

the Theravada. In Tibetan Buddhism, the three yanas also symbolise successive stages of the path for an individual, from the model of individual progression to enlightenment, to one of universal enlightenment, to the apparently antinomian anarchy of the Vajrayana. The most helpful aspect of Sangharakshita's separation of these three usages is that it discourages us from unreflectively importing assumptions from one of these senses to another. Everything the Mahayana and Vajrayana do is not necessarily superior to the practice of Basic Buddhism, nor are more 'advanced' practices necessarily more helpful.

This is also an area where Sangharakshita's thinking has developed over the course of his life, from a position that tended to accept Tibetan chauvinism to one that questioned it. Whilst he accepts that the historical development of the yanas marks two points of necessary reform in Buddhist history, where Buddhism had become caught up in scholastic formalism, this did not prevent the reformers in each case also becoming formalistic in their turn. Even the Vajrayana, Sangharakashita points out, developed a scholasticism.[7] By 'scholasticism' I assume he means a form of absolutisation: the belief that Buddhist rules, rituals, and goals are ends in themselves rather than ways of seeing one's whole experience in a bigger context. Each new revolt, in any tradition, reasserts the value of lived experience, with its uncertainty and complexity, against dead metaphors that form the basis of absolute principles. Sangharakshita evidently recognises that such revolts are a necessary basis of growth in any tradition, through the open feedback loop process of challenge leading to reformulation.

As in all his other interpretations of the Buddhist tradition, then, Sangharakshita's account of the yanas offers us a way of relating traditional Buddhist concerns to creativity, provisionality, integration, and individuality. What it does not do is show that the three yanas, as an empirical phenomenon represented by historically successive schools of Buddhism, are essentially unified. The yanas are similar in following the same modes of development found in the histories of every tradition, and indeed of every individual, but not identical in some unique way that is identifiable solely in the terms of top-down Buddhist doctrine. If we apply the Middle Way

---

7 Ibid. p. 45. Subhuti quotes a discussion that I have been unable to trace directly.

prescriptively as the basis of interpretation, we can take Theravada, Mahayana, or Vajrayana as the basis of its practice, and find many resources there that will support it. But it is this interpretation, in line with the open spirit of reform, that is the source of the creativity rather than the yana itself.

Though this remains one of the most contradictory areas of Sangharakshita's teaching, it is hard not to respond positively to the passion with which he writes of the unity of Buddhism:

> All Buddhist schools, whether of the Mahayana or of the Hinayana, were concerned not with the theoretical determination of truth as an end in itself, but with its practical determination in life. What divided them, therefore, was not differences of opinion over what was true and what was untrue in the scientific, descriptive sense of that term – for all agreed that truth being indescribable was a matter for personal experience – but differences regarding which doctrines, as well as which ethical observances and which meditational techniques, could in practice function as the means for the attainment of enlightenment.[8]

This view can be easily accepted if only one removes the 'Buddhist', and ceases to try to support universal claims with exclusivist arguments. Buddhists are not the only people who have ever recognised the truth as 'indescribable', though the extent to which they can continually describe its indescribability is probably unsurpassed. Any convergence in the way they describe the goal is of little significance if we take its indescribability seriously. But variations in techniques to make progress towards these common, universally available but indescribable goals-that-are-substitutes-for-awareness clearly do not stop at the boundaries of the Buddhist tradition.[9]

To make any sense of Sangharakshita's claims about the unity of Buddhism, then, we have to interpret them as claims about the unity of the Middle Way or the spiritual path, rather than the unity of Buddhism. We also have to constantly interpret this 'unity' prescriptively and avoid any conflation of this with beliefs about the essential unity of the empirical Buddhist tradition. Sangharakshita's ideas here, then, may for some have offered a stand-in or a substitute for an understanding of the unity of the path itself, but hardly a clear or consistent one.

---

8 Sangharakshita (1987a) p. 232.
9 For an account of ten alternative sources of the Middle Way beyond Buddhism, see Ellis (2019) section 7.

4.f. Faith and Going for Refuge

The centrality of 'Going for Refuge' is one of Sangharakshita's most distinctive teachings in his interpretation of Buddhism. The declaration 'I go for refuge to the Buddha, ...to the Dharma, ...to the Sangha' is the one that is often considered formally constitutive of Buddhist identity. It is a mark of conversion to Buddhism, but also a constantly renewed declaration of Buddhist commitment, stated in the context of ritual. Sangharakshita stresses its role as the unifier of all Buddhists and dissolver of the monastic-lay division. For him, it marks the centrality of *commitment* in a practical Buddhist life.

The centrality of commitment makes basic sense in relation to the practical emphasis in Sangharakshita's approach and thus in that of Triratna. One can only undertake practices, particularly deeply challenging ones, by being committed to them. Sangharakshita's central intention in emphasising Going for Refuge thus has an obvious relationship to the Middle Way and an obvious universality. Regardless of the nature of the spiritual practices one undertakes, they will have little effect without consistent application, and this also requires consistent motivation. Formally stating one's commitment (and indeed, doing so publicly), helps to maintain that commitment with the support of the *ottapa* conscience – one's awareness of others' expectations as a means of providing objectivity of perspective. 'Going for Refuge', however, is also a process of inner awareness and ongoing work with one's motivations.

Sangharakshita's ideas about levels of Going for Refuge have also become central to the development of the Triratna Order, with 'effective' Going for Refuge being the central requirement for ordination. The idea of 'effectiveness' in Going for Refuge long predates the foundation of the Order, and can be found in the *Survey of Buddhism*:

> *Formal refuge, which is held to constitute one a member of the Buddhist community, can be taken simply by repeating after any ordained monk the refuge-formulae and the five precepts. But effective refuge, of which the formal refuge is at once the expression and the symbol, can be taken only by one who has an understanding of the true nature of the Triple Gem. The deeper this understanding goes, the more effective will be his refuge.... The refuge is complete when one's understanding of Buddhism is complete, that is to say, when one attains enlightenment. Then, paradoxically enough, there is no going for refuge: the Enlightened One is his own refuge.*[1]

1 Sangharakshita (1987a) p. 446.

This idea of the effectiveness of Going for Refuge was later elaborated into a scheme of five levels of Going for Refuge: cultural, provisional, effective, real, and absolute.² Cultural going for refuge consists in the formalistic recitation of the formula in traditional Buddhist societies, in order only to fulfil social expectations. Provisional going for refuge, already mentioned in 2.c above, does involve a sincere intention to change one's life by practising, but one that is not yet put fully into effect. Effective going for refuge means committing oneself with sufficient integration to maintain that commitment. 'Real' going for refuge is identified with stream entry – the idea of irreversible progress, as discussed above in 4.b. 'Absolute' going for refuge is then the attainment of enlightenment.

The further 'upwards' one goes with this scheme, the more metaphors become rigidified and reified, and the more an important awareness of ambiguities is lost. Sangharakshita certainly puts his finger on the differences between going through the motions for social reasons, unintegrated commitment, and more integrated commitment. However, given the phenomenon of asymmetry of integration, 'effective' commitment is extremely hard to determine, and its institutionalising in ordination tends to impose a simple discontinuity on the complex increments that are involved in spiritual development. If that's the case even with 'effective' going for refuge, it's even more so for 'real' and 'absolute' going for refuge. I have already discussed the problems involved in treating both enlightenment and stream entry discontinuously, rather than as symbols of integration in our own experience.

Sangharakshita's levels of Going for Refuge, then, have tended to create a rigid hierarchy from what started out as a valuable insight into the importance of relationship between commitment, practice, and integration. If we cannot and should not in fact distinguish any actual cases of the top three stages in this hierarchy, it would be better left only as a two-stage hierarchy. In human experience, there is formalistic 'cultural' commitment, and then there is provisional commitment with some measure of awareness of the value and demands of what one is committing oneself too. Everyone from that point onwards can only be said to be provisionally committed, and the fact that they recognise this is one indication of the strength of that commitment in practice. Far from achieving 'absolute'

2 Sangharakshita (1983) pp. 22-4, (1988b) pp. 101-2.

commitment, the person with the most effective commitment is the one who is most consistently provisional – in their view of their own and others' achievements as well as in other respects. Anyone who claims to have 'absolute' or 'real' going for refuge is thus regressing, at least in some respects, to the formalistic level at which absolutized beliefs substitute for experiential engagement with the uncertainties of practice.

Sangharakshita actually takes the levels of 'Going for Refuge' even further than this, by talking about the 'Cosmic' as a sixth level of 'Going for Refuge' – sort of.

> Cosmic Going for Refuge was not exactly another level of Going for Refuge but referred to the evolutionary process, that is, referred to the Lower Evolution and the Higher Evolution. First came the amoeba, then the mollusc, then the fish, the reptile, the bird, and the mammal. Finally there came man – homo sapiens. Looking at this process, what one in fact saw was a Going for Refuge. Each form of life aspired to develop into a higher form or, so to speak, went for Refuge to that higher form. This might sound impossibly poetic, but it was what one in fact saw. In man the evolutionary process became conscious of itself; this was the Higher Evolution. When the Higher Evolution became conscious of itself (and it became conscious of itself in and through the spiritually committed individual) this was Going for Refuge in the essence of effective Going for Refuge. Through our Going for Refuge we are united, as it were, with all living beings, who in their own way, and on their own level, in a sense also went for Refuge. Thus Going for Refuge was not simply a particular devotional practice or even a threefold act of individual commitment, but the key to the mystery of existence.[3]

This is vintage Sangharakshita – soaring and satisfyingly synthetic, almost casually offering an entire theory of the universe in one paragraph; but also half-baked, obviously not run through any kind of careful critical process either in his own or anyone else's mind. 'Going for Refuge' started off as a formal process of commitment in the context of Buddhist tradition; this has then been conflated with commitment to spiritual development in general; this commitment has then been conflated with aspects of human development that are not self-conscious in the same way; this in turn has then been conflated with the tendency of living organisms to adapt to new circumstances by developing greater complexity; this tendency of living organisms has then been projected onto the universe as a whole, including non-living elements, and then claimed to be

3 Sangharakshita (1988b) pp. 102–3.

Interpreting Buddhist Tradition

'the key to the mystery of existence'. When anyone has begun to point out what a conceptual mess this is, Sangharakshita's standard response is to claim that it is intended to be 'poetic', and should not be taken 'literally': but this is really not the way he has framed it. 'It was what one in fact saw,' he writes here, suggesting that he does indeed intend it to be taken seriously as a basis of belief. He really has no excuse of being unable to anticipate that hundreds or even thousands of his devoted followers would take a statement framed in this way 'literally'.

Subhuti, in writing about this, makes a valiant attempt to save his teacher's credibility:

> *How are we to resolve the gap between what we once were [before self-consciousness] and what we now are? What has brought us to the point of Going for Refuge? We can either see that process as fortuitous or as itself having a purpose. Taken literally, both are equally untrue, since they are applying limited concepts drawn from our ordinary sense experience to the universe as a whole. However, from a spiritual point of view, the metaphor of the entire universe as having a purpose is far nearer the truth and far more helpful. It comes nearer to expressing the Buddha's insight into the essential interconnectedness of all things. The individual's spiritual efforts are not... entirely isolated from everything else: they take place within a vast context.*[4]

Subhuti, unlike Sangharakshita, at least here makes some attempt to apply the Middle Way and some awareness of human uncertainty, but his assertions about 'a spiritual point of view' still seem to take Sangharakshita's absolutisations for granted. How can he know what is 'nearer the truth' from 'a spiritual point of view' except in practical terms? In what way is it 'far more helpful' to assume an essential meaning to the universe on the basis of a series of conflations and projections? If we are aiming to overcome our delusions, surely it is most spiritually helpful to acknowledge that we know nothing about these matters? Surely our inspiration and commitment, far from relying on such delusions, depends on our bodily and mental states, including perhaps our relationship to archetypal symbols? The recognition of the bigger context of our spiritual efforts is, of course, helpful, but we do not require speculative beliefs about the universe as a whole to recognise such a bigger context – indeed speculative beliefs are likely to shrink our awareness of that context into merely conceptual reassurances.

4 Subhuti (1994) p. 103.

As I have already discussed in relation to conditionality (4.b above), the Buddha's teachings about conditionality can be projected into a 'top-down' absolutisation about the nature of the universe or interpreted much more helpfully as a prompt to reflection on specific conditioning. A belief in 'Cosmic Going for Refuge' clearly does not help us reflect on specific conditioning, but rather pre-empts any such reflections by leading us to assume that we know about them all already. Rocks, planets, slugs, and starlings are indeed all parts of systems, and we can helpfully reflect on the ways that they are interdependent with other specific things. This seems to have no particular helpful relationship with the idea that rocks, planets, slugs, and starlings are all committing themselves to the path laid down by Buddhist tradition.

Going for Refuge is directed towards the Three Jewels or Gems, which may also be interpreted as different dimensions of the commitment to practice. However, Sangharakshita's treatment of all of these is ambiguous, tending to conflate universal principles on the one hand with the authority of the Buddhist tradition on the other. The Buddha represents the ideal of enlightenment. This can be interpreted in archetypal terms, but also in relation to Sangharakshita's traditional claims about the revelatory status of the Buddha's achievement. The Dharma represents the teachings – ambiguously either those of the universal Middle Way or of the Buddhist tradition. The Sangha represents the community, but again on the one hand this may represent any supportive community that aids practice, or on the other the Arya Sangha of stream-entrants whose enlightenment is supposedly guaranteed, making them traditionally reliable sources.

For the full flavour of this ambiguity, let us contrast Sangharakshita's two different passages, to show his more experiential alongside his more traditionalist explanation of the significance of the three refuges:

> *(1) Committing oneself to the Buddha does not mean...blindly obeying the Buddha. It means taking the Buddha as one's ideal, taking* **Buddhahood** *as an ideal.... It means recognising Buddhahood as a practical ideal for all human beings, and actually devoting all one's energies towards the realisation of that ideal.... Committing oneself to the Dharma means actually following the path in order to realise the goal.... It means committing oneself to the process of one's development as an individual by whatsoever means.... The Sangha is the spiritual community – that is, the community of the*

spiritually committed.... We can enjoy spiritual fellowship with all members of the Sangha in different ways and in differing degrees. This is what we mean by committing ourselves to the Sangha.[5]

(2) Though the minimum degree of understanding that would enable one to take effective refuge in the Triple Gem is naturally difficult to estimate, we may at least assert with confidence that the conviction that the Buddha has attained the Transcendental, that the Dharma is the means to the Transcendental, and that the members of the Sangha, by which is meant in this context the Arya Sangha, have gained the Transcendental Path, are indispensable elements of such refuge. One who denies, or even seriously doubts, the existence of such a state as Nirvana, or the possibility or desirability of its attainment, is naturally precluded from taking refuge in any of them.[6]

The language of 1 (though I have edited it somewhat for brevity) is a good deal more open and universal. In the terms of 1, someone who was not committed specifically to the Buddhist tradition (such as myself), but who was committed to a practical path of development, in co-operation with others who were similarly committed, could be said to be 'taking refuge'. In the language of 2, however, 'taking refuge' becomes very clearly a matter of accepting certain beliefs that are specific to Buddhist tradition. These beliefs, moreover, are concerned with claims beyond our experience, and thus (as argued above) involve absolute assumptions.

Can these two ways of understanding going for refuge ever be reconciled? Not by simply asserting one or the other to be correct. If we take the more open version to be definitive of Sangharakshita's view, we will have to ignore a great deal of absolutising material that will continue to conflict with our motivations whenever we encounter it. If we take the closed and absolutising version to be correct, then all the universal insights to be found in Sangharakshita's approach to Buddhism are betrayed. One way of attempting to reconcile them that I have heard from some Order members involves a kind of supererogation: the basic form of commitment to spiritual practice is available to all, but the specific Buddhist version goes beyond it as a kind of optional extension. Not only does this introduce an unacceptable discontinuity between the universal and traditional kinds of commitment, but it puts the cart before the horse

---

5 Sangharakshita (1990a) pp. 79–81.
6 Sangharakshita (1987a) p. 446.

by getting things precisely the wrong way round: it is those who deny the universal and focus on an exclusive type of commitment that have the less adequate, more constrained, and thus morally and spiritually inferior type of practice, not the other way round. I can see no way of reconciling the contradictions in Sangharakshita's view of the refuges, but they are created by his more general tendency to inconsistently absolutise the Buddhist tradition.

The difficulties with Sangharakshita's account of Going for Refuge are interdependent with those in his view of faith (*saddha*), one of the five spiritual faculties of Buddhism. Sangharakshita gives a detailed exposition of his view of faith in *A Survey of Buddhism*.[7] 'The connotation of the word is not cognitive but definitely emotional,'[8] he begins, rejecting the use of the term 'confidence' as 'rationalising'. In the context of Buddhism, he defines faith as 'the act (expressed by "taking refuge") or state (condition of being established in the refuge) of acknowledging unquestioningly that the man Gautama, or what appears as the man Gautama, is in possession of Full Enlightenment'.[9] Faith is thus focused on the Buddha refuge, with the Dharma and Sangha being subsidiary, but he also insists that, despite its emotionality, it is 'not blind faith'.[10] Instead, he says, it is grounded on intuition, reason, and experience.

The intuitive response to enlightenment is one that Sangharakshita compares to a sympathetic vibration.[11] We encounter the Buddha, he says, whether personally or in imagination, and something deep within us resonates with the enlightenment in him. However, Sangharakshita offers no reason at all why the inspiration of this sympathetic resonance needs to be attached to a belief in the enlightened status of the person with whom one resonates. He merely assumes this – in a way that is completely inconsistent with his use of archetypes in discussing the Buddha (see 4.d). This sympathetic intuitive response can be readily understood, as well as deeply appreciated, as the response to an archetype – but one that is all the more fully engaged with if it is recognised to be an aspect of our experience rather than projected onto a person. We might also presumably have this kind of resonant response to someone who is

7 Sangharakshita (1987a) pp. 312–22.
8 Ibid. p. 312.
9 Ibid.
10 Ibid. p. 313.
11 Ibid. p. 314.

merely highly integrated without having the concept of enlightenment projected onto them: and, as long as we clearly separate the meaning and inspiration of that resonance from our beliefs about the person concerned, this is safe enough. The emotionality of this response is not reduced or threatened by a clear separation from beliefs about a specific person, but rather given a safe space in which to operate without disrupting our lives with delusion.

Faith is also justified by reason, Sangharakshita argues, because 'there exists an invariable concomitance between Enlightenment, on the one hand, and various moral, spiritual and intellectual qualities on the other'.[12] Since this merely tells us *a priori* about the ways that Sangharakshita and other traditional Buddhists define enlightenment, it tells us precisely nothing – like the information that a dodo is a flightless bird, it tells us nothing to justify a belief in the existence of dodos. Logic is only ever as good as the assumptions it begins with, and only relevant when those assumptions bear some relationship to our experience.

Sangharakshita then finally claims that faith is justified by experience, because when we follow the Buddha's advice and attain 'a certain stage of the path' we know 'beyond all possibility of doubt that the Buddha attained it'.[13] This does identify a feature of the path – namely that confidence in it grows incrementally with practice and progress, but this is marred yet again by Sangharakshita's reliance on an absolutisation of enlightenment. This is also completely inconsistent with Sangharakshita's suggestion that enlightenment may not consist of a fixed point. We cannot rely on there being a specific point in a path that we haven't trodden yet at which we will become absolutely certain of the rightness of that path, because the nature of the path itself is one of acknowledging embodied uncertainty rather than clinging to certainty. Nor can we rely on a judgement that someone else has reached such a point of certainty – as opposed to a practical recognition of a relatively high degree of progress.

Sangharakshita's writings on faith identify a core point of insight that is connected to the one he has about Going for Refuge: that practice to develop our integration and individuality requires commitment, and commitment in turn requires gathering confidence of

12 Ibid. p. 315.
13 Ibid. p. 316.

a kind that is indeed not 'just intellectual'. However, I've already discussed the problems caused by Sangharakshita's tendency to employ a false dichotomy between 'reason' and 'emotion' in 3.a. No 'emotion' operates without beliefs and reasoning of at least an implicit kind, and no 'reason' occurs without an emotional motivation. It is far more practically relevant to ask whether our judgements are absolutising than it is to ask whether they are 'rational' or 'emotional'. *Saddha* as faith or confidence is a vital part of spiritual development, as the Buddhist tradition of identifying it as a spiritual faculty attests, but Sangharakshita's tendency to identify it with absolute beliefs at the same time constantly undermines the practicality of that faith.

A fear of relativism again seems to lurk behind this tendency to take refuge in traditional absolutes, expressed in Sangharakshita's trenchant rejection of 'rationalising'. But there is nothing 'rationalising', and not necessarily any negative absolutes, reductionism, materialism, or relativism, in the recognition of uncertainty – a recognition that is profoundly explored and symbolised in Buddhist tradition. It is hard not to feel that the faith in the path first stirred in the mind and heart of the sixteen-year-old Sangharakshita when he read the *Diamond Sutra* – a document almost ridiculously excessive in its pronouncement of constant uncertainty – has received a deeply flawed expression in his later writings and utterances on the subject of faith, which constantly betray living, experiential faith for the very 'rationalising' absolutism Sangharakshita apparently fears elsewhere.

5. Controversies

5.a. Sangharakshita's Personal Authority

We now reach the final phase of this book, in which I'm moving from the assessment of Sangharakshita's general teachings to their specific application in issues that have created controversy. Overwhelmingly, the application of Sangharakshita's ideas has occurred within Triratna, and the controversies are thus about practice within Triratna. My aim is to put these controversies in the widest possible context by placing them at the end of my more general assessment. In some cases, these controversies have created a great deal of polarisation, and treating them in a consistently balanced and equanimous way is not at all an easy task, but I nevertheless feel compelled to attempt that task.

The issues that may spring to mind first for many involve sex and gender, and I will come to these in due course. However, first I must consider an equally controversial question central to nearly all Triratna practice at a social level – namely, the status to be given to Sangharakshita himself within the Order and movement that he founded. This is now clearly an even more important issue following Sangharakshita's recent death. The sexual abuse allegations against Sangharakshita have also impacted many people's personal assumptions about his integrity and authority, throwing open questions about it to a much greater degree within Triratna. The question of Sangharakshita's status involves the question of authority, which I will discuss in this chapter, but also involves the symbolic or archetypal use of his image, which I will discuss in the following chapter.

The development of Sangharakshita's thinking about his own status needs initially to be put in the context of his responses to the guru tradition in Buddhism, offered in his 1970 lecture 'Is a Guru Necessary?' Here he tries to head off various misunderstandings, as he sees them, of the role of a guru:

> *The guru is not the head of a religious group, he's not a teacher, he's not a father substitute, and he's not a problem-solver. But that means – one must be careful to see – that means that the guru as such is not any of these things. The guru per se is not any of these things. But that does not mean that he may not at times, or from time to time, function in these different ways.*[1]

He then goes on more positively:

> *The guru is one who stands on a higher level of being and consciousness than ourselves, or to put it in a word, one who is more aware; one who is more evolved, one who is more developed. In the second place, the guru is one with whom we are in regular contact.*[2]

His account of the guru, then, is a development of his account of 'vertical friendship' as discussed above in 3.d. It depends entirely on the idea of there being a person who is more integrated than oneself, who may need to stimulate one towards spiritual growth in ways that may be deeply challenging and quite unpredictable. To evolve without the aid of such a person, he says, is 'extremely difficult', making a guru practically necessary for most people. However, he acknowledges the difficulties in finding a guru who is genuinely more advanced, and that it may be quite a haphazard process, in which the guru may choose the disciple as well as the disciple choosing the guru.

In a further lecture in 1990 Sangharakshita reflected back on this material:

> *In the East, I suggested, the guru was sometimes overvalued; in the West, usually undervalued. The proper course was to follow a middle way between the two extremes, simply recognizing that there were others more highly evolved than ourselves and that we could evolve through contact with them. What was required was not absolute faith but contact and receptivity. In this way did I attempt, in effect, to revise the guru concept and rid the word 'guru' of its unpleasant connotation. The tide was against me, and now, twenty years on, I would drop the guru concept and, as I said, preferably not apply the word 'guru' to myself nor have it applied to me by others. We have in Buddhism the wonderful term 'spiritual friend' and this I am more than content to apply to myself and to have applied to me by others. Indeed, there are times when I think that 'spiritual friend' is almost too much and that just 'friend' would be enough.*[3]

---

1 Lecture 90.
2 Ibid.
3 Lecture 172.

Controversies 169

This marks a change in terminology from 'guru' to 'friend', and also a clarification that what was required of the disciple was not 'absolute faith'. However, there is no substantial change in underlying approach, and it still leaves me in doubt about how far Sangharakshita really appreciates the limitations of the guru-style relationship. As I have already mentioned in relation the Sangharakshita's ideas about vertical friendship (3.d above), the main factor that he does not seem to take sufficiently into account is the asymmetry of integration – a phenomenon that is well supported by recent psychological studies. There also seems to be little acknowledgement that a disciple will need to exercise critical thinking in checking out a potential guru. Asymmetry may mean that the guru may be one-sidedly integrated, and that his/her appearance of impressive integration in one context may be misleading if taken as a guide to his/her total integration. This puts all the more emphasis on the need for the disciple to avoid absolutising the authority of the guru, but, as often, it is not entirely clear to what extent Sangharakshita appreciates this point. As we will see, his more recent utterances particularly cast doubt on how far he consistently wishes his disciples to develop critical thinking in relation to his teachings.

In 2009, Sangharakshita met a group of senior Order members and answered a series of their questions on the nature of the Order, including ones that closely concerned his authority in it. The answers were published in the form of a document called 'What Is the Western Buddhist Order?' In this document,[4] which Sangharakshita says 'may...be seen as my Last Will and Testament for the Order', he comes across as far more blunt and unequivocal than he had previously been about the question of his authority over the Order.

He defines the Order as 'the community of my disciples' and asserts that 'the duty of my disciples is to adhere faithfully to the teaching they have received from me, to practise faithfully in accordance with that, and to do their best to hand it faithfully on to others.' He later issued a postscript conceding that the term 'disciple' might be interpreted by some to imply 'an unrealistically intimate, uncritical, or reverential view of me'[5] and thus suggesting that other

4 Sangharakshita (2009a).
5 Sangharakshita (2017).

language could be used – but, like his earlier change of approach to the word 'guru', this seems to be largely an attempt to avoid triggering unnecessary reactions to a word rather than a substantial change of view.

He offers both traditional and pragmatic justifications for this approach to the definition of the Triratna Order. To begin with the traditional justification:

> In founding the Order in this way, I was simply following an ancient pattern that we find again and again when we look at the history of Buddhism. We find that teachers arise, they study whatever Dharma teachings are available in their time, they then give their own presentation and that attracts people, and that develops into a Sangha, into a school or a tradition. At the highest level, this is the pattern that was established by the Buddha himself.[6]

As an appeal to tradition, this is fallacious. Whatever may have happened in Buddhist tradition, it has no necessary implication for what would be the right thing to do in the modern context. Of course, a model from the tradition might be examined and adapted, with critical awareness, to the modern context, but then further justifications are needed for doing so.

Sangharakshita also does have a pragmatic justification:

> My approach stems from the nature of spiritual life itself. For commitment to be strong it has, in a sense, to be narrow. It is only through intensity of commitment and practice that you achieve any results. You will not achieve that intensity if you try to follow different teachers and their different teachings and practices at the same time. You need to follow a particular set of teachings and practices within a particular framework under a particular teacher in order to experience any real progress. And you must have confidence in that teacher and his teaching otherwise you will not be able to apply yourself consistently and successfully.[7]

The causal claims here are highly contestable. He asserts that narrowness of focus, using one particular well-defined framework, is necessary to achieve intensity of commitment and thus of practice. However, this surely depends on the nature of the task one is undertaking, and on how one understands the nature of spiritual practice. To perform a practical task, such as, say, carpentry, it is obviously correct that one needs a clear framework of assumptions about the goals, the methods and tools to be used, and so on, to improve one's

6 Sangharakshita (2009a).
7 Ibid.

skill and thus to develop. The development of creativity, integration, provisionality, and individuality, however, is a practice that actually depends on the ability to question the frameworks that we are using. Intensity here may depend not on a narrowing of assumptions, but on the contrary on our ability to gather together a wider range of ideas and inspirations and synthesise them, seeing how different perspectives could inform the ways in which we respond to conditions, and focusing energy from different sources within ourselves.

Our integrative development does not merely consist in one type of practical task, but in the ongoing development of our judgement in relation to all tasks. It thus demands a fundamentally different framework of assumptions. This provisionality of frameworks is emphasised again and again in the Buddhist tradition in relation to the Middle Way, anatta and Emptiness, but for some reason does not seem to figure at all in Sangharakshita's thinking where his relation to the Order is concerned. Instead, a process of abstraction seems to predominate in the thinking of both Sangharakshita and his leading followers: the practical experience of increasing integration that actually depends on bringing together different influences becomes associated with the Buddhist language of enlightenment and stream entry, and the sense of what this actually means in relation to experience seems to be lost when this language is conceptually applied to judgements involving authority and tradition. I've also observed something similar in the changes of Sangharakshita's mood face-to-face: at one moment, he can be fully acknowledging the limitations of his outlook, but then in the next, abstract beliefs have come to predominate, and his demeanour assumes a narrow trenchancy that it did not previously have. This reflects a general human tendency to shift between narrower states over-dominated by the left hemisphere and more open and aware states – but a tendency that one would expect a teacher promoting integration to have addressed more effectively.

Even if we were to interpret the spiritual path as a well-defined task in a sense in which it clearly is not, it would not follow from this that confidence in one sole teacher was a requirement for its completion. Given that any teacher will be imperfect in their response to conditions, and that their influence and example may not actually be the one best adapted to our specific needs, an awareness of alternatives is vital to making an appropriate judgement about how to act. If we depend on only one source, it is most likely to influence us only to act in one way, or at least within a limited repertoire of ways, and thus to lead us into closed feedback loops in our response to conditions. To learn we have to be challenged, and challenge comes from a variety of influences, not just one influence. Even if I am learning how to do a particular piece of carpentry, once I have learnt the basics I might get more and different tips from other carpenters beyond the one I began with as an instructor.

Sangharakshita goes on:

> Dharma needs to be made specific to a particular Sangha. It needs to hang together, doctrinally and methodologically, if it is to be the basis of a Sangha or Order. Everybody needs to be following the same founding teacher, be guided by the same doctrinal understanding of the Dharma, and undertaking broadly the same set of practices. If they do not do that they will not have sufficient in common to be an effective Sangha and will not be able to make progress together on the Path.[8]

Sangharakshita here seems to be very specific in his practical expectations about what constitutes an acceptable Sangha, and everything he has said about individuality (2.e) seems to have gone out of the window. It is he who has discussed the authentic individual and the ways in which the helpful community consists of a group of individuals. For these individuals to work together without being merely motivated by the group mind, they need to be following a universal integrative path that they recognise as similar in each other, rather than the beliefs and practices prescribed by the group. If there is no such universal integrative path, and it cannot be accessed through Buddhism, what is the point in a Westerner becoming a Buddhist? They could easily follow the teachings of any other group with defined teachings and practices that 'hang together' and get the same social confirmation.

In parallel with Sangharakshita's anxieties about relativism, anxieties about 'effective Sangha' seem to be at issue here. For a community to be 'effective', like an individual who is 'effectively' going for refuge, it presumably needs to be supporting people on the path with sufficient consistency. However, in the case of the spiritual path, that consistency does not depend on everyone believing the same things or performing the same practices. Rather it depends on the community offering the kind of stimulus and support that is

---

8   Ibid.

required for individuals to sustain beliefs and practices appropriate to them, which will then also enable them to relate helpfully to the group. Where specific beliefs and practices are dominant in the group but wrong for the individual, an insistence on homogeneity in the group may actually work against the spiritual development of the individual, not for it. For instance, people in Triratna may struggle for years with devotional rituals, feeling that they ought to be making them part of their practice, but remain alienated from them. An 'effective Sangha' is not one that insists that devotional practice must be the way forward for such people, but rather one that encourages them to find other practices that fulfil the same integrative functions.

Thus far, it could be stated that Sangharakshita's claims about his own authority at least have an impersonal justification. He is not claiming to be a special, exceptional guru who should be followed because of his unique revelation, but rather arguing that the community needs to unite around something to be effective, and that contingently he has ended up being that something. However, the following response seems to make the claims rather more personal:

> *Q: But there are, of course, other versions around of what defines the Order, or even of who defines it, especially the view that could be summed up as that the Order is what Order members collectively think it is – the Order collectively decides what the Order is.*
>
> *S: I wouldn't agree with that. My version is that, directly or indirectly, I decide. The Order cannot be redefined democratically.*[9]

If one had any remaining hopes that Sangharakshita's motives have an underlying pragmatism, this blunt response seems to defeat them. It is apparently a direct attempt to dictate what the Order should be by appeal to authority, without any reference at all to the value of other perspectives, to the need to create consensus, to the Middle Way, individuality, or any other of the values that the Order should supposedly be run on. Even if one accepts that practical leadership requires a unity of perspective, it does not follow from this that the unified perspective has to be entirely his perspective, unmodified by learning or consultation.

As previously noted (in 2.e), Sangharakshita also here apparently fails to appreciate that 'democracy' is not a single fixed system

9 Ibid.

based on some sort of naïve egalitarianism, but rather a way of integrating political perspectives that has formed an essential part of the necessary conditions for the development of Buddhist movements in the West. The contrast between the Order as 'democracy' and as dictatorship is thus a false dichotomy. Democratic norms are already part of the societies in which Triratna operates, and have given rise to the expectation of autonomous judgement that he himself has greatly encouraged. Such norms do not exclude leadership, but subject it to appropriate limitations. Of course the Order could be 'redefined democratically' – if it wanted to be.

Sangharakshita's words here are also inconsistent both with the values expressed by many of his actions, and with the empirical reality of Triratna, especially after his death. Since the 1990s he has gradually handed on all formal responsibilities as head of the Order. If this means anything at all, then presumably it means that he is not the person who 'decides'. If you no longer run something, you have to expect that the people who take it over may make decisions that are not the ones you would make. Consensus between them is by far the most likely basis for decision-making, not only about short-term issues, but also about the most basic values on which those decisions are made. Even if in practice later in his life, he was still consulted about major questions of value, this can no longer be the case after his death, when the Order can only be entirely free to make itself autonomously into whatever it wishes to be.

In the question of the basis of the Order, then, Sangharakshita seems to not only be claiming authority but attempting (in a somewhat Lear-like deluded fashion) to wield power. Of course, this power can be easily disavowed, because it is not supported by any sanctions beyond those of group approval or disapproval, but the psychological power associated with group approval should not be underestimated (as Sangharakshita himself has previously told us). The Order is presented as a matter of take-it-or-leave-it, but in practice, that judgement is not made in the abstract. One only leaves the Order (as I did in 2008) with reluctance, by abandoning a great many sunk costs. This is a point that needs to be borne in mind when it is presented simply as a matter of choice:

> Q: *To what extent are we at liberty to disagree with what you teach?*
>
> S: *That depends on whether you mean liberty as a disciple or as a human being. As a human being you are at liberty to disagree, but if you disagree*

> beyond a certain point as a disciple you cease to be a disciple. Of course, I don't expect people to follow blindly and uncritically whatever I have said or taught, but I expect them to take me very seriously and think very carefully about it, as most Order members do. If Order members find themselves disagreeing with me on significant issues, I expect them to discuss that with me, while I am still available, or with their own teachers within the Order. Otherwise being a disciple doesn't mean very much.[10]

What he means by 'take me very seriously and think very carefully' is amplified by the following answer:

> The criticism should take place in the context of an assumption that something is being said by the teacher that is of spiritual significance. If you cannot make sense of what your teacher says or cannot agree with it, you should first assume that you may have misunderstood or not got it clear yet, and then you should try to understand through intelligent, critical discussion and inquiry. If you cannot make that assumption you have probably already ceased to be a disciple.[11]

This makes it clear that what he is expecting is more than just giving him credibility, which will mean that what he says is worthy of attention. Nor is he just expecting a charitable interpretation, which would also be reasonable. Rather, he is expecting the disciple to exercise extreme confirmation bias, in which he/she stretches every sinew to interpret what has been said positively, even when the possibility of it being mistaken, irrelevant, or inapplicable presents itself as a much greater probability in the light of experience. The disciple is also apparently under no intellectual obligation to compare what he says with any other source of information – which is the most basic starting-point for trying to avoid confirmation bias. The penalty for continuing disagreement with Sangharakshita here is (apparently) ceasing to be his disciple, which in practice means the loss of a social position and of a great many vested interests and sunk costs, for every disciple who might be in that position. Any pragmatic disciple concerned with maintaining continuing conditions for his or her spiritual development (not just worldly advantage), might well think twice if they took this seriously, and self-censor rather than following through a genuinely critical line of enquiry.

10 Ibid.
11 Ibid.

If this was the only way in which an organisation like Triratna could possibly operate and do the degree of good that it does, or the only way in which the path could be followed, perhaps this approach could be pragmatically justified. However, this is clearly not the basis on which Triratna actually operates, let alone the basis on which it should operate, and it is certainly not the basis on which a path of developing creativity, integration, provisionality, and individuality is followed. Any organisation aiming to support people on that path needs to be a learning organisation, which means that statements made by the teacher that are not adequate to experience cannot be pursued endlessly on the assumption that they must be right if one only has enough confirmation bias. Instead, it must be possible for the organisation to contradict the teacher – which is what has in fact happened, as we will see in the later chapters of this section. Those who are responsible for contradicting Sangharakshita have also apparently managed to turn a blind eye to the possibility that they are no longer his disciples because of it. The fact that they have found it necessary to do so is a sad indictment of the incoherence of Sangharakshita's position.

In my experience, in practice, a much more liberal regime operates in the Order than the one that one might expect if one was going on Sangharakshita's words, and people within it are quite willing to criticise him on important issues, without consulting him on every one of them, and without necessarily giving him every benefit of the doubt. That's probably because members of the Order, in many cases, have followed a path of integration inspired by the best parts of Sangharakshita's teaching, and in fact do recognise the value of synthesising different values. In practice, the integrity of that path is supported, not by the authority of Sangharakshita, but by the process of developing awareness created by pursuing the path itself. The theory is just not up to the level of the practice.

Finally, there is also a question of the compatibility of Sangharakshita's approach to his own authority with the Middle Way. Sangharakshita obviously thinks it is compatible, because his main way of practising the Middle Way in this context (as in many others) is to emphasise the opposite view to the one that he takes to be over-dominant in the context. It's a compensatory approach. The following answer illustrates this strongly:

> *Q: In what you have said so far, Bhante, there is a strong emphasis on what might be called conservation: making sure that the Order remains faithful to its founding principles, embodied in the teachings, practices, and institutions established by you. In your interview with Mahamati, shown at the Bodhgaya Order Convention, you mentioned an, as it were, balancing factor to conservation: development – responding creatively to new circumstances and needs. Why are you stressing conservation here and not development?*
>
> *S: The general mood of the times favours constant innovation, and that influences us, and the mood has to be resisted. There is, however, room for development – depending on what one means by development. If it means considering a new way of communicating the Dharma, that is to be encouraged: the development of Buddhafield was an example of that. It may be useful for there to be developments in terms of the medium used and the manner of presentation, but there should not be any development that is inconsistent with whatever teachings, practices, and institutions we already have and there should not be innovation in terms of principles.*
>
> *Although I certainly see an important place for development in this sense, I feel the need to stress sticking to our basic principles and basing ourselves firmly in my particular presentation of the Dharma. That is because I detect, within the Order and movement at present, that the voices raised loudest seem to be in favour of, what could be called, innovation. I don't hear equally strong and numerous voices being raised in favour of conservation, to call it that. I therefore see that innovation is the current danger, especially in view of the general climate around us and the craze for what is new and different – the new for new's sake.*[12]

It's not just that Sangharakshita may be misjudging where the balance between innovation and conservation should lie here, but rather that his more general method, when he thinks one extreme is being over-emphasised, is to over-emphasise the other in compensation. Such an approach does not help others to identify where the Middle Way lies in the longer term, and carries the danger of simply perpetuating a series of oscillations. It is as though the Buddha, rather than discovering the Middle Way, had rebounded from the forest back to the palace, and then probably back again to the forest. Although Sangharakshita does acknowledge the importance of creative development here, it is confined in a way that prevents that creative development from changing the established order: 'there should not be any development that is inconsistent with whatever

---

12 Ibid.

teachings, practices, and institutions we already have and there should not be innovation in terms of principles'. In other words, there can be change as long as we don't actually change anything important.

The integration of beliefs about the importance of conservation with contrary beliefs about the importance of development can only occur when the sets of assumptions animating each are respected even-handedly, and a new position is adopted that clearly maintains what is important in each. It is only in that way that a position that is sustainable in the longer-term can be accepted. That requires a critical process to establish what is most important in each of the conflicting priorities, of the kind that I have been trying to model in this book. One cannot stipulate in advance of such a process what can be changed and what cannot, or one ends up in rigid and absolute positions that have failed to take one's degree of ignorance into account.

To attempt to maintain one's own authority over what the Order should be after one's death, especially after having already handed on that authority, and to attempt to do so through blunt assertions that depart from the values that inspired your movement in the first place – this is not the balanced, aware, inspiring action of a spiritual leader, but unfortunately looks very much more just like the perverse act of a stubborn old man. I hope that its resemblance to King Lear goes no further than that, and that its consequences will not bear any further resemblance to that tragedy.

5.b. 'The Bearer of the Archetype'

One of the features of Triratna centres that has startled me in the past, and I suspect many others, is that when one goes into the shrine room, where meditation, ritual, and quite often talks take place, somewhere on the shrine next to the Buddha image is quite often a photo of Sangharakshita. Other devotional acts may also take place in relation to Sangharakshita at times, such as the chanting of the White Tara Mantra with the insertion of his name to wish him long life. As I have already mentioned in 3.b, Sangharakshita's image also appears on the 'Refuge Tree' of Triratna, visualised in meditation along with Buddhas, bodhisattvas, and past teachers by those preparing for ordination, who then prostrate themselves numerous times before it. Another occasional practice, the Guru Yoga, involves the visualisation of a line of gurus culminating in Sangharakshita as one's immediate guru, with the visualisation of light emanating from the guru and conveying his wisdom and bliss.[1]

From the point of view of outsiders, it may seem that Triratna Buddhists are worshipping or idolising Sangharakshita, and it may well be assumed that this can hardly be compatible with maintaining a balanced and potentially critical attitude towards his teachings. Of course, Triratna Buddhists are likely to respond that this is a misunderstanding, and they have a justification for this practice at hand. In some ways this justification can be rooted in Sangharakshita's teachings, though in others it seems to have an equivocal relationship to them.

This justification is based in the adoption of Tantric practices from the Tibetan tradition of Buddhism, in which the guru figure stands for a more immediate and embodied version of the Buddha refuge. In this approach, there is a lineage from the Buddha to the Guru along which there is a 'transmission of energy' – an inspiration that cannot be reduced to a particular formula.[2]

> *So far as the Tantra is concerned, therefore, the Guru is the Buddha. The Tantra points out, one has never met the Buddha.... Buddha is only a concept for one.... But one has contact with, one is in touch with the Guru.*[3]

---

1 This practice is described in general (without any reference to who the guru is) in Lecture 106.
2 Lecture 106.
3 Ibid.

If the Buddha is a source of archetypal inspiration (as discussed in 4.d), and archetypes are universal, there is of course no reason why the practitioner of the path cannot seek that archetypal inspiration elsewhere. On the face of it, seeking that inspiration in a living person with whom one has actual contact might just seem a way of making that inspiration more powerful. However, in that very power lies the danger of projection: of seeing only the archetype in a living person and thus having a deluded view of them that does not engage with them or appreciate them as a person. Similar projections occur when we fall in love or when we demonise, but a projection on the guru would be a tendency to assume complete integration when only asymmetrical integration can be found.

The basic justification for the use of Sangharakshita's photo on shrines, then, is that he is 'the bearer of the archetype'. Sangharakshita has himself introduced the idea of the guru as the bearer of the archetype from Buddhist tradition, but he has also shown awareness of the dangers involved.

> *In the case of the person who is the bearer of the archetype it's as though you take it almost on faith, on trust, that he is the bearer of that archetype; even though it might not be actually manifested in his life. I think if you regard a living person (especially if he's an imperfect person) as the bearer of a particular archetype, you can get into difficulties, he can get into difficulties. On the whole it's safer to regard figures of the Path or mythological figures as bearers of archetypes, rather than living persons.*[4]

However, although he shows awareness of those dangers in general, he does not explain any of the nature of those 'difficulties'. In the more specific case of his own image being used in public Triratna centres, there is also a resounding silence, with no public comments having been made at all (with the possible exception of the rather indirect one quoted at the end of this chapter). This is odd, and perhaps disingenuous, because if he perceives dangers in the practice, one would have expected him to at least warn others about them. If one looks more closely at the words used here they are also quite equivocal: it may be 'safer' not to use living people, but of course that doesn't offer a clear discouragement from the practice, or show that he might not think the risks worthwhile.

In the same seminar, Sangharakshita offers two other ideas that seem to have been latched onto by Triratna devotees, but that are

4 Seminar 134.

neither developed nor explained fully: these are the ideas that the projection onto the guru is 'positive', and that there is a distinction between 'the bearer of the archetype' and 'the embodiment of the ideal'.

> *I think whether a person becomes the bearer of an archetype, I think there is inevitably a sort of projected element there, even though of a positive nature, and that is incompatible with a 'real', in the sense of intimate and realistic personal relationship. That's different from regarding someone embodying an ideal, because that ideal will find expression in his actual life and the way in which he relates to you.*[5]

The idea that projection can be 'positive' sounds very much like an *ad hoc* rationalisation. Projection is deluded by definition, as it involves attributing qualities to a person that they do not have. Of course, a person may be inspiring in certain respects even if one has a clear-eyed understanding of their weaknesses, but then one is no longer projecting. To get into contact with an archetypal inspiration we do not have to project it, but just become aware of the archetype in relation to mythic forms that can be clearly distinguished from projections. Perhaps projection is practically unavoidable in some circumstances, and can only gradually be unpicked, as in the case of a young child's projections onto his/her parents, but that does not give any excuse for creating optional conditions that are likely to encourage projection.

The idea of the embodiment of an ideal also seems to be an unhelpful idealisation, since nobody in practice completely embodies an ideal. If you really think that they do, you are probably not taking nearly enough account of the uncertainties accompanying your interpretation of your experience of them. The distinction between the embodiment of an ideal and the bearer of an archetype is thus of no practical help.

In another place in the same seminar, Sangharakshita discusses traditional Tibetan methods of distinguishing between a living person and the bearer of an archetype:

> *Yes, well they've got all sorts of manners and customs and traditions, and social observances which helps them to do that. For instance, if you've got a magnificent shrine, there's a great throne there, and there's your guru sitting there all in his robes, well then you can regard them as the bearer of the archetype; but if perhaps you were discussing logical grammar with him while you*

5   Ibid.

> study, it's open for you to disagree or dispute with him, in fact that might even be encouraged. It's a different situation and they set up these different situations much more definitely and strongly than we do, and those differences for instance call forth the appropriate behaviour.[6]

This obviously provides the basis of another possible defence of the use of Sangharakshita's photo on public shrines: that we all have the capacity to make a distinction between two different contexts. If you see his photo on the shrine, you relate to him as the archetypal guru there, but if you meet him in person, then you will treat him as a person. In practice, it might be argued, people do switch between projective ways of relating to others and much more complex nuanced ones in different contexts: relating to someone entirely as a sex-object whilst masturbating to their image in private might be a parallel example, as that does not necessarily imply that we won't treat them in a complex, socially acceptable way when we meet them face-to-face. The human capacity for compartmentalisation shouldn't be underestimated.

In practice, however, although such compartmentalisation often takes place, it is not watertight, and cannot always be sufficiently relied upon. The ways in which we habitually imagine a person do have an effect on how we respond to them when we meet them, even if social mechanisms of suppression often override the most obvious changes in the short-term. What's more, Buddhists generally recognise this. The metta-bhavana meditation, for instance, is entirely premised on the idea that the way we imagine others (in this case, cultivating loving-kindness towards their image) affects how we subsequently feel about them, so that we build-up loving-kindness towards them. The common attitude to Sangharakshita's image in Triratna shrine rooms seems to be inconsistent with the assumptions made in basic meditation teaching there.

Nor is the Triratna Buddhist's encounter with Sangharakshita likely to be so neatly divided between archetypal devotion to an image on the one hand and encounter with the living person on the other, especially after his death when there will be no more such encounters. Rather, the Triratna Buddhist is much more likely to encounter Sangharakshita through his writings, or through audio and video recordings. It is in these contexts where it is actually most important to maintain a balanced critical perspective, but where a habitual idealisation is most likely to make itself felt.

6 Ibid.

There is also an issue of group-repression at stake here, of the kind I mentioned in relation to ritual in 3.g above. In the context of a shared, public shrine room, a photo of Sangharakshita on the shrine sets up an expectation that the group norm is to venerate Sangharakshita's image. Anyone who feels differently, by feeling indifference or even dislike towards it, is then likely to be placed in a quite unnecessary position of conflict. Even if the photo has a value in practice for some, its public prescription is in conflict with Sangharakshita's ideas about individuality and about the Middle Way, in accordance with which an individual needs to judge their own practices autonomously to address their own situation and develop as an individual. The individual, in most cases, is most unlikely to have come to the shrine room because of a choice to venerate Sangharakshita's image as a practice, but rather to learn or practice meditation.

In a private setting, such as a shrine in a private house or room, a photo of Sangharakshita is likely to have a quite different significance. A visitor is not likely to feel that they have to share any veneration of Sangharakshita, and the photo may not even represent such veneration, perhaps merely being a positive symbol, like a picture of a grandchild on the mantelpiece. The same dangers of projection apply to the individual, if they go on to visualise Sangharakshita in meditation, or otherwise cultivate an idealisation of his image, but the same social issues do not arise from the mere display of his photo.

Sangharakshita has also made some attempt to defuse this issue by making a distinction between his role as a 'Teacher of the Present' and the status of the refuges:

> *I do not see myself as being an object of refuge to anyone. So far as I am concerned, there are only three refuges, namely, the Buddha, the Dharma and the Sangha. If my picture is put on the shrine, I am there only as one of the Teachers of the Present. In any case I do not see the Teachers of the Present as being objects of Refuge.... Yes, a shrine is meant for worship, so that we should place on the shrine only those objects that symbolise what we worship, i.e. The Three Jewels. If the 'Teachers of the Past and of the Present' [including Sangharakshita, ed.] are included they should, in my opinion, occupy a lower level so as to illustrate the difference between that to whom we go for refuge and that which we respect.*[7]

7 https://thebuddhistcentre.com/system/files/groups/files/triratna_controversy_faq_-_version_2.0.pdf (accessed 2018).

However, this is very much a technical distinction that makes little difference to the issue of idealisation. Sangharakshita may not be treated as himself a refuge, but he is still placed on shrines as an object of worship with the attendant danger of idealisation. That danger of idealisation is not necessarily created by him being confused with the refuges, but just by him being there on the shrine.

In general, then, Sangharakshita's ideas about 'the bearer of the archetype' need to be treated with a good deal more caution than they actually seem to be habitually treated with in Triratna. It is a basic part of the practice of working positively with archetypes that their 'bearers' *are not* living or recently dead people, and perhaps not even people whose intellectual work we need to examine critically. To at least some extent, Sangharakshita seems to have recognised this, but he has failed to follow through the implications, and has failed to discourage his followers from venerating his image in public centres. This surely must have contributed (though to what extent it is difficult to say) to the uncritical approach to Sangharakshita's work that is all too common in Triratna, and the mere lip-service to 'critical thinking'.

5.c. *Women, Men and Angels*

In early 2017, a statement appeared on the Triratna website from Subhuti, often seen as Sangharakshita's closest literary collaborator and author of several books presenting his teachings:

> *I want to make it quite clear that I very much regret the publication of my book, Women, Men and Angels, which I think was a serious mistake. I am happy that the book was long ago withdrawn from distribution by the publisher and that all remaining copies were pulped for recycling about 10 years ago.*
>
> *Unfortunately, the book drew attention to a relatively peripheral aspect of Sangharakshita's thinking, giving it a status it did not warrant and having effects that I did not anticipate....*
>
> *So far as I am aware not many Order members these days would be willing to back Sangharakshita's sense of the issues the book discusses. What this indicates to me is that we are free to disagree with our teacher, without disloyalty, on such matters that are not directly connected with the nature of the goal and the following of the Path. That surely is a sign of maturity.*[1]

This statement is perhaps one of the major pieces of evidence for the ways in which the Triratna Order has been obliged to explicitly depart from Sangharakshita's stated views because of his intransigence. In a survey of Order Members made in 2007, 75% of female Order members and 40% of male Order members said they disagreed with the book.[2] Yet Sangharakshita told me face-to-face in 2018 that he did not agree with Subhuti's withdrawal of the book, which was always stated to be an amplification and development of Sangharakshita's views, and that he still found nothing to object to in it.

Sangharakshita's continued avowal of the views that *Women, Men and Angels* represents is not the only reason for still considering the book and its ideas worthy of evaluative discussion. It should be noted that in the statement above, Subhuti nowhere says that he no longer believes the things he wrote in the book: rather he states that he thought its publication a mistake because of the effects of that publication.[3] His brief statement does nothing to indicate

---

1 Subhuti (2017).
2 Order Survey (2007) https://www.freebuddhistaudio.com/ftpusers/lokabandhu/Report%20-%20Order%20unity%20and%20change.pdf (accessed 2018).
3 In a subsequent videoed interview (https://thebuddhistcentre.com/adhisthana-kula/maitreyi-interviews-subhuti-women-men-and-angels, accessed

re-examination of the assumptions on which that book was built, but re-reading the book now I find it a revealing source for many of Sangharakshita's unhelpful assumptions. These are assumptions that may well be applied to other judgements, and seem likely to still be ones maintained by Subhuti and others. The idea that they are 'not directly connected with...the following of the Path' seems to be a convenient and unconvincing rationalisation for disagreeing with Sangharakshita, as the book has many implications for how one follows the Path, some of them stated explicitly within the book itself. The book cannot be completely nullified simply by being withdrawn, while the intellectual superstructure that created it remains intact and effectively unexamined by those who were responsible for it.

In what follows in the remainder of this chapter, I am going to work on the assumption that Subhuti's book represents Sangharakshita's view. This is something that Subhuti has stated many times, including in the book itself, and something that Sangharakshita has confirmed. Sangharakshita's only reservation when he said this was that he might possibly find himself disagreeing with the way in which some things were worded if he read it again with care, but it seems that he could not really imagine any substantial disagreement with it as a representation of his views. Sangharakshita's own direct public utterances on the subject are scattered and far less clear than *Women, Men and Angels*. The book is so revealing, that it is in some ways fortunate that I have a copy available to me dating from before the book was pulped.

Women, Men and Angels[4] consists in a defensive argument for two claims that Subhuti had previously included in his book about Sangharakshita:[5] 'Women generally [are] at somewhat of a disadvantage, at least at the commencement of spiritual life' and 'The feminist reading of history as the story of Woman's oppression and exploitation by Man belongs not to history but to mythology.'[6] The

---

2019), Subhuti does show acceptance that one of the premises of the book – that is, the belief that it is of practical relevance to make judgements about the relative 'spiritual aptitude' of the sexes – was mistaken. It is a shame that he has not also done this clearly in published writing. This video is full of expressions of regret for the practical effects of the publication of the book, but does not offer any reconsideration of the other assumptions discussed in this chapter.

4 Subhuti (1995).
5 Subhuti (1994).
6 Subhuti (1995) pp. 10–11.

major part of the book focuses on the first claim, and rests on an appeal to Sangharakshita's experience and his superior spiritual status as requiring his disciples to consider the views he believes to be supported by that experience: the same apparently open-ended advocacy of conscious confirmation bias that we saw in 5.a. At the same time, though, he puts forward commonsense (rather than scientific) claims about the respective biologically conditioned attributes of men and women and their implications for the spiritual aptitude of each, as well as defending both the truth and the practical value of such generalised comparison.

Women have, on average, less spiritual aptitude at the beginning of the spiritual life, Subhuti argues, because 'though woman has self-consciousness, she tends more to serve the purely biological ends of reproduction than does Man',[7] due to her much closer involvement in childbirth and childcare.

> Sangharakshita points out two aspects to the lesser aptitude women generally have for spiritual life. Firstly, the woman's form, her 'psycho-physical complex', already gives greater expression to interests and concerns that have little to do with spiritual life. Her consciousness is therefore, from the outset, likely to be more limited because it expresses a more limited predisposition. Secondly, the form once taken as the manifestation of previous volitions now exercises its own influence on consciousness, tying it down and limiting it to a far greater extent than does a male form.[8]

Sangharakshita and Subhuti also stress that women have the same *potential* in the spiritual life as men, i.e. they can reach just as far. The comparative difficulties are said to be concentrated at the beginning, when men are said to be able to imagine more new possibilities, and to be able to give more energy to realising them.[9] On the whole Sangharakshita and Subhuti also seem to think that this supposed difficulty in getting started is no justification for discrimination of any kind against women – except, perhaps, in the prioritisation of resources when setting up a new centre.[10]

If this was indeed an inconvenient truth based on a careful interpretation of experience, as Subhuti depicts it, one that it is important for people to understand to deal with the conditions created

---

7 Ibid. p. 28.
8 Ibid. p. 30.
9 Ibid. pp. 45–7.
10 Ibid. p. 79.

by sexual difference, even if it is hard to accept, his argument could be admitted as a courageous one consistent with a provisional approach to the path. However, instead it is an argument formed, not from experience, but from the interpretation of that experience solely in the terms of the kind of top-down approach to the interpretation of Buddhist teachings that I have already noted as interfering greatly with the practical value of Sangharakshita's teachings in other areas.

One thing that needs to be noted particularly is the way in which this frame of reference forces us to interpret the Path. Instead of being the most effective way of responding to any set of conditions at any moment, the Path is seen as a set of targets to be reached, starting at one particular point of initial commitment, and culminating in Stream Entry and Enlightenment. Subhuti tells us that women have more difficulty in getting started on this Path than men – a point that may or may not be correct – but even if it is, one needs to ask where 'starting' begins. For instance, women might need to spend more time in preparation for any practical effort than men, but that preparation time would still be part of 'the Path' because it would be part of a balanced and adequate response to the conditions that an individual has encountered. In broader terms, any biological disadvantage (if there is one) needs to be interpreted in the same terms as any other disadvantage: as simply the context in which one makes better or worse judgements. If 'the Path' is a universal human function rather than a specific Buddhist artefact, it cannot start in any other place than the place you are in now, and it certainly can't be reduced to a formalistic set of descriptions of a track with certain external staging posts marking its beginning, middle, and end.

Again, then, we see the contrast between the potential helpfulness of the best teachings Sangharakshita offered in adaptation to the West, and the fixed ideas he has become attached to in the Buddhist tradition. The practice of creativity over reactivity is not a practice that begins at a certain point, as though a starting pistol had been fired – it simply happens when one is aware enough to make judgements creatively rather than reactively. Nor is the development of individuality, which is an extension of the process that all maturing humans go through: if it had a starting point it might be birth, or even fertilisation! Integration, particularly, requires that we do not simply reject a previous set of conditions in order to set out on a discrete 'Path', but that we gradually transform those conditions into something better. Whoever makes a judgement in greater awareness than they had before, then – whether woman, man, or angel – is already on the Path, however little 'progress' may appear to result from it.

One of the other major questionable assumptions in Sangharakshita and Subhuti's whole approach to this topic is the Platonic one[11] that reactivity is linked to biology and that creative mental states involve an 'ascent' from biology into a state dependent only on the mind. This Platonic assumption is also found in the traditional Buddhist cosmological hierarchy of the *kama-loka* (world of desire), *rupa-loka* (world of form), and *arupa-loka* (formless world).[12]

> Clearly, the greater the preoccupation with the physical body and the concerns of dimorphic sexual reproduction, the lower the level on the hierarchy. Sangharakshita follows Buddhist tradition in arguing that women, being generally more involved with these concerns, will generally be lower on the hierarchy than men.[13]

However, the assumption that reactivity is somehow 'more physical' and creativity 'more mental' is an unnecessary and unjustified conclusion to draw from the conditions of creativity. It is the complexity of human mind-brains giving them the capacity for self-consciousness that enables the development of awareness found in more creative responses. However, greater complexity and awareness does not make us any less physical than we were before, and, more importantly, biological imperatives are not the only source of reactivity: we can get caught up in proliferation that depends very much on abstract beliefs rather than only more obviously 'biological' drives such as anger, anxiety, or sexual desire. Being a floating mind in the *arupa-loka* (if it were possible) would be no guarantee at all of having a creative, integrated, or individual mind.

Such a Platonic interpretation of Buddhism also departs completely from the Middle Way, having a closer relationship with the attitude of the ascetics that the Buddha left behind as he discovered the Middle Way. The Buddha was able to move on from asceticism by recognising his embodiment, and thus move on from the alienated attempt to force the will of the 'mind' on the supposedly

11 E.g. in Plato *Phaedo* sections 64 ff., Plato (1993) pp. 116 ff.
12 Subhuti (1995) pp. 27–8.
13 Ibid. p. 28.

separate 'body', typical of the ascetics. That embodiment is strongly symbolised by the Buddha's acceptance of food when he stopped starving himself, and the recognition of embodiment is a vital starting point of meditative awareness.[14] As discussed in 3.f above, the very meaning of our language and other symbols also depends on the body (as shown in the work of Lakoff and Johnson).[15] Platonic thinking, on the other hand, tends to assume that meaning consists only in a cognitive relationship between words and reality. The Middle Way, if one is to take it seriously, requires an embodied standpoint that strongly challenges such thinking.

The greater involvement of women than men in reproductive processes, then, has no necessary implications at all for them being, even generally or on average, more prone to reactivity or less integrated. It may, on the contrary, allow women to be more *aware* of their bodies, which is one of the basic conditions of mindfulness. This link with their bodies might also have the effect of releasing the imagination from the dominance of closed feedback loops that are strongly *mentally* driven. But even the question of whether women are in fact more generally invested in the body because of their reproductive processes is a complex one. There could well be other factors that make men invested in their bodies when women may not be – for instance competitiveness in physical prowess as shown in sport. Subhuti's argument that men are able to *imagine* more freely is, at the very least, not obviously correct.

In addition, Subhuti's approach in this book involves a major misunderstanding of the working of equality in modern society, as it objects to the assumption that men and women are 'equal' on the grounds that they cannot be so if their conditioning (and thus their supposed spiritual aptitude) is so different. As I discussed above in 3.d, though, equality in a democracy 'is a formal, social relationship governing the way in which people seek to interact, not a complete description of a quality shared by two people'. No amount of information about how people are descriptively different (in for example their abilities, intelligence, or aptitude) makes any difference to the practical case for formal equality in a modern democracy, so Subhuti's objections to 'pseudo-liberal egalitarianism' are evidently based on a confusion about the justification of what he is objecting to.

14 See Ellis (2019) 1.e and f.
15 Johnson (2007).

Once again, too, that objection to basic values of modern society seems to show no awareness of the way that those basic values are essential to Sangharakshita's thinking and Triratna's existence. The value of individuality is socially respected only because of the formal equality of the modern democracy, which limits power relationships, and prevents the stronger interfering grossly with the freedom of development of the weaker. The development of Triratna's women's wing, particularly, would be impossible in a more traditional society in which women are not given any scope or resources to develop their individuality.

It is these assumptions, rather than the empirical claims made, that in my view make *Women, Men and Angels* such an unhelpful document. Subhuti's case for the value of generalisation and comparison seems to be a sound one. Though of course one needs to be aware of how one communicates them, the putting forward of empirical views about the spiritual aptitude of women as compared to men, or about the degree of truth of historical claims about the oppression of women is fair enough – provided these views are genuinely provisional and capable of modification in the light of further evidence, or of the pointing out of assumptions made. However, the lack of genuine provisionality here seems to be shown by both Sangharakshita and Subhuti's complete lack of interest in surveying the scientific evidence, their failure to revise their views after a good deal of warranted criticism, and their failure to recognise the ways in which the *a priori* assumptions they are making dictate their conclusions. How can one claim to be supporting spiritual development if one lacks basic awareness of the limitations of one's understanding?

The second empirical claim in Subhuti's book, that the feminist reading of history as a story of oppression of women by men 'belongs not to history but to mythology', is a vast one that is treated very briefly. It is fairly unclear, despite Subhuti's laboured explanation of 'what exactly is being said', what exactly is being said. Is it being claimed that the interpretation of history as patriarchal oppression is actually false, or just that it is unproven? On the question of male versus female power, Subhuti writes:

> One would have to be able to show that either men or women generally were less able to achieve what they wanted because the other sex had been able to dominate them. Were there more hen-pecked husbands than mouse-like wives? I doubt if it is really possible finally to say, since one would have to

examine a very large number of human relationships in history, many of them completely unrecorded.[16]

All this tells us is that the claim is unproven, not at all surprising in one of such magnitude. Subhuti here seems to be subject to a combination of two fallacies: the nirvana fallacy and the straw man. The straw man sets up an easy version of the opponent's position to knock down: in this case 'feminism' is presented as making an absolute claim about the whole of history, which unsurprisingly cannot be proven. The nirvana fallacy rejects an imperfect answer or solution simply on the grounds of its imperfection, with an implicit comparison to a perfect version. Yes, there is no perfect, unbiased evidence of the history of women's oppression by men. There is, however, a massive weight of imperfect evidence that should lead us to take it far more seriously than Subhuti does.

Without attempting to survey that vast weight of evidence here, perhaps I can give a brief impression of it, by mentioning some of the aspects of female oppression that Subhuti fails to mention and apparently fails to consider, limiting his attention to 'hen-pecked husbands and mouse-like wives'. There is the history of male violence against women, both in the home and elsewhere; there is the history of male rape, sexual assault, and sexual harassment of women, much of it unreported and unprosecuted until recently; there are culturally sanctioned assaults such as female genital mutilation; there are marriage conventions that give women no power in the direction of their lives, with dowries and bride prices meaning they are effectively bought and sold; there are vastly differential education levels until recently; there have been vastly different rights where the expression of sexuality is concerned; and there have been vastly differential levels of personal freedom until recently: to travel, to leave relationships, to pursue a profession, or to own property and transact business. Many of these things have changed significantly in the modern Western world, but remain largely unchanged in the Islamic world and in other more traditional societies. Not all of them have changed sufficiently even in the West.

Subhuti also fails to give any attention to the positive effect of these changes for the whole of society where they have taken place. In a society where men no longer have to oppress women,

16 Subhuti (1995) p. 84.

men too are liberated. The model of individuality becomes not just a male one, but one of the individuality of human beings in general. Reactivity fuelled by conflict can be replaced by creativity in relationships. Conflicts can be resolved that were previously only repressed: resulting in more divorces, but also a lifting of the lid previously placed on the sexual, physical, and psychological abuse of both women and children that accompanied unchallenged patriarchal power. The liberation of women has also allowed them to make an ever larger economic, cultural, and intellectual contribution to society. Where women have been given more political and social power, violence and corruption in society has demonstrably decreased. Where women have control over their own fertility, excessive population levels rapidly decrease to a more sustainable level, removing another source of conflict in the struggle for resources.[17]

So this is yet another instance of Sangharakshita engaging in poorly-informed historical theorising, like the examples discussed in 2.e. As in the previous examples, his interpretation of very selective empirical information is dictated by large unquestioned *a priori* assumptions, but he and his more uncritical followers have then presented his views as a matter of special experience and insight. Once again, his historical assertions are completely unnecessary, because they have no necessary practical connection with the integrative practices he allegedly wants to support by making them.

According to Subhuti, the purpose of making these claims about the history of women's oppression is to discourage women from adopting a victim mentality in which they blame men for their difficulties, rather than taking responsibility for their own lives.[18] However, there is no necessary connection between such a victim mentality and the belief in past patriarchal oppression. Women can believe that they were oppressed in the past but still feel empowered today, or they can deny past oppression but still adopt a victim mentality fuelled by immediate personal experience. It is indeed possible to use past history as an excuse for a lack of responsibility in one's present life, but the way to remedy this is to make people aware of the bias they are indulging by doing this, not to rewrite the history.

17 Pinker (2011) pp. 827 ff.
18 Subhuti (1995) pp. 91–2.

Women, Men and Angels does not merely mark a tactical mistake in the publicising of Sangharakshita's views in a world unready for them, as Subhuti seems to regard it. It is a more profound marker of the intractable conflicts in Sangharakshita's view of the world. Sangharakshita has in fact done much to promote the rights and opportunities of women, especially in India, but he has also greatly undermined this work through his continued attachment to the false certainties represented by absolutes, even when these are in direct conflict with the values that he first promoted in the development of Triratna. These absolutes are clearly not restricted to Buddhist tradition, but are also found in his idealisations of traditional society generally, his Platonic opposition to the body, and his apparently ignorant disregard of any kind of social science when making pronouncements about empirical issues long studied by social scientists. They lead him to continually bite the liberal Western hand that feeds him and sustains his followers, resulting in a deeply confused and incoherent account of how to approach the modern world.

5.d. The Single-Sex Idea

From the nadir of bad argument represented by *Women, Men and Angels*, it is a relief to turn to another aspect of Sangharakshita's approach to relations between the sexes where the arguments appear to be much more genuinely based on experience rather than dogmatic assumptions. What became known as 'the single-sex idea' in Triratna seems to have had its origins in experiment, and its defiance of modern social norms seems to have been motivated by creativity rather than absolutisation. It consists broadly in the idea that single-sex activities can be beneficial to the spiritual path.

According to Subhuti's account, when Sangharakshita returned to the UK initially and founded the FWBO, all activities were for men and women together, following the prevailing custom in the surrounding society.

> *After some time, he began to see that the constant proximity of the sexes was not necessarily advantageous to the spiritual life, even perhaps to ordinary human life. For a start, an element of sexual attraction was present in the mixed situations he organised, especially since many of his disciples were quite young. This introduced a tension into the atmosphere that was inimical to the cultivation of meditation – at times even to the simple study of the Dharma. Then he saw that the sexes' broadly different approaches to life in general applied also to the spiritual life. He encouraged experiments with retreats and other activities for men and women separately. By chance a residential community was formed that consisted only of men, proving particularly successful and being ancestral to the many current single-sex communities within the movement. Within a few years of the founding of the FWBO, many of its activities, beyond the beginners', were for men and women separately, and the 'single-sex idea', not without much debate and some conflict, an established part of Sangharakshita's teaching and of the practice of the movement he founded.*[1]

Despite these apparently tentative experimental beginnings, the 'single-sex idea' seems to have become quickly entrenched quite strongly in Sangharakshita's teaching. It was not applied inflexibly, and did not prevent friendships (and indeed sexual relationships) between men and women in the movement. It was not, and still is not, normally applied to beginners' meditation classes. However, it is pretty much the non-negotiable basis of most Triratna activities for

---

1   Subhuti (1994) pp. 162-3.

those who are ordained or preparing for ordination. Sangharakshita has stated this basis quite clearly:

> For those individuals who go for Refuge, or who seek to go for Refuge, the best lifestyle – circumstances permitting – is one that contains a strong single-sex element, either by virtue of the fact that one lives in a single-sex spiritual community and/or works in a single-sex cooperative or by virtue of the fact that one is a regular participant in single-sex retreats, study groups, etc.[2]

The justifications for this principle seem to be roughly threefold: sexual distraction, sexual polarisation, and commonality of interest.

The first of these, sexual distraction, is the most obvious, and it is mentioned by Subhuti in the quotation above. We have many social mechanisms for suppressing sexual distraction in social relationships, so that, for instance, even if we have to work closely with someone whom we find sexually attractive (but with whom we are not likely to start a relationship), most of us have enough awareness of the negative consequences of expressing it to avoid doing so. However, spiritual or integrative practice requires us to engage beyond that level of social suppression, acknowledging our feelings and working with them, for example in meditation or in quite intimate discussion. In those circumstances, if the object of our attraction is present, it is likely to make it much harder to go through that process.

However, if the single-sex idea was only about sexual distraction, it might be rather a blunt instrument for avoiding it. It applies only to some of us some of the time, and seems more likely to disproportionately affect men (because of their greater tendency to respond instantly to merely visual attractiveness), younger people who are not yet in settled relationships, and heterosexuals.

The other arguments seem to apply much more fully to all members of each sex, whatever their age and sexuality. The argument about sexual polarisation is much more concerned with the unconscious projections that all men and women may place on each other, just because of their habitual social relationships. For example, socio-linguistic analysis shows that in mixed conversations, men are more likely to dominate and interrupt.[3] Men are on average likely to become more competitive in the presence of women, and women to become more passive in the presence of men. To be in

---

2 Sangharakshita (1990d).
3 Thorne & Henley (1975).

a single-sex environment that is also an environment of reflective practice allows us at least the opportunity to become more aware of these unconscious assumptions. Usually it is only by temporarily withdrawing from something that we become more conscious of its effects on us. Just as temporary solitude can have the effect of making us more aware of the effects of others, the withdrawal of the opposite sex allows us to see the effects of our relationship with that sex.

For Sangharakshita, the avoidance of sexual polarisation is presented as part of an ideal of 'spiritual androgyny' – of transcending the limitations of gender altogether:

> *To the extent that one ceases to think of oneself as being a man or a woman in any absolute and exclusive sense, to that extent one will cease to speak and act as though one was a man and nothing but a man or a woman and nothing but a woman, i.e. one will cease to behave in that sexually ultra-polarised fashion which for Buddhism is exemplified by the figures of the male and female asuras. Male asuras are fierce, aggressive, and very ugly, rather like the orcs in* The Lord of the Rings. *The female asuras are voluptuous, seductive and very beautiful....*[4]

Just as it is not necessary to 'believe' in Enlightenment to follow the Path, it is similarly not necessary to 'believe' that spiritual androgyny is possible in any final sense, to see the value of overcoming sexual polarisation in the way that Sangharakshita describes. The Platonism that I criticised in the last chapter may well be being applied in the way he thinks about this, since sex is a feature of human bodies that is being 'transcended' by the reduction of polarisation; but the more immediate practical focus in the single-sex practice is one of avoiding the absolutisation of sexual identity, and thus recognising the wider potential in one's embodied situation. This is a compensatory process, also discussed by Jung in his writings about the anima (feminine archetype of a man) and animus (masculine archetype of a woman). A man, for instance, is more likely to be able to accept and integrate his anima if he first ceases to project it onto women and thus seek it beyond himself.

The third type of argument suggests that we should concentrate more on relationships with those of the same sex because of our commonality of interest with them: as Subhuti puts it above, 'the sexes' broadly different approaches to life in general also applied

---

4 Sangharakshita (1989) p. 74.

to the spiritual life'. Here there is a more positive use of some the distinctions made in the last chapter, not to make claims about differing degrees of spiritual aptitude, but only to recognise differing needs. If women have some basically different physiological conditionings to men, and this has a variety of psychological effects, then it follows that men and women respectively will be able to support each other better in those conditions they have in common with each other in a single-sex context. Single-sex contexts also allow the development of more depth of friendship with members of the same sex than might otherwise occur.

Commonality is, of course, only a starting point for friendship, but we all experience how much easier it is to begin a friendship with someone with whom we have something in common than with someone that we have little in common with. There are also lots of other possible bases for commonality that cut across sexual divisions – for instance race, nationality, class, profession, or interests – but sex provides one of the most important. Compared to the case based on avoiding polarisation, then, that based on commonality is relatively weak, because it doesn't provide any reason why we shouldn't treat sex just like other forms of commonality.

This area is rather interdependent with Sangharakshita's view of marriage, which I will return to in 5.f. Sangharakshita has, as we will see, quite a negative view of marriage on the whole, and is convinced that marriage is largely based on compensatory polarisation rather than friendship. However, he accepts that friendship may also develop in marriage, particularly as a couple mature. But surely, if commonality is an important part of the single-sex idea, that commonality applies to an even greater extent within a married couple? They often share the same social and economic challenges, the same environment, and of course the same children – they are thus likely to develop in parallel. Not all our commonalities, including those related to spiritual development, are with members of our own sex.

On the whole, then, the arguments from sexual distraction and commonality do apply quite well to some people some of the time, but are a relatively weak basis for the strength of Sangharakshita's statement about it. The argument about polarisation is stronger, both because it is more widely applicable, and because it is difficult for us always to be aware of when it is applicable. Nevertheless, it is an empirical argument that needs to be subject to empirical investigation. In 2.c, I noted some of the ways that Sangharakshita advocates empirical approaches, even advocating 'experiment' as one of the 'Pillars of the FWBO'. The single-sex idea is also regularly defended on the grounds that it has developed from experience. It thus needs to be much more rigorously investigated. Does putting people in single-sex environments actually work in supporting their integrative development? If it does, does this apply equally to a wide range of people of different ages, sexualities, and cultures? Does it apply equally in all kinds of single-sex environments, both temporary and long-term?

As far as I can ascertain, no research has been undertaken by social scientists into the effects of single-sex environments on the development of adults. There is a great deal of research into the effects of single-sex schooling, which seems to have been inconclusive in showing its benefits, but the issues are rather different for children because they are at different stages of psychological development. Researchers such as Igor Grossman have developed ways of charting and measuring wisdom (often based on degrees of bias) which can be at least indicative, though of course its presuppositions need close scrutiny. To conduct a study of the effects of single-sex environments, one would simply need to apply these methods at different points in time to a study group who were exposed to them, in comparison to a control group who were not. Such studies do not provide any certainties, but they do give a more rigorous indication of the conditions at work than either personal anecdote or Sangharakshita's over-generalised pronouncements.

Any overall conclusions about the correctness of the single-sex idea will not only need to estimate how well it works in practice, but also take into account the drawbacks of single-sex activities, because they involve costs as well as potential benefits. One of those costs is the loss of the stimulus that comes from the different perspective of the other sex. The more one emphasises the difference between the sexes (as Subhuti does), the more this cuts both ways, because we need to be able to consider and integrate different points of view. One of the features of single-sex male environments in Triratna, in my own experience, is a male groupishness in which unreflective prejudices about women could develop unchallenged. It would probably be an overstatement to call this misogyny, or to accuse the single-sex idea of promoting misogyny, but there is nevertheless the loss of a female perspective that is required to help form our judgements, and a danger of absolutising shared male assumptions.

Spiritual development involves facing up to the challenge of the other, so as to be able to integrate it, just as much as it involves avoidance of polarisation towards the other. It is thus probably the *contrast* between single-sex and mixed situations that provides the benefits of single-sex ones in a world that is mainly mixed. In a more traditional, and more segregated, society, however, it would probably be men and women being brought into closer contact with each other, and being forced to explore their differing views in ways that were not stereotyped by tradition, that would be of spiritual benefit. In the Western context, that perhaps suggests that short-term single-sex environments (such as single-sex retreats) are more likely to be beneficial than longer-term ones (such as single-sex communities). But I offer this only as a suggestion – the whole matter needs fuller investigation.

Another possible drawback is one of potential discrimination. In some circumstances, separation of different groups provides the conditions for discrimination against one of those groups, as classically illustrated by Apartheid South Africa. The argument that separation does not necessarily imply discrimination *can* be used as a cover to rationalise that very discrimination, though I am not suggesting that this is any part of the intentions of Sangharakshita or Triratna. The absolutising responses of external critics, however, often involve assuming that the single-sex idea is merely a way of discriminating against women.

In practice, separation involves discrimination when resources are unequally distributed between the two groups. This seems to have happened quite markedly in the early years of Triratna, as Vajragupta records:

> *The men seemed to develop single-sex activities and facilities more quickly than the women – at least initially. This created some tension between them at the Archway Centre. Some people didn't like the men 'pulling away' and the prospect of segregation. The single-sex idea was hotly debated.*
>
> *[Vajragupta then describes the development of the men's wing in London, and the founding of the men's retreat centres in Padmaloka and Guhyaloka.] The women's wing did...develop similar facilities, but it took longer. In the early days, it seemed that classes in Buddhism and meditation drew in larger numbers of men than women (whereas the opposite is true in many centres today).... This meant that the men's facilities developed faster, which*

attracted more men...and a self perpetuating situation evolved. Sometimes, women lost their confidence by making unhelpful comparisons with the success of the men.[5]

It took until 1977 for the first women's community to be founded, and until 1985 for the first permanent women's retreat centre, Taraloka, to be founded – some nine years after the purchase of Padmaloka for men in 1976. In the meantime, it could well be argued that far fewer resources were going into the women's wing of Triratna than into the men's wing. Of course, the advantage of leaving women to develop their own wing of the movement was that they were forced to take initiative, and in the process overcome their own limitations. Sangharakshita's attitude throughout seems to have been to encourage women to develop their own facilities, and to encourage men to get out of their way. It seems not unreasonable to suggest that Sangharakshita could have taken more of a Middle Way on this, by helping to divert more resources to the women's wing of the movement at an earlier stage, even if it was women who were entirely in charge of how those resources were used.

These kinds of practical difficulties with the application of the single-sex idea seem to illustrate some of the ways that it can very easily become an end in itself rather than a helpful approach rooted in experience of practice. There are numerous anecdotal examples of such rigidity, some of them mentioned by Vajragupta, such as 'Sometimes the only woman Order member in a particular city wouldn't be allowed to join the local Order chapter, as the men in it wanted to keep it single-sex, and she would be left feeling isolated and alone.'[6] Again, this appears to reflect an over-generalised understanding of the principle based on authority and group pressure, rather than an approach that was adopted and applied provisionally, and perhaps attributable in part to Sangharakshita's insufficiently provisional ways of presenting it.

On the single-sex idea as a whole, though, I would conclude that the jury is, and should, still be out. If it works, it should be an inspiration for other groups, but as far as I'm aware it has not been much adopted by other groups, apart from those practising traditional Buddhist or Christian monasticism (who only apply it to the

---

5   Vajragupta (2010) pp. 72–3.
6   Ibid. p. 78.

monastics themselves), and those working on a radical feminist or masculinist agenda. But there is insufficient evidence of how well it works. It seems most likely that it works in some ways and not others, probably better in the shorter term than the longer term, and that where it is used its benefits need to be weighed consciously against its costs. My own personal experience of it is also mixed – it worked for me in some ways when I joined single-sex retreats and lived for a while in a single-sex community, but not others. I await further evidence.

5.e. Sex and Scandal

We now come to the heart of the controversies surrounding Sangharakshita. On the one hand, there has been a trail of public denunciation of Sangharakshita since the publication of the 'FWBO Files' on the internet in 1999[1] and of Madeleine Bunting's critical article in *The Guardian* in 1997.[2] According to the allegations of these critics, Sangharakshita is a serial sexual abuser (who has also lied about his past and distorted the teachings of Buddhism). On his own account, though, Sangharakshita engaged in a series of homosexual relationships between 1967 and 1988 that he sincerely believed at the time to be fully consensual, and, although admittedly reticent, he has never sought to hide these.[3] In general terms, he has apologised for any aspects of them that were not as consensual as he thought.

It is not the purpose of this book to examine any specific allegation against Sangharakshita, nor to attempt to reach any moral (let alone legal) judgement on whether Sangharakshita merits the label of 'sexual abuser'. The evidence on that is complex, and would require a book in itself to be examined properly – but I am not aspiring to the role of investigative journalist. The question, instead, that I want to ask here in relation to Sangharakshita's thought is this one: 'Are Sangharakshita's sexual transgressions to any extent the result of his thought? Does his broader thinking justify them in any way, and thus make them more likely to happen again in future?' To examine that question, we'll need to consider Sangharakshita's attitudes to sex and sexual relationships. His personal conduct is relevant to this, but only insofar as his personal conduct gives an indication of attitudes that may be a model for others, or may reflect on the integrity of his teachings.

Although I have already remarked on the extent of Sangharakshita's confirmation bias, it is as nothing compared to the extremely one-sided material of his most trenchant accuser in the 'FWBO Files'. This (anonymous) person gives complete credence to unsubstantiated old rumours, and interprets every possible piece of evidence as negatively as possible without any attempt to consider the wider context. This author's animus against Sangharakshita is

1 http://www.ex-cult.org/fwbo/fwbofiles.htm (accessed 2018).
2 Bunting (1997).
3 Sangharakshita (2009b).

closely associated with defensiveness of the purity of traditional Buddhism. As one of the FWBO's responses points out:

> The author has a view of Buddhism that is so at odds with that of the FWBO that he is convinced the FWBO's view is a wilful and dangerous misrepresentation. The FWBO is founded on the belief that Buddhism needs to be re-expressed in the context of modern Western Society. The FWBO Files and the Refutation seem to have no interest or sympathy with this approach. The FWBO's core project of establishing the basis for Buddhist practice within the conditions of Western culture (indeed, within modern culture in general) while staying true to the core of the Buddha's teaching, is therefore quite alien to the author.[4]

The author of the 'FWBO Files' seems to represent Sangharakshita's Shadow, in that he ironically shares some of Sangharakshita's absolute commitment to the Buddhist tradition. However, he lacks the awareness required to be inconsistent about it in the ways that Sangharakshita is, being unable even to consider the possibility that Buddhism might offer a way into a practice that is universal in nature and not merely confined within the terms of one tradition. Sangharakshita's sexual transgressions thus seem to him to be proof of a departure from an absolute set of expectations, rather than what they must be from the standpoint of the Middle Way – human transgressions. The many who seem to regard Sangharakshita's teachings as entirely undermined by those transgressions seem to me to have similarly inappropriate absolute expectations – ones that entirely miss the point of what Buddhist practice might offer, and substitute an abstract reification for it.

Sangharakshita's teachings are not a fragile object that can suddenly vanish and be replaced by pure evil because of its author's transgressions, and the first requirement for any helpful approach to the subject is to see them in proportion. If you cannot see the value of even trying to do that, but insist on an absolutized moral response (as do many critics of Sangharakshita that I have communicated with), then I'm afraid we must part company here. What is good and what is bad in Sangharakshita's thought and work do in my view have *some* connection to his sexual transgressions, and it is this that I will be seeking to explore in the remainder of this chapter: but you will be in no position to judge the extent of this connection if you start off by assuming either that his human failings make

4 Vishvapani & Cittapala (1999).

everything he said bad, or that he must have been entirely innocent and that everything he says and does must be good. Either of these polarised approaches is simply fallacious. The introduction of the word 'abuse' tends to do little to clarify any of the issues around Sangharakshita and sex, because it is associated with the inappropriate importation of absolute legal judgement to an ethical discussion. You are either guilty of 'abuse' or not guilty – but human frailty lies, instead, on an incremental scale.

For Sangharakshita, any discussion of sexual ethics begins with the third of the five moral precepts, which give a basic expectation for lay ethics across the Buddhist tradition. He translates that precept as 'I undertake the training principle of refraining from sexual misconduct', and summarises its implications as follows:

> *There is a personal aspect and a social aspect. One must avoid sexual behaviour which is socially disruptive, and one must at the very least avoid engaging in sexual behaviour of any kind to such an extent that one's ethical and spiritual progress is seriously impeded.*[5]

If there is a potentially damaging ambiguity here, it seems to lie in the term 'socially disruptive'. How should we judge which sexual activities are 'socially disruptive'? Some may fall back on traditional social rules to judge this, such as those that try to confine sex to heterosexual activity within marriage, but this is now a very old-fashioned attitude for most people in the West. Others may try to use evidence of harm resulting from some forms of sexual activity to judge social disruption from observable consequences. On this basis it is very difficult to make a very convincing case for the wrongness of any kind of activity between consenting adults that does not result in obvious harm. It is this kind of reflection that has supported both the legalisation of consensual homosexual activity in the West, and the widespread loss of any shame about pre-marital sex. It is obvious from Sangharakshita's discussions of sex that he accepts and indeed prefers this modern Western attitude to sexual ethics,[6] regardless of his sentimental attachment to traditional societies in some other respects. As an acknowledged homosexual himself, it would be surprising if he held any other view.

5   Sangharakshita (1987b).
6   'Luckily, by the time I founded the Order, homosexual acts between consenting adults in private had been decriminalised, thanks to Roy Jenkins, Home Secretary in the Wilson government.' Sangharakshita (2009b) p. 9.

At the same time, Sangharakshita adopts what he takes to be a traditional Buddhist view that sexual desire is intrinsically 'an unskilful mental state':

> I suppose the Buddha's view was that sexual desire is a form of craving. Craving is, of course, an unskilful mental state, and unskilful states hold us back from gaining Enlightenment. For Buddhism...sexual desire is thus axiomatically unskilful. I doubt very much whether it is anywhere considered that you can engage in sexual activity without, at least to some extent, that activity being the expression of an unskilful mental state.[7]

This seems to be a contradiction of what is understood by the term *skilful* (*kusala*) in the context of Buddhism. Skilfulness suggests a way of working practically with the materials at hand, like a craftsperson working with a piece of material such as a block of wood. The concept of skilfulness is an expression of the Middle Way, because it involves both a full acceptance of the starting conditions in any given situation, and the maintenance of a model of how those starting conditions can be helpfully changed. Many Buddhists thus emphasise the distinction between this type of 'skilfulness' and traditional morality, and Sangharakshita unfavourably contrasts this Buddhist view of sex with a theistic view of sex as good because given by God.[8] However, sexual desire is undoubtedly an aspect of our starting embodied conditions if anything is, so there cannot possibly be anything intrinsically *unskilful* about sexual desire. Indeed, the idea of *any* type of desire or action being intrinsically unskilful is contradictory, given that skilfulness is supposed to involve a flexibility in relation to our starting position, in which no rule about how to respond to it can be absolute.

The idea that sexual desire can be intrinsically unskilful only makes sense in the terms of Sangharakshita's Platonic model of spiritual progress transcending embodiment – already discussed in the previous chapter. In his exposition of the Third Precept in *The Ten Pillars of Buddhism*,[9] Sangharakshita places heavy reliance on this model and its justification in terms of a hierarchy of three increasingly disembodied realms found in Buddhist cosmology. As I have already explained, this model is based on a confusion between there being complex mental conditions for the self-consciousness needed

7 Sangharakshita (1987b).
8 Ibid.
9 Sangharakshita (1989) p. 71.

in creative responses, and those conditions being in some way disembodied. Where sex is concerned, however, this Platonism has the potential to create a great deal of confusion. It implies, not just that we shouldn't idealise sex, but that our sexual feelings are basically wrong and unacceptable, because we are gross physical beings and we really shouldn't be. If we are to actually take this seriously, it can only be productive of irrational guilt and conflict proceeding from unconscious cognitive dissonance. The language of 'skilfulness' and the attacks on theism are only a rhetorical distraction from a view that implies old-fashioned sexual guilt in the same fashion as the worst forms of theistic sexual repressiveness.

This also raises deeper issues about the treatment of desire in Buddhist tradition. I have argued in more detail elsewhere that the traditional Buddhist distinction between craving and the desire for enlightenment (or skilful desire) is incompatible with the Middle Way.[10] It is only within a framework that presupposes the desirability of believing in rebirth that there can be particular types of desire, including sexual desire, that are considered intrinsically cyclic and intrinsically bad. In the framework created by belief in rebirth (or its desirability), even the desire to continue to live by itself (*bhava tanha*) has to be seen as ultimately bad, because it leads to rebirth. Sexual desire also has to be considered bad, because it also contributes to rebirth, which is assumed to be reactive. However, if we consult our experience rather than traditional dogma, it seems far more likely that there are no particular objects of desire that make desire necessarily reactive. Rather it is the beliefs that accompany desire (whether they are absolutising) that create the closed feedback loops of reactivity. We can experience the 'stickiness' and power of sexual desire, and this may make it more likely that our accompanying beliefs about what we desire will be absolutising and reactive, but that does not necessarily imply that *all* sexual desire is unhelpful craving. Sexual desire is just an aspect of the embodied conditions we start with that can then be diverted in one direction or another according to our practice, even if it is often associated with a strong weight of conditioning that it is particularly hard to push back on. It is a condition that can be associated with new openness to another as well as with powerful attachments.

10 Ellis (2019) 6.c.

Sangharakshita's Platonic view is used to justify the ideal of spiritual androgyny, which in turn is supposed to justify Sangharakshita's opposition to a range of sexual projection and polarisation in the modern world. However, it is not necessary to believe that spiritual androgyny is possible, or that sexual desire is necessarily 'unskilful', in order to recognise that projection and polarisation are unhelpful. Indeed, the avoidance of projection and polarisation are simply part of the Middle Way, which involves the reduction of delusion by the avoidance of both positive and negative absolute beliefs.

It is on this basis, then, with a theoretical and traditional justification that is actually not needed, together with an underlying basis of conflict, that Sangharakshita sets about criticising 'neurotic' sexual relationships in Western society. Some of these criticisms have had a practical value, but if there was also commonly overstatement and absolutisation, we can attribute it to the underlying conflicts in his view. The frequently used term 'neurotic' seems for him to involve a psychological idea of craving going beyond normal desire. In relationships, he recognised that some degree of dependency was inevitable and healthy, but also asserted that 'neurotic' dependence went beyond that (into what I would call an absolutized belief about that relationship).

> *Well sometimes the line of division between what is objective dependence, as I call it, and subjective dependence is very difficult to detect, exactly where one ends and the other begins. But there is a difference, a distinction between the two things. You can expect quite reasonably as a human being, a certain amount of consideration and warmth from others and this is necessary to you, just as an ordinary human being. So there is this possibility without it being a neurotic dependence. But when you have to have it all the time and you are very unhappy if you can't have it in the way that you want it, then that becomes subjective and neurotic.*[11]

Sangharakshita sees this distinction between healthy and neurotic relationships as cutting across different forms of sexual practice (celibacy, monogamy, or promiscuity). There are thus 'three lifestyles, each one having both a healthy and a neurotic possibility. ...You could be healthily married, and neurotically married; healthily promiscuous and neurotically promiscuous; and healthily celibate and neurotically celibate.'[12] In some ways this sixfold

---

11 Seminar 61.
12 Seminar 118.

categorisation just involves an extension of Sangharakshita's well-known dictum that 'commitment is primary, lifestyle secondary', all of which suggests that one can practise universally in any set of circumstances. Sangharakshita thus emphasises that celibacy by itself is of little value without an effective re-direction of one's energies away from sex, and conversely, he seems to have a positive view of promiscuity when practised without hang-ups. In between, he recognises that monogamy may provide people with helpful emotional stability, but is often sharply critical of its 'neurotic' effects on married couples who are prevented from developing individuality apart from each other.

It is in this positive view of 'healthy' promiscuity that we can seek to explore the possible links between Sangharakshita's views about sex and his personal mistakes in that area. His discussions of sex in the seminars and recorded discussions focus very much on his own motives for promiscuity, and very little on his partners. He was obviously very clear in his own mind that his own reasons for being involved in sexual activity were not 'neurotic', and that he was morally considerate of his partners without being unduly attached to them, or necessarily expecting anything from them beyond that context. In one lecture we can find an attempt to justify this approach through the juxtaposition of casual sexual relationships with committed non-sexual ones:

> *It is quite impossible for all the relationships of one's life to be continuous. But some of them must be continuous. Otherwise one will not be self-conscious, one will not be an individual, at least not to that extent. One will not continue to grow as an individual. One's sexual relationships can be non-continuous only if one has strong non-sexual relationships which are continuous, i.e. in relation to which one practises fidelity. Obviously in such a case these non-sexual relationships must be very important to one. They must come very near the centre of one's mandala. Otherwise if one's non-continuous, i.e. promiscuous, sexual relationships are more important to one than one's continuous non-sexual relationships, one is in a very difficult position. However I didn't really intend to say so much about promiscuity. I just wanted to guard against possible confusion.*[13]

However, if we apply Sangharakshita's own account of sexual ethics, it seems that there is very little emphasis in his thinking on the question of whether what he was doing was 'socially disruptive'

---

13 Lecture 155.

as opposed to whether it was holding back his own spiritual development. See, for instance, this conversation where he is explaining on what basis he set up his promiscuous sexual relationships with young male Order members:

> *Sangharakshita: No, so far as I was concerned, there had to be a definite sexual frisson and it certainly seemed to me there was one in each case, so far as I can remember. I went on instinct and mutual chemistry and even the look in the eye. In this sort of situation one knows, or thinks one knows. There were many young Order members and others around with whom I did not have sexual relationships because I did not feel that frisson between us.*
>
> *Subhuti: As far as you are concerned, everybody you had sex with had some degree of response on some level and was a willing partner?*
>
> *Sangharakshita: I did not feel I was forcing anybody and would have regarded that as a quite wrong thing to do. Perhaps in a very few cases they were not as willing as I had supposed at the time – that is possible. It is not always easy to find out what is going on in someone else's mind, especially if you don't know them very well.*[14]

However, there is often a marked discrepancy between Sangharakshita's account of these encounters and those of his partners – a discrepancy that seems to take Sangharakshita by surprise.

Mark Dunlop's account in the *Guardian* report gives a flavour of what it might have been like from the partner's perspective:

> 'I was very in awe of Sangharakshita,' he says. 'He represented Buddhist ideals. But he was petulant and controlling. He doesn't boss people about but suggests something isn't spiritually appropriate. I thought he was an important spiritual teacher and I ought to do whatever I could to help him.... He would want to have sexual contact about twice a week on average. He usually said something like, "Let me just lie beside you for a while." I dreaded hearing this but felt mean and selfish if I thought of refusing. It was distressing, but some of the other Buddhist practices I had recently learned were themselves strange, such as meditation, but there were apparent benefits. He would get into my bed and perhaps stroke my chest for a while. Then he would get on top of me and rub himself against my stomach until he had an orgasm. I found the whole business repellent but at least it didn't take very long – only about four or five minutes usually. I was completely passive throughout, just waiting for him to finish.'[15]

---

14 Sangharakshita (2009b).
15 Bunting (1997).

Sangharakshita was attracted to younger men, and all of his partners were much younger than him. One would thus expect this kind of view of the situation to be the rule rather than the exception.[16] Whether or not Sangharakshita thought he was being controlling, the younger men were quite likely to interpret his actions as controlling because of the nature of the social relationship between them. It seems that only a marked lack of imaginative empathy would prevent Sangharakshita recognising this – a lack of imaginative empathy that would be surprising in Sangharakshita, who is known for his sensitivity.

The reasons for this 'blind spot' in Sangharakshita are likely to remain mysterious, perhaps even to him. However, it seems to me that in the contradictions of his view of sex we have at least a plausible hypothesis for it: namely unconscious cognitive dissonance created by on the one hand by a deeply rooted belief that all sex is 'unskilful', alongside the more recently developed belief that sex, even promiscuous sex, is acceptable. It is a feasible, though far from certain, explanation that this inner conflict had the effect of blocking the moral awareness he might otherwise exercise.

This would probably not be a speculation worth making, as it would have no further practical relevance, if it did not potentially contribute to an understanding of the relationship between Sangharakshita's ideas and his actions. Sangharakshita's ideas on sex have been very influential on a large number of other people, and indeed, the *Guardian* article based its criticism of the FWBO on a parallel between Sangharakshita's behaviour towards Mark Dunlop and that of a man labelled 'the head of the community' (probably Padmaraja in Croydon) towards young men in his context.

The danger, it seems, lies not just in the abuse of power, which is obviously part of the situation, but the ways that such abuse can be rationalised by the presence of absolutes in the ideologies that support it. In a context like the Roman Catholic Church, it is fairly clear how explicit absolutes can facilitate abuse by supporting an

---

16 An online statement from the Adhisthana Kula, set up to deal with the controversies in Triratna, says that they managed to contact 25 men who have had sexual relationships with Sangharakshita. Of these 5 were 'very unhappy', and of the remaining 20 some were 'quite happy' and others 'less happy' – though there is no clear indication of the proportion who were 'less happy', and also of whether the whole sample excludes some who were so unhappy that they would not have responded to the contact. (https://thebuddhistcentre.com/node/14140#id.668jwjih5jx).

unquestionable structure of authority. In Triratna, by contrast, the absolutes seem to be disruptive rather than formative, releasing practitioners from a full sense of the moral importance of sexual behaviour through a background sense that all sex is wrong in any case, and creating a disjunction between the individual integrity that one can believe one possesses and the social effects of one's actions.

It is in compensation for the effects of our actions that we are *not* aware of and do not anticipate that deontological ethics (that is, allegiance to general moral principles) comes into play and is able to reveal its strengths. In other areas of ethical practice, such as avoidance of violence, or even of coarse language, Sangharakshita is very supportive of fairly traditional moral principles, whether these are derived from Buddhist tradition or from society.[17] In the case of principled moral disapproval of promiscuity, though, it seems that he has quite a different approach, somewhat to his cost. Promiscuity has the drawback that one does not know much about the mental states and beliefs of the person one is having sex with, and thus is not in a very good position to judge whether one might be harming them in unexpected ways. Despite Sangharakshita's tendency to treat 'non-neurotic' promiscuity equivalently with 'non-neurotic' celibacy or monogamy, in many respects promiscuity, even of a 'non-neurotic' type, is not equivalent to the other two options: not because it is always necessarily wrong, but because practising it takes account of our degree of uncertainty far less than other forms of sexual activity.

In addition to Sangharakshita's attitude to promiscuity, there is also some controversy over his attitude to homosexuality. In the *Guardian* article, Mark Dunlop reports that Sangharakshita's rationalisation for having sex with him was to help him overcome 'anti-homosexual conditioning',[18] and there have been accusations that this was a regular part of Sangharakshita's ideology, used to justify the sexual abuse of reluctant heterosexual young men.

It's certainly the case that Sangharakshita thinks that fear of homosexuality is a problem inhibiting Western men from developing depth of friendship:

17 Sangharakshita (1989) thoughout.
18 Bunting (1997).

> For most people in the West it would seem that physical contact occurs in association with sex. We consequently seem to confuse the two, or to regard the two as inseparable. Purely physical contact is therefore quite difficult for people to obtain, especially, I think, for men to obtain from other men. Normally, in the case of other men, there's no 'danger' of sexual involvement. Even so, men find it quite difficult to experience physical contact with other men because of their fear of homosexuality.
>
> I've observed cases where men are even afraid to give each other a brotherly hug! It may take them years to get through that. And when they succeed in doing it, they are quite overwhelmed and overjoyed, as though they've had a real breakthrough! This illustrates the terrible mess we've got ourselves into; such a simple thing has become an enormous problem.[19]

This certainly accords with my own experience of specifically British society, and that of many others, though it may apply much less to other Western societies. After becoming involved in Triratna, as a young man, I had to teach my father to hug. However, whether fear of homosexuality is the only factor in this fear of physical contact, particularly among British heterosexual men, is another question. Even if unconscious fear of homosexuality is indeed one factor, then engaging in homosexual activity with a reluctant heterosexual is not obviously the best way to overcome it effectively. Even if intended as 'therapy', such a procedure would be difficult to distinguish from abuse.

However, Sangharakshita denies that this is what he was doing:

> *Mahamati:* You weren't having sex for therapeutic reasons?
>
> *Sangharakshita:* No, I was having sex because I was attracted to the person and saw, or thought I saw, an answering response. However, I did see the benefits of it and I remember seeing those benefits quite concretely in a number of cases. I formed the view – and I still think it is true – that many men are afraid of getting too close to other men emotionally, fearing that this will slide into homosexuality. That was my thinking in those days, 30 or 40 years ago. Though that is not so much the case today, there is still a homophobic element in society and some men will be affected by this fear.[20]

Though Sangharakshita's motives may well have been mixed, there is limited evidence that Triratna has ever taught such 'therapeutic homosexuality' to be a justifiable approach in any systematic way. I can find no reference to it in Sangharakshita's lectures or

19 Sangharakshita (1987b).
20 Sangharakshita (2009b).

seminars. The five quotations given at the end of the *Guardian* article, obviously intended to show the scandalous nature of Triratna teachings on sex, are mainly about neurotically attached couple relationships contrasted with the possibility of promiscuity, with the exception of the final one. This quotes Subhuti in 1986:

> *Sexual interest on the part of a male Order member for a male mitra (novice) can create a connection which may allow kalyana mitrata (spiritual friendship) to develop. Some, of course, are predisposed to this attraction, others have deliberately chosen to change their sexual preferences in order to use sex as a medium of kalyana mitrata – and to stay clear of the dangers of male-female relationships without giving up sex.*[21]

Subhuti does not clearly advocate this way of acting here, or suggest any institutional expectation that it should be followed. However, he does seem to suggest this kind of 'therapeutic homosexuality' as one possible kind of acceptable practice, in the process apparently assuming a spiritual superiority for homosexual relationships over heterosexual ones, and also showing no awareness of the likely effects of the power imbalance in the relationship. Triratna critics have found other similar quotations from other prominent male Order members, but none of them are given in contexts that indicate that this was a general policy or belief followed in the organisation as a whole. It seems very unlikely that any such practices continue in Triratna now, following the introduction of safeguarding procedures and the spread of much wider awareness of the effects of social power imbalances on sexual relationships.

Linked to this is the idea that Sangharakshita teaches 'Greek love': that is, that a homosexual relationship between an older and a younger man can be spiritually advantageous. Again, this is an approach that may have been adopted by some Order members, but Sangharakshita denies that it played a part either in his motivations for sexual relationships, or in his teachings:

> *Mahamati: I was wondering whether you thought in terms of 'Greek love'. I seem to remember that in the Greek tradition the younger partner was not supposed to be aroused or something like that. Was this in your mind?*
>
> *Sangharakshita: I had forgotten about that tradition. Greek love was not what many people seem to think it was. It was supposed to be an aspect of an educative relationship, in which an older man would help to educate and mature a*

21 Subhuti (1986).

youth through an intense friendship in which sex played its part. The youth was supposed to satisfy the desire of the older man out of gratitude or affection, but without being sexually involved himself. That does seem to have been the old Greek pattern. As far as I remember from what I have read, the ancient Greeks regarded sexual relations between two grown men as rather laughable. They definitely saw the healthy variety as asymmetrical, as we would say. At least that was the classic form of that relationship among men.

Mahamati: *Do you think that influenced your thinking?*

Sangharakshita: *I doubt it very much. My principal thinking in this area was that fear of homosexuality seemed to prevent some men from forming strong or deep friendships with other men, because they were afraid of sliding into homosexuality – which of course they feared and despised. I think that was the point I was more concerned with.*[22]

Sangharakshita's critics may ask here why we should believe him. Since my aim here is not to put Sangharakshita himself on trial, either morally or legally, but rather to put his ideas on trial, I don't see that question as practically relevant. Sangharakshita's account of his motives appears clear and coherent, but that is no guarantee against self-deception. He may be self-deceived to some extent, and as I have already suggested, may have been subject to unconscious conflicts, but the bigger question is whether the legacy of his ideas can be taken to be one that promotes unethical sexual practices.

In my judgement, his view is guilty of promoting a rather naïve account of the justification of promiscuity that fails to take into account our degree of ignorance of others' feelings, but not of promoting 'therapeutic homosexuality' or 'Greek Love'. If Sangharakshita himself denies that he was motivated by these things, he did not publicly teach them, and most others in Triratna agree that they are unwise, that is sufficient to conclude that they are not a legacy that is particularly likely to undermine the ethics of Triratna as a whole. No future Buddhist will be able to justify sexual abuse by appealing to Sangharakshita's teachings on homosexuality specifically, at least not without a good deal of unfairly selective interpretation. However, that does not rule out the possibility of the interpretation of his teachings that facilitated abuse still being found amongst some of his followers. Any such cases will need to be considered individually.

22 Sangharakshita (2009b).

5.f. Marriage and Family Life

Sangharakshita's attitudes towards the roles of men and women, the use of single-sex environments, and sex itself all tend to combine into a critique of marriage and the family. For him, women's lower spiritual aptitude is bound up with their desire to have children, and the ways in which he sees this as interfering in their spiritual development. The married couple and the 'nuclear family' of couple plus children offer a model of social organisation that is in conflict with his views about the benefits of single-sex environments. He also regards the 'couple' as predominantly an institution that promotes 'neurotic' dependency. This has led him to propose alternative non-familial arrangements for bringing up children, and, though not denying that people can develop spiritually when living in families, to regard families as a regrettable second-best arrangement. All of these views seem to depend on a great many contestable assumptions, in addition to the ones I have already discussed in the last few chapters.

Sangharakshita's critique of the 'couple' depends on a perception that monogamy often takes a 'neurotic' form:

> The 'couple' is the enemy of the spiritual community. By the couple, in this context, one means two people, usually of the opposite sex, who are neurotically dependent on each other and whose relationship, therefore, is one of mutual exploitation and mutual addiction. A couple consists, in fact, of two half-people, each of whom unconsciously invests part of his or her total being in the other: each is dependent on the other for the kind of psychological security that can be found, ultimately, only within oneself. Two such half-people, uneasily conjoined as a couple, can no more be part of a spiritual community than Siamese twins can be part of a corps de ballet. Their 'presence' within a community can only have a disruptive effect.[1]

Sangharakashita's way of expressing himself here is characteristically extreme: a classic instance of his rhetorical excess. The degree of 'neurotic' dependence that he presents here may be present in some, perhaps many, couple relationships, but he presents it as ubiquitous, in a sweeping generalisation. There is no balancing mention at all either of the ways that some couples may not be so mutually dependent, or that monogamous relationships may have pros as well as cons. His first sentence, particularly, is extremely

---

1 Sangharakshita (1986) p. 180.

polarising in effect, and can easily be misread as meaning that no actual couples should be part of any actual spiritual community – though more charitably, it is probably intended to mean that no neurotic couples can be members of an *ideal* spiritual community. Characteristically, too, this is presented in absolute terms. There is no recognition that too much mutual dependence in couples is a matter of degree, or that spiritual communities may be exactly the place they need to avoid any extremes of mutual dependence. It is very hard to recognise here the Buddhist teacher who also sets store by the Middle Way. For large tracts of his teaching, especially where subjects that involve sex are concerned, he seems to entirely forget that there was ever such a thing as the Middle Way in Buddhism, or that it might be relevant to him expressing himself in a more appropriate way that puts any specific problem into a wider context.

As we saw in the previous chapter, Sangharakshita does not actually think that monogamous couples have a monopoly on 'neurotic' relationships. He also thinks that celibacy and promiscuity can have 'neurotic' forms. He does discuss 'neurotic' celibacy in a number of places: for instance where people have become celibate 'out of guilt, or for the sake of some material advantage'.[2] However, he also recognises that most people are not yet ready to enter a state of celibacy in a 'non-neurotic' way. That leaves promiscuity as the only alternative option, but although he recognises in principle that promiscuity can be practised in a 'neurotic' way, you will look in vain in his writings for any warnings about the dangers of promiscuity equivalent to his attacks on 'the couple'. In general he seems to think that promiscuity is harmless for men even if it can be psychologically disruptive for women:

> *This, as I say, is my thinking aloud; it's not my definite conclusion but it's the way my thinking is tending at present. It seems that it doesn't do a man much psychological harm, probably none at all, to just gaily scatter his seed around here and there. It doesn't seem to matter in his case, but I think in the case of a woman to come to the point of conception and then the whole process is interrupted, and again it happens and again – this seems to do her harm both physically and mentally.*[3]

He goes on to remark that he's surprised at how many ailments women seem to get, and to associate these with their promiscuity.

2 Sangharakshita (1987b).
3 Seminar 118.

The connection between promiscuity and health levels for each sex is clearly an empirical matter needing research, but as usual Sangharakshita is happy to rely on anecdotal evidence and speculation to provide the justification for comments whose implications go far beyond that context. But there is no recognition at all here that promiscuity might be bad for men as well because of the lack of awareness one is likely to have of one's partner's mental states. There thus seems to be a nirvana fallacy (or fallacy of perfectionism) here: he attacks monogamy without showing recognition that, like democracy, it may be overwhelmingly the least worst option of those available in most cases, despite its many faults.

In the same seminar, Sangharakshita offers the view that the only point of marriage is to provide a stable context for rearing children:

> *I don't really see the point of getting married, you being a man, if you don't intend sooner or later to start a family. That seems to be the point, really, of getting married and settling down with one woman and undertaking to look after her: well, why should you look after her rather than she look after you? – well, you can look after each other – unless you're going to have children. And, if you have children, it becomes incumbent on you to look after her, at least for the time being, rather than the other way round, for obvious reasons. So it would seem to me that the only reason for proposing to yourself to stay with one and the same woman for some 15 or 20 years is that during that period you are going to be raising a family which will need your joint attention for pretty well that period. So therefore it seems to me quite pointless to get married, or the equivalent, if you're not thinking in terms of having a family.*[4]

Again, the one-sidedness is striking. He does not mention the other advantages of marriage in providing a rooted sense of security and basic support for both partners. Statistically, married people are less prone to health problems such as cancer, heart attacks, and stroke, have lower stress levels, are less prone to mental illness or unsafe behaviour, and will live longer.[5] These advantages may be slightly better, or at least similar, for men than for women – according to empirical research in the wider population, rather than anecdotal claims justified only with reference to one person's experience in the Triratna community. In other areas he seems happy for people to make formal undertakings to incentivise helpful practice

---

4 Ibid.
5 Siegler et al. (2013), Simon (2002). Wells (2016) provides further links to a variety of other sources.

– but not, it seems, where monogamous relationships are concerned, except for the purpose of having children.

Whether Sangharakshita even thinks that marriage is desirable for having children, is, however, also debatable, because he often makes one-sidedly negative comments of a similar kind about the family, especially the 'nuclear' family consisting only of parents and their children.

> You see, the trouble nowadays is, from a certain point of view, we find ourselves belonging to groups which are either much too small, or much too big. On the one hand there is the nuclear family into which we are born, mother, father, maybe one or two brothers and sisters. But this sort of nuclear family is a quite late, a quite recent development in human history, and even now it's by no means found everywhere in the world. And it's so late and so unusual, this sort of nuclear family, so sort of exceptional and aberrant, that it's not surprising that psychologists say that it's a sort of breeding ground for neurosis. On the other hand, groups nowadays are so big that we can't possibly have contact with all the members of them. Especially, we think of the nation state. That's the biggest group of all, perhaps. So here we are as it were, suspended almost, between a group which cramps us, i.e. the nuclear family, and a group which is so big as to be meaningless, i.e. the state, with a number maybe of other very large equally unsatisfactory groups of which we have a sort of partial and intermittent membership which don't really satisfy us. But what man wants, or all man wants sometimes is just a group that he can belong to as in the good old days, when he roamed the forests or lived in the little village. All he wants is 30, 40, 50, or maybe if he's very ambitious and greedy, 60 other people with whom he's in real live contact all the time, whom he knows personally, with whom he has a genuine sort of relationship on that sort of group level.[6]

Again, the weakness in his approach here is not that these negative aspects of the nuclear family are necessarily incorrect, but that they are not set against positive aspects, nor compared realistically with alternatives. They are also absolutized, because they are not dealt with as a matter of degree. Nuclear families can be more or less isolated, and there are various possible ways of embedding them more effectively in wider communities without dissolving them. The nuclear family also has advantages compared with alternatives such as the extended family, such as greater flexibility and freedom from the patriarchal authority that tends to predominate in extended families. Whilst its relative isolation may create conditions

6 Lecture 91.

for too much mutual dependency, these are also conditions where individual freedom can be maximised whilst maintaining some family support both for adults and children. That individual freedom, once again, is essential for the development of individuality.

Even in relation to the family in general, Sangharakshita always seems to focus on its disadvantages for spiritual life, whilst saying nothing about its relative advantages. Subhuti, for instance, represents his view as follows:

> Perhaps the most crucial disadvantage of raising children from a spiritual point of view is the extent to which family life tends to absorb one in a narrow world whose deep and largely unrealised attachments can easily become embedded in one's personality, rendering spiritual progress very difficult indeed.[7]

Does family life always 'absorb one in a narrow world'? Obviously it can have that effect, but in my own experience it can also have the effect of stretching one's world by obliging one to meet new kinds of demands that one would never have tried to meet without it. Its effects are quite unpredictable, because they are deeply rooted in the body and its instincts. Bodily instincts, contrary to Sangharakshita's Platonic assumptions, are not necessarily reactive or narrow, but merely part of the set of conditions we are working with. Facing up to bodily conditions, like facing up to social or political conditions, can never be negative for spiritual growth, even if it is difficult and uncomfortable. The ways in which family life limits our available time and energy for institutions outside the family should not be confused with spiritual growth itself, which depends on our responses at each moment regardless of our circumstances.

Sangharakshita's suggested alternative to the family is that children should be brought up in single-sex communities, initially with their mothers, until boys become old enough to join their fathers in men's communities. The practical difficulties of this scheme become clearer even in the discussion about it in the seminar on the *Sigalovada Sutta* – for instance, how old should the boys be when they transfer, and why should men in men's communities devote time to looking after someone else's child?[8] From the psychological point of view, there is also the issue of ensuring that a child is

---

7   Subhuti (1995) p. 41.
8   Seminar 118.

securely attached so as to secure its long-term psychological well-being, the family being a well-established institution for doing this. Research into the effects of communal child-rearing in the Israeli kibbutzim suggests mixed results: that communal caregiving can be positive in its psychological effects compared to conventional family life, as long as it does not extend to communal sleeping, which can have the effect of making attachments insecure.[9] Even if there were no doubts about its effects on the children, though, there are serious issues as to whether adults without family ties can in fact be induced to support others' children adequately. The practical difficulties can also be judged by the ways in which Triratna Order members have voted with their feet: in a 2007 survey, 50% of them lived with their partners, a third were married, and about 22% had children. More men than women also expressed a wish to marry or have children in the future.[10]

Sangharakshita's radical proposals for dismantling 'neurotic' family life have thus been unsuccessful even amongst his own followers, who, like modern Catholics, have increasingly ignored theoretical pronouncements on sex and family life from on high that have not been adequately considered in relation to the complexity of their lives. As with the other issues related to sex in the last few chapters, there is an underlying reason for this lack of success, which is that they are based on dogmas rather than considered in a sufficiently broad experiential fashion. They begin with the Platonic rejection of embodied experience, assuming that experiences motivated by basic biological drives must thereby be reactive and spiritually negative – when there are no grounds for believing this. They are pursued with one-sidedness, fallacy, and bias, which means that there is no attempt to realistically weigh up the pros and cons of different options. As with Sangharakshita's other pronouncements on social issues, there is also no attempt to consult the perspective of the social sciences to provide realistic information on what actually works for a broad range of people. If you really want to transform society, it pays to do some research so that you properly understand the conditions you are trying to transform.

9 Aviezer et al. (1994).
10 Order Survey, 2007: https://www.freebuddhistaudio.com/ftpusers/lokabandhu/Report%20-%20FWBO%20and%20the%20Three%20Cs%20for%20web.pdf (accessed 2018).

6. Conclusion

6.a. Review of the Argument

At the end of this process of evaluation, it is clear that Sangharakshita's contribution to humanity is profoundly mixed, but also very substantial. The mixed nature of his contribution can easily obscure the substantial ideas and example that have inspired many in practical progress that has helped to transform their lives. It can also obscure the depth of understanding and engagement that at times illuminates his work.

I started off this book with a focus on the most helpful, distinctive, and universal syntheses that Sangharakshita identified between Buddhist tradition and the best of Western thinking. Perhaps the most important of these is the distinction between creative and reactive mind as an interpretation of Buddhist conditionality. If we were to forget the rest of Sangharakshita, but only focus on developing the open feedback loops of creativity rather than the closed ones of reactivity, we would have learnt something of universal value. This emphasis on creativity also requires provisionality and an experimental attitude, connecting with the best aspects of scientific method, which are ideas theoretically present in Sangharakshita's teaching but unfortunately often not applied. It supports integration, a concept widely used in Triratna that links Sangharakshita's thinking with psychotherapy. It also implies the development of individuality – a concept closely linked to freedom and democracy in Western liberal tradition, but which Sangharakshita used in deeply contradictory ways, showing little positive appreciation of that tradition.

Sangharakshita's attitude to the Middle Way encapsulates these strengths, and the contradictions that accompany them. Nearly everything helpful and positive that he offered can be seen as an aspect of the Middle Way, forcing people to consult and develop their experience rather than relying on dogmatic or absolute beliefs imported from authorities. At times, some of his best practical strategies were recognised as applications of the Middle Way – as in his talk 'Twenty Years on the Middle Way'. However, Sangharakshita's thinking is extremely inconsistent in its application of the Middle Way, and often worked directly against it, by placing too much emphasis on appeals to the Buddhist tradition that can be easily interpreted as absolute appeals. His theoretical account of the Middle Way itself also does little to clarify the contradictions found in the Buddhist tradition.

When considering his attitude to practice – of meditation, ethics, friendship, social organisation, the arts, and ritual – I found a common pattern of Sangharakshita promoting helpful practices that enable people to work towards greater integration in experience. This is particularly the case in individual practices like meditation, ethics, and the arts, but even here, Sangharakshita's views are often marred by rigid attachment to tradition, hierarchy, and idealised concepts. The more socially-mediated practices become, the more his views tend to reveal unhelpful rigidities. His political attitudes also begin to emerge as a disruptive factor here, particularly resulting in the one-sided rejection of approaches effectively established by liberal democracy, even when his whole movement takes the social practices of liberal democracy for granted in other respects. His linear thinking and prescriptiveness become increasingly evident in the rigidities of his approach to vertical friendship, to the Order-trustee system, and to ritual, in a way that often undermines the creativity that initially seems to characterise his approach to these areas.

When we get on to Sangharakshita's interpretation of Buddhist teachings, his adherence to Buddhist tradition comes to dominate much more explicitly, at the expense of any experiential understanding of spiritual progress. Although he offers interpretations of enlightenment that emphasise it as a process rather than as a final state, these interpretations are never applied to any other teachings, with the concept of enlightenment instead being typically used as a justification for top-down authoritative deduction from traditional Buddhist formulations. Such top-down interpretations tend to predominate, at least in theory, in his accounts of conditionality, karma, rebirth, the authority of the Buddha, the unity of Buddhism, and the importance of Going for Refuge. In all these teachings, there are experiential points to be made and potential relevance to integrative practice (or its archetypal inspiration), but Sangharakshita generally insists on the top-down approach, assuming that the tradition offers access to an 'enlightened' perspective even when he has also raised our awareness of how problematic the reification of that perspective is. His formal interpretations of Buddhist teaching thus represent a major failure of the critical thinking that he theoretically supports.

When we come to the areas of greatest controversy, then, we see an accentuation of the same patterns by which Sangharakshita undermines the best of his own teachings, but this time with more obvious and immediate practical implication. His absolutising appeal to his own right to decide the basis of the Order he founded apparently reflects not only the trend of top-down certainty, but also traces of the incoherent reaction against liberal democracy and failure to apply the Middle Way that we saw in other respects. His failure to object to his image being used in ways that he explicitly recognises as dangerous is disturbing, as is his inability to learn from the objections of his own Order to his views on the spiritual aptitude of women. On gender roles, the effectiveness of single-sex environments, on marriage, on the family, and above all in relation to his own sexual conduct, he showed a dangerous over-confidence in his own intuitions, bolstered by direct or indirect claims to authority, and rationalised rather than scrutinised by the more experiential and critical aspects of his teachings.

The scandals and disputes surrounding Sangharakshita are thus not incidental to his teachings, but have emerged explicably from the weaknesses and contradictions in those teachings. More than anything, they appear to be the outcome of what we could call blind spots, domain dependence, or just inconsistency. His temperament and self-directed education have given him insights, but have not trained him to think consistently about the application of his beliefs in one area to another one. The possibility of some deeply-rooted cognitive dissonance disrupting his thinking also cannot be ruled out. Whatever the reasons for his inconsistency, its result is that the creativity, depth, and inspiration of his thinking appear to have far outstripped his ability to synthesise it all effectively or to engage in effective self-critical questioning.

6.b. Responses to the Argument

I am expecting some strong reactions to this book. Whenever one attempts to intervene in a polarised debate, my experience is that a common reaction is for both sides to attack one for daring to question their assumptions, and for each to identify one with the other side. My motive is a sincere attempt to find the Middle Way, but it is unfortunately likely that some will not even respect that intention as sincere. However much you may disagree with particular aspects of my argument, I would ask you to respect that intention.

My argument is provisional, in the sense that anything I have said about Sangharakshita's life, views, motives, or behaviour may be wrong. I have tried to reference my empirical claims, and to make it clear in my wording when I am speculating to any extent, or when I am drawing on my own experience or other anecdotal information. Here, provisionality markers such as 'seems' or 'apparently' have been used deliberately and should be taken seriously. I am happy to be corrected on any specific points that can be clearly evidenced, or where I have misrepresented a wider position through partial treatment.

However, the most important work of this book is critical and philosophical, and consists in pointing out inconsistencies and dogmatic assumptions in Sangharakshita's work. I am expecting that most of the likely objections will come from those who want to defend his assumptions, with perhaps a few from those who feel that I am letting him off too lightly. I am going here to try to list the most likely of these anticipated objections:

- 'It is unfair to treat Sangharakshita's work as theory when it consists in spiritual insight'
- 'Sangharakshita was not a philosopher, so should not be judged by philosophical standards'
- 'Sangharakshita's positions, however unacceptable they may seem, are justified by his experience'
- 'You have no personal authority to criticise Sangharakshita or the Buddhist tradition'
- 'Sangharakshita's views need to be interpreted within a framework of faith'
- 'Sangharakshita's insights are synthetic, so should not be over-analysed'
- 'You are a rationalist'

- 'You are a materialist'
- 'Sangharakshita's work should not be given this amount of credence, given his abusive behaviour, betraying his responsibilities as a spiritual teacher'

Some of these objections may be based on misunderstandings, others on dogma. I am going to offer some responses to each of them here, so that the misunderstandings can be pre-emptively cleared up and the dogmas identified.

'It is unfair to treat Sangharakshita's work as theory when it consists in spiritual insight'

This kind of criticism normally results from the assumption of a false dichotomy between theory and insight. 'Insight' refers to the way in which we may personally come to understand what we then tend to express in the form of beliefs, not to a special form of infallible belief that is beyond criticism. As discussed in 2.c, scientific theories may also be arrived at through intuitive means that we might call 'insight' – a 'eureka' moment in which we bring together ideas that have previously been separated. This way of coming to understand something does not justify any assumption that the beliefs we formed in this way are necessarily correct, or that their consistency, applicability, or justification in experience or evidence should not be investigated. 'Dharma' is theory, and needs to be treated as such.

On the other hand, because a set of beliefs are treated as theory, it does not justify them being investigated only in a particular narrow way prescribed by scientific specialists, for example with the elimination of first-person experience. Narrowing of the form of investigation can easily pre-determine the results, and again involves unnecessary dogmatic assumptions about the kinds of experience that can justify our beliefs. There are a wide range of ways of potentially investigating the compatibility of theory with experience: through empirical science, through personal experience, or by more negatively identifying ways that theory can exclude experience (which is the particular focus of my own work). As long as the limitations of each of these ways of investigating theory are recognised, they cannot be simply dismissed.

'Sangharakshita was not a philosopher, so should not be judged by philosophical standards'

This related objection is one of a kind I have often heard in Triratna, and involves a false dichotomy between 'philosophers' and everyone else. 'Philosopher' is just a term for someone who gives greater attention than average to the clear and consistent justification of beliefs, including ones that are of a more basic and general kind and thus likely to be taken for granted in everyday life. 'Philosophers' are also likely to be people who accept a responsibility to justify their beliefs carefully. However, anyone who offers general teachings about how to live our lives, as Sangharakshita did, is subject to these responsibilities. There is obviously no justification for engaging in philosophical types of claims but not accepting the philosophical responsibilities that come with them. Sangharakshita was indeed a philosopher in the sense that he made philosophical claims, but not in the sense that he always faced up to his philosophical responsibilities. Given that he began his engagement with philosophy by reading Kant's extremely daunting and complex *Critique of Pure Reason* at the age of sixteen,[1] it is also difficult to realistically claim that Sangharakshita did not have the intellectual ability to face up to his philosophical responsibilities.

'Sangharakshita's positions, however unacceptable they may seem, are justified by his experience'

There is no justification for denying anyone else's experience, the full nature of which is beyond our knowledge. It is very likely that Sangharakshita had profound and insightful experiences. However, the interpretation of these experiences in absolute terms, as though they justified the ultimate truth of a particular set of claims or beliefs in words, cannot be justified by any such experience without dogmatic assumptions. Anyone's reports of their experiences need to be weighed in the balance with other factors, even if they are apparently unique, and the assumptions they make when interpreting an experience need to be taken into account. Experience of any kind cannot be just directly translated into true beliefs.

---

1 Sangharakshita (1996) p. 65.

'You have no personal authority to criticise Sangharakshita or the Buddhist tradition'

The concept of 'authority' can either be used in an absolute way, to assume that someone's views must necessarily be correct because of their status, or in an incremental way (as a matter of degree), to help us to judge where best to bestow our limited attention, or whom to trust when we have no other evidence. For the incremental sense in which 'authority' is used, I prefer the term credibility.

Absolute authority is implicitly invoked whenever no scope is allowed for weighing up one source against another when making a particular judgement (as in 5.a): in other words, when we are asked to just take a particular person's word for it. To claim that either Sangharakshita or the Buddhist tradition has absolute authority is a dogmatic position, beyond all experiential justification. I certainly also claim no such authority for myself. No such authority is needed to point out the limitations of dogma. Doing this is a sceptical process that involves no absolute claims, whether positive or negative, but only a recognition of the limitations of our claims, and the limitations of their justification, due to the embodied nature of our position in the world and the embodied dependency of our language. Embodiment is not the same as materiality, but involves a recognition of the bodily basis of our *experience*.

Credibility judgements, on the other hand, can only be made by individuals deciding where best to bestow their attention. Incremental judgements of credibility can be supported by considerations like reputation, access to information, expertise, bias, vested interests, or corroboration and conflict with other sources. If you have got this far into this book, you have presumably already decided that the book is credible enough to warrant your attention, and I have no need to establish 'authority' beyond the point where you will read and consider my arguments. I would not suggest that you need to trust me personally beyond that point, because my arguments do not depend on any appeal to my personal status or insights, even though they would not have been developed without such insights.

'Sangharakshita's views need to be interpreted within a framework of faith'

Those who make this kind of objection tend to interpret religious language as sealed within a particular context, where it is made meaningful by the practices of a particular group. This is a kind of view particularly associated with the linguistic philosophy of Wittgenstein. 'Faith' is interpreted in this way of thinking either as a set of foundational beliefs, or at least as a set of implicit assumptions that create a *form of life*. It may then be argued that it is illegitimate to criticise one form of life in the terms of another, so that Sangharakshita's views should only be interpreted within the form of life created by the Buddhist tradition.

I argue that the Wittgensteinian view of the meaning of language assumed here is dogmatic.[2] Although the *social conventions* with which we interpret language (not the same as *meaning*, which is embodied) are affected by forms of life, these forms of life cannot be assumed to be 'sealed units' completely separated from each other (the absoluteness of this 'seal' is the key indicator of dogma here). Sangharakshita's career itself is almost a demonstration of this – that 'the West' is not a sealed unit in which the meaning of our language is completely separated from that of the Buddhist tradition. Rather, the social conventions we employ constantly evolve, interacting with our immediate experience of the meaning of the language and of the other symbols that we use. Our individual capacity for meaning, and for engaging with new and strange forms of it, also evolves and develops. Sangharakshita's work marks a stage in the synthesis of different traditions that can only be judged in relation to its relevance and helpfulness to human experience in general, not solely in the terms of one tradition judged in isolation.

'Sangharakshita's insights are synthetic, so should not be over-analysed'

This is a misunderstanding that can only be due to insufficient attention to how much both synthesis and analysis are used in all sorts of contexts. Sangharakshita's insights are indeed often synthetic, and he remarks himself on his capacity for both synthesis and analysis.[3]

2 See Ellis (2013b) 3.c, and (2001) 4.e.
3 Sangharakshita (2009b).

Nevertheless, many of my criticisms in this book involve pointing out a *lack* of synthesis in Sangharakshita's thinking: i.e. that he fails to apply beliefs that he expresses in one sphere to his views in another. At many other points, indeed, he does synthesise, but in a way that conflates different ideas that need to be separated – for instance in his ideas about Cosmic Going for Refuge (see 4.f).

Synthesis and analysis both need to be employed at different points, either to bring together ideas that have been unhelpfully separated, or to separate ideas that have been unhelpfully conflated. Of course, the key issue is then the basis on which one decides when each can be helpfully used. The basis I have used in this book is that if either an analysis or synthesis is not provisional (i.e. it is assumed to be absolutely correct, without any scope for comparison with alternatives and thus modification), it is unacceptable. There needs to be a *pragmatic* justification for both our analyses and our syntheses, not a dogmatic one. Of course, there is continued scope for argument about any positive claim about pragmatic value, but it is relatively easy to identify absolutized analyses or syntheses that are interfering with our ability to adapt to new conditions.

'You are a rationalist'

A 'rationalist', in the sense in which Sangharakshita seems to use the term, is someone who puts too much emphasis on reason to the exclusion of emotion. However, the very use of this distinction is inadequate, as I argued in 3.a., and Sangharakshita often places far too much reliance on it. The use of reasoning (i.e. the justification of one claim by linking it conditionally with another) is not necessarily an indicator of 'rationalism', since even those apparently influenced by very strong and distorting emotional states can employ such reasoning. The assumptions with which we begin to reason are based on a complex mixture of justification from other assumptions and emotional motivation, and it is the *justifiability* of those assumptions that is far more significant than whether reasoning is employed, or whether an argument is 'logical'. That justification depends on the integration of *both* our cognitive and emotional states. It depends on the degree of awareness we have of our assumptions and the ways that they could be questioned.

It is thus probably a misunderstanding to call me a 'rationalist' – a misunderstanding that is in turn dependent on a false dichotomy.

I employ reasoning, but the main way in which I do so is to point out limitations in assumptions. I do not expect reasoning to create certainties, even negative ones. The pragmatic standpoint that this leads me to is one that can only be developed through a process of emotional integration as well as intellectual discussion.

'You are a materialist'

This accusation can only be based on a misunderstanding of scientific theory and its use, and of the way in which I have at times employed scientific perspectives in this book to either corroborate or criticise Sangharakshita's views. As discussed in 2.c, the way in which Sangharakshita characterises science as 'reductionist' or 'mechanistic' is a caricature, and the use of scientific theory does not require one to adopt any such assumptions. Scientific theory makes generalisations about the universe that are justifiable by the evidence so far. Most scientists recognise that scientific statements are provisional and always subject to revision in the light of new evidence, even if there are variations in the degree to which they consistently apply this view. This recognition is the most important way of avoiding the metaphysical claims implicit in materialism (the view that the universe is ultimately only predictable matter), reductionism (which involves the privileging of one type of explanation as final), or mechanism (which implies that a particular type of causal explanation is final).

All references to scientific theory in this book, as in any of my other work, are offered on the basis that this theory is provisional, and that it is precisely because it is provisional that it is likely to be credible and informative. In many cases, scientific theory can be positively contrasted with dogmatic claims that do not adopt the same provisionality. In terms of my personal view, I decisively reject materialist, reductive, and indeed most naturalistic interpretations of science.

'Sangharakshita's work should not be given this amount of credence, given his abusive behaviour, betraying his responsibilities as a spiritual teacher'

This dogmatic perspective against Sangharakshita is one I have discussed in 5.e. It involves an assumption, first of all, that a spiritual teacher should be judged by standards of moral perfection that would not be applied to other humans. That our expectations should be higher of those who claim to exemplify ethical standards is fair enough, but this does not imply that infractions of those ethical standards should be judged to absolutely destroy the credibility of their teachings. It is only when a person's authority has been assumed to be absolute in the first place that it becomes as fragile as this, whereas if Sangharakshita is recognised as a flawed human being with asymmetrical integration to begin with, our expectations can still be relatively high without being absolute. His hypocrisy does undermine his credibility, and this should be weighed in the balance, but it does not destroy an absolute authority that he should never have been credited with in the first place.

The assumption that anyone's faults, even serious ones, completely destroy the justification of the rest of what they have to say is an *ad hominem* fallacy, though unfortunately one that I have often found amongst Sangharakshita's critics. In fact, I would go so far as to say that my attempts to engage with Sangharakshita's critics in researching this book were seriously impeded by the prevalence of this fallacy amongst them.

Short of completely dismissing him like this, of course, those who have not yet engaged with Sangharakshita may still be justifiably put off by the damage to his reputation. However, there are also many positive reasons for considering him credible enough to engage with at least to some extent. These include his obvious expertise, his access to insight through long experience of practice, the way in which his intersecting role between traditions makes him relatively free of the vested interests of any of them, and the degree of corroboration (noted in section 2 of this book) between his best ideas and those from other sources, not just in Buddhist tradition but beyond it. It is easy for us to identify negative factors impacting credibility and use them as a basis of dismissal, but credibility is a matter of weighing up many different factors, including positive ones, and attempting to give them a weight proportional to their actual importance. As David Hume wrote, 'A wise man proportions his belief to the evidence.'[4]

---

4   Hume (1975) § 87.

6.c. Sangharakshita's Legacy

Sangharakshita's death, occurring at the very time I have been writing this conclusion, opens up a new chapter for the way in which we choose to respond to and interpret his ideas, both within and beyond Triratna. Triratna, relieved of his immediate influence, now has more genuine choices about its direction. Beyond Triratna, the force of many people's reaction against the organisation following the abuse allegations may be mitigated now that they can no longer perceive it as dominated by him.

Sangharakshita's legacy is profoundly mixed, yet that mixedness confers a responsibility of interpretation. We can choose to emphasise the helpful aspects of his teachings, and use them as a source of positive inspiration, or we can focus on his absolutisations, and use these as a prompt for one-sided acceptance or rejection. A positive focus will be far preferable in its practical effects, yet it needs to be accompanied by acknowledgement of the extent of Sangharakshita's limitations. Particularly it needs to be accompanied by recognition that he was not simply a good thinker who failed to practice some of what he preached through 'weakness of will' – it is the contradictions within his thinking itself that help to make him so mixed. I would argue that a deliberately positive interpretation, accompanied by a full critical acknowledgement of the limitations of Sangharakshita's teachings, is the response that fits the best of those teachings themselves.

I hope that Sangharakshita's legacy beyond Triratna will be a body of work that at least becomes better known and somewhat better studied. I hope that it will be recognised that Sangharakshita is a pioneer in the Western interpretation of Buddhism, and that his work needs to be understood and built on rather than either dismissed or idealised. I hope that it will be realised that his core project, of adapting and synthesising, cannot be ducked, and cannot be replaced simply by the importation of authority assumptions from traditional Buddhist schools. I hope that it will not only be Buddhists who engage to some extent with his work, but also those beyond Buddhism: Christians, Jungians, Humanists and others can all learn from it.

One problem for those beyond Triratna seeking to engage with his written legacy is its wide extent, disorganisation, and variable quality. The publication of *The Essential Sangharakshita*[1] has helped with this to some extent, but this compendium contains a mixture of his more practical and absolutising material. Perhaps the two books I would recommend most to those approaching his thinking for the first time would be *A Guide to the Buddhist Path*[2] and *The Ten Pillars*,[3] as in both of these works the focus is *mainly* practical, and they contain some of his most creative material.

Obviously, though, the biggest manifestation of Sangharakshita's legacy is the Triratna Buddhist Order and Community itself. After studying and reflecting on Sangharakshita's work as intensively as I have during the past year, I have reached some reasonably clear and justifiable conclusions about ways in which aspects of it have damaged Triratna, and thus of the direction that Triratna needs to take to rectify that problematic legacy.

In the remainder of this conclusion, then, I am going to list five key things that I conclude Triratna needs to do in order to embrace the helpful aspects of Sangharakshita's legacy but cast off the unhelpful. I do not expect to have any personal role in making these things happen, so they are not offered from a position of responsibility. However, I hope they can be seen as the advice of a reasonably disinterested but sympathetic outside advisor: one that would like to see Triratna continue to prosper and do good in the world.

1. Take full responsibility for its own destiny

There is now a danger that Sangharakshita's writings will start to be treated as absolute authorities, and that appeals to his expressed wishes will be seen as the basis of judgement. Such absolutisation of his words is unlikely to take the form of direct or blatant fundamentalism, but instead may take the subtler forms of open-ended confirmation bias (see 5.a) or of denial of alternative interpretations. As with any text, religious or otherwise, this type of use of authorities diminishes responsibility, because it fails to take into account that every use of a text is actually the use of a particular interpretation of it, for which the interpreter needs to take responsibility. Without Sangharakshita, the Order can now decide what it stands for and

---

1 Sangharakshita (2009c).
2 Sangharakshita (1990c).
3 Sangharakshita (1989).

where it is heading. It's important to do so on the basis of the best estimate of the conditions and how to address them, not even on the implicit assumption that Sangharakshita's extremely mixed output gives reliable instructions as to what to do.

2. End the ambiguity about what the Order stands for

This is the most crucial issue for the Triratna Order. It stands at the intersection between two interpretations of Buddhism with a conflict of priorities: on the one hand a universal path in which the specific Buddhist language is recognised as contingent, with its guidance investigable through experience and illuminable from many possible sources; and on the other an exclusivist Buddhist path, known only through Buddhist tradition and described in ways that take Buddhist language to be unique and essential. Hitherto it has not been clear which of these takes priority, and there has been no attempt to clarify this issue in principle. Instead, the Order has relied on (and idealised) Sangharakshita's judgement as to which takes precedence in any particular case. Given the demonstrable fallibility and divisive effects of Sangharakshita's judgement, this temporary solution to the dilemma needs to change, and cannot be substituted by absolutising his surviving words (see point 1).

It also cannot be pretended that there is no conflict between these priorities: this book has identified and discussed a large number of them, from karma and rebirth to the spiritual aptitude of women. Almost every chapter in this book indicates a conflict of this kind. It is not that Buddhist tradition cannot always be interpreted in ways that fit our best understanding of the universal path, but that using the authority of the Buddhist tradition as an absolute basis of judgement conflicts with the provisionality that is needed on the universal path.

There are at first sight three different possible ways of resolving this conflict: agree clearly that the basis of the Order is the universal path, agree clearly that it is Buddhist tradition, or find some other consistent principles that enable judgement between them. However, the third option is actually a version of the first. If you find consistent and helpful principles that are not ones ultimately justified by the Buddhist tradition, you will be developing the universal path. The universal path is not necessarily an abstract or solely 'intellectual' path, and it can be quite consistent with a profound love of and faith in the Buddhist tradition – it simply involves the recognition that no given interpretation of the path can be absolute, and an attempt to follow through the implications of that recognition.

The alternative option, of choosing the Buddhist tradition as an absolute starting point, is a potential reactionary disaster. Not only will Triratna then have little relevance or appeal to the vast majority of people in the modern world, but it will also be based on the pretence that there is one true and authoritative interpretation of the Buddhist tradition. This absolutisation of the tradition is then likely to become the basis of power-play, as the person or people who know the 'true' interpretation can gain power from doing so. Everything practically valuable in Sangharakshita's teachings may then quickly unravel.

The only feasible option, then, is to choose clearly that the universal path is the basis of the Order, making the 'dharma' an ongoing provisional theory to which all kinds of sources may potentially contribute, and that is justified by its practical effects in developing increasingly integrated perspectives. Such an approach does not prevent the Buddhist tradition continuing to be a major source of inspiration, archetypal meaning, and practical guidance, and thus does not threaten the justified retention of the name 'Buddhist' in any way. It also does not prevent a practical recognition that the stages of psycho-spiritual development (as identified, for instance, by Robert Kegan)[4] may require different conceptions of what 'Buddhism' means to a given individual at different stages. What it does is clarify the meaning of the term 'Buddhist' in ways that Sangharakshita has failed to do.

Such a move would in my view not involve an abandonment of Sangharakshita's work, but rather a development of the best of it. At his best, Sangharakshita himself was not limited by assumptions about what was 'Buddhist' and what was not, or indeed what was 'religious' and what was 'secular'. Where these conflicts appear, it is important not to take sides (I am not recommending 'secularism'), but rather to support a dialectical process to resolve them, investigating the assumptions being made over whatever timescale people are capable of understanding them. The development of that process is the Middle Way – a concept deeply embedded in Buddhism, and

---

4   Kegan (1982).

offering interpretations of it that are capable of gradually resolving these false dichotomies.

3. Learn from the sciences

If Triratna begins to more clearly prioritise universal interpretations of Buddhism when there is a conflict, one implication of this is that it will need to be more open than at present to learning about that path from a wide variety of sources outside the Buddhist tradition. Whilst Triratna has followed Sangharakshita by engaging strongly with the Western arts as a source of inspiration, it has tended to set up barriers against any other sources that may potentially challenge its core beliefs. Although in recent years the strength of discouragement of those involved from participating in alternative movements has reduced, it is still present, with new mitras (those undertaking a formal but provisional commitment) still asked to publicly declare that Triratna is the main context for their practice.[5] Study sources are still usually Sangharakshita's (or Subhuti's) works or Buddhist scriptures. With only occasional exceptions, institutional engagement with outside input tends to be limited to other Buddhist groups, such as those gathering in the European Buddhist Union. Triratna is still an extremely introspective, self-contained organisation, and this needs to change if it is to develop in a way that addresses modern conditions and that actually practises provisional belief and critical thinking, rather than using these terms for virtue signalling.

The biggest lacuna in Triratna's lack of engagement with the wider human world, however, lies in its neglect of the sciences. In Sangharakshita's work there is almost no attempt to engage with the sciences, beyond the early ideas of 'higher evolution' and the Jungian elements such as integration and archetypes: but science has moved on massively since then. I can list at least six developing areas of science[6] that have major implications for the topics tackled in the thought of Sangharakshita – topics such as mindfulness, meaning, delusion, objectivity, provisionality, and conditionality

---

5 https://thebuddhistcentre.com/system/files/groups/files/becoming_a_mitra_new.pdf (accessed 2018).

6 For a more detailed account of each of these see Ellis (2019) section 7, where detailed references for them are also given.

– but that have been completely ignored by him and thus also have no central place in Triratna and its teaching.
1. The falsificationist philosophy of science of figures like Popper, Lakatos and Kuhn[7]
2. Systems theory, e.g. Maturana and Varela[8]
3. 'Cognitive linguistics' or embodied meaning theory, e.g. Lakoff and Johnson[9]
4. Several aspects of neuroscience, including the work of figures like Paul Gilbert on compassion[10] and of Iain McGilchrist on brain lateralisation[11]
5. The cognitive psychology of bias, e.g. in the work of Kahneman and Tversky[12]
6. The psychological research into mindfulness of Ellen Langer[13]

None of these, incidentally, involves any requirement of reductionism or mechanism of any kind, but they rather give reasons for believing that science cannot justifiably be interpreted in that way. They do not require the replacement of an understanding of personal experience with some kind of abstractly clinical outside view, but rather offer amazing resources with which to supplement and challenge our understanding of personal experience. They are all concerned in some way with practical judgement – so I have not included other oft-cited scientific areas such as quantum physics, which are of purely theoretical interest and have no evident application to judgement.

The fact is that the path is about *humans* and how humans operate and respond to things. If a spiritual community is intended to help humans to develop, it needs to provide not only inspiration, support, techniques, and values but also maximally helpful information based on evidence about how humans actually operate. There is no excuse for instead offering half-baked speculations about these things, and presenting them as insightful truths with only a formalistic nod towards provisionality. Even when more careful explorations have been made of Buddhist psychology, there is also no

---

7 Kuhn (1996), Lakatos (1974).
8 Maturana & Varela (1992), Capra & Luisi (2014).
9 Johnson (2007).
10 Gilbert (2010).
11 McGilchrist (2010).
12 Kahneman (2011).
13 Langer (1997) and (2014).

Conclusion 239

excuse for relying only on traditional Buddhist sources and failing to compare them with more rigorous recent investigations that are of obvious relevance.

Again, the main barrier here seems to be perceptions around labels: that Buddhism is 'religious' and that 'science' is opposed to religious insight in some way. Both Buddhism and science consist in complex traditions, and both of those traditions are rapidly evolving, often in response to each other. To participate in a tradition is a matter of rootedness, but trees grow in the direction of the light, not necessarily only in the direction first pointed by their trunks. A full engagement with scientific sources offers a fulfilment of Buddhism's most important motivations as they are interpreted by Sangharakshita, and as they were explored in section 2 of this book.

4. Teach critical thinking systematically as part of core practice

A standard way for people to begin engagement with Triratna is through a meditation class, and meditation is normally considered the most important core practice. There is also a recognition that this needs to be supplemented with practice that works with ideas and concepts, but the way of doing this normally consists in 'study'. 'Study', as advocated by Sangharakshita and practised in Triratna, may well mean individual reading and reflection on a text, followed by group discussion of it.

In comparison to meditation as a practice working immediately to transform mental states and emotions, 'study' does little to work systematically with concepts and beliefs. Instead, the student may incidentally develop some intellectual skills in the course of discussing various issues, but may also alternatively have prejudices reinforced by the study group. Through critical thinking training, it is quite possible to work much more directly and flexibly to help increase a practitioner's awareness of his or her assumptions, and to question those assumptions in comparison with alternatives, thus greatly improving their objectivity of judgement. In the context of modern society, critical thinking is just as vital a skill as meditation, and just as generic and flexible in its implications for every situation. Sangharakshita seems to have theoretically advocated critical thinking,[14] but done little to actually promote it as an institutional expectation.

14 Sangharakshita (2009c) p. 155.

If it is to be concerned with the Buddhist path interpreted in terms of integration and individuality, Triratna needs to make the teaching and learning of critical thinking for personal development a core practice. 'Study' may also be necessary to provide a cultural starting point, but even for beginners it might just provide a springboard from which more serious critical thinking training can be introduced when people are ready for it. I'd suggest that it should be a normal expectation for those preparing for ordination, or otherwise entering more seriously into practice. Critical thinking teaching can be adapted for different prior levels of education or aptitude, just as meditation can be adapted for people with different needs and circumstances, and there may also be ways of adapting existing study frameworks to gradually introduce more critical thinking elements.

5. Recognise asymmetry of integration

As I have identified at various points in this book, one of the biggest weaknesses of Sangharakshita's views of integration, spiritual progression, and spiritual hierarchy is that they did not sufficiently take into account the asymmetry with which people actually advance. Rather, Triratna was set up on the assumption that 'a degree of integration' in general could be readily recognised, and thus provide a key basis for ordination with its 'effective going for refuge' (reliability of commitment to practice). In practice, however, people can be much more developed in, say, meditation than in thinking, or in social interaction than in self-motivation, or in creativity than in consistent application. This makes them reliable in some respects and not in others. Both the idea of the highly integrated spiritual teacher, and that of the effectively integrated Order member, are thus misleading. The ideal of 'vertical friendship' is thus also made simplistic.

The implication of asymmetry of integration is thus that we cannot justify general social institutions that require the pretence that integration is always symmetrical. Instead of one guru, then, there need to be many gurus who challenge and inspire us in different ways. Instead of one kind of Order member, there also need to be a variety of social recognitions of different kinds of achievement, implying different kinds of integral reliability in different areas of experience. In the process, the cliff-edge of the current ordination system could be softened, so that there is not a sudden and discontinuous change in social status, but rather a series of specific social recognitions and challenges better adapted to reflect an individual path.

It is not for me to devise the details of a new system to replace the current ordination system in Triratna, merely to point out that asymmetry of integration does have important practical effects, and that Triratna's social arrangements need to take this into account. In effect, members of the current Order need to reflect on what the function of that Order is in terms that are adequate to experience, rather than only in terms of idealisations. Taking account of more of the complexity of how humans actually operate (and thus taking into account scientific perspectives), they then need to think again about how those functions could be best fulfilled with the minimum of collateral projection.

Conclusion

To summarise the most important aspects of the legacy of Sangharakshita for Triratna, then, we could say that it positively consists in a uniquely synthetic institution attempting to meet the spiritual needs of human beings through a rigorous emphasis on spiritual practice. In that respect his legacy is impressive. However, his legacy also consists in various defects in that institution, such as an implicit tendency to appeal to authority, a fatal ambiguity of identity, an introspective tendency, a lack of systemic critical training, and a flawed model of human spiritual development. All of these defects could potentially be overcome through determined practical action by the Order.

The home page of the website for Adhisthana,[15] the retreat centre where Sangharakshita lived and is now buried, carries a quotation from Gustav Mahler: 'Tradition is the handing on of the flame, and not the worship of ashes.' Now that Sangharakshita has departed, we will see what the use of that quotation actually means.

---

15 https://adhisthana.org/ (accessed 2019).

Bibliography

Asch, Solomon (1956) *Studies of Independence and Conformity: 1. A Minority of One against a Unanimous Majority*. Psychological Monographs.
Aviezer, Ora, Ijzendoorn, Marinus, Sagi, Abraham, & Schuengel, Carlo (1994) '"Children of the Dream" Revisited: 70 Years of Collective Early Childcare in the Israeli Kibbutzim'. *Psychological Bulletin* 116(1): 99–116. https://doi.org/10.1037/0033-2909.116.1.99
Batchelor, Stephen (1994) 'A Thai Forest Tradition Grows in England'. *Tricycle*. https://tricycle.org/magazine/thai-forest-tradition-grows-england
Batchelor, Stephen (2015) *After Buddhism*. Yale University Press, New Haven.
Bodhi, Bhikkhu (1998) 'A Look at the Kalama Sutta'. *Access to Insight (BCBS Edition)*, http://www.accesstoinsight.org/lib/authors/bodhi/bps-essay_09.html
Bodhi, Bhikkhu (2000) *The Connected Discourses of the Buddha: A New Translation of the Samyutta Nikaya* (2 vols). Wisdom Publications, Boston.
Bowker, Julie, Stotsky, Miriam, & Etkin, Rebecca (2017) 'How BIS/BAS and Psycho-behavioral Variables Distinguish between Social Withdrawal Subtypes during Emerging Adulthood'. *Personality and Individual Differences* 119: 283–8. https://doi.org/10.1016/j.paid.2017.07.043
Bunting, Madeleine (1997) 'The Dark Side of Enlightenment'. *The Guardian* 27 October 1997. Reproduced on https://medium.com/@eiselmazard/critique-of-sangharakshita-triratna-fwbo-archived-e76008fc03e1 (accessed 2018).
Capra, Fritjof & Luisi, Pier Luigi (2014) *The Systems View of Life: A Unifying Vision*. Cambridge University Press, Cambridge. https://doi.org/10.1017/CBO9780511895555
Chabris, Christopher & Simons, Daniel (2011) *The Invisible Gorilla*. HarperCollins, London.
Dhammadinna & Suvajra (eds) (1999) *Puja: The FWBO Book of Buddhist Devotional Texts*. Windhorse, Birmingham.
Ellis, Robert M. (2001) *A Buddhist Theory of Moral Objectivity*. PhD Thesis, Lancaster University. Also published by Lulu, Raleigh as *A Theory of Moral Objectivity*.
Ellis, Robert M. (2012) *Middle Way Philosophy 1: The Path of Objectivity*. Lulu, Raleigh.
Ellis, Robert M. (2013a) *Middle Way Philosophy 2: The Integration of Desire*. Lulu, Raleigh.
Ellis, Robert M. (2013b) *Middle Way Philosophy 3: The Integration of Meaning*. Lulu, Raleigh.
Ellis, Robert M. (2015) *Middle Way Philosophy 4: The Integration of Belief*. Lulu, Raleigh.

Bibliography 243

Ellis, Robert M. (2018) *The Christian Middle Way: The Case against Christian Belief but for Christian Faith*. Christian Alternative, Alresford.

Ellis, Robert M. (2019) *The Buddha's Middle Way: Experiential Judgement in His Life and Teaching*. Equinox, Sheffield.

Fordham, Frieda (1953) *An Introduction to Jung's Psychology*. Penguin, Harmondsworth.

Gilbert, Paul (2010) *The Compassionate Mind*. Constable, London.

Grossmann, Igor & Brienza, Justin (2018) 'The Strengths of Wisdom Provide Unique Contributions to Improved Leadership, Sustainability, Inequality, Gross National Happiness, and Civic Discourse in the Face of Contemporary World Problems'. *Journal of Intelligence* 6(2): 22.
https://doi.org/10.3390/jintelligence6020022

Hume, David (1975) 'Enquiry Concerning Human Understanding' from *Enquiries Concerning Human Understanding and Concerning the Principles of Morals*. Oxford University Press, Oxford.
https://doi.org/10.1093/actrade/9780198245353.book.1

Ireland, John D. (1990) *The Udana: Inspired Utterances of the Buddha*. Buddhist Publications Society, Kandy.

James, William (1905) *Principles of Psychology* (2 vols). Macmillan, London.

Janis, Irving L. (1982) *Groupthink: Psychological Studies of Policy Decisions and Fiascos*. Houghton Mifflin, Boston.

Johnson, Mark (2007) *The Meaning of the Body: Aesthetics of Human Understanding*. University of Chicago Press, Chicago.
https://doi.org/10.7208/chicago/9780226026992.001.0001

Jones, Dhivan Thomas (2012) 'The Five Niyāmas as Laws of Nature: An Assessment of Modern Western Interpretations of Theravāda Buddhist Doctrine'. *Journal of Buddhist Ethics* 19.

Jung, Carl (1959) *Aion: Researches into the Phenomenology of the Self: Collected Works Volume 9, Part 2*. Routledge, London.

Jung, Carl (1960) 'On the Nature of the Psyche' from *Collected Works Volume 8*. Routledge, London.

Jung, Carl (1968) *The Archetypes and the Collective Unconscious: Collected Works Volume 9, Part 1*. Routledge, London.

Kahneman, Daniel (2011) *Thinking Fast and Slow*. Penguin, London.

Kegan, Robert (1982) *The Evolving Self: Problem and Process in Human Development*. Harvard University Press, Cambridge Mass.

Kuhn, Thomas (1996, 3rd edn) *The Structure of Scientific Revolutions*. University of Chicago Press, Chicago.

Lakatos, Imre (1974) 'Falsification and the Methodology of Scientific Research Programmes' from *Criticism and the Growth of Knowledge*, ed. A. Musgrave & I. Lakatos. Cambridge University Press, Cambridge.

Lakoff, George & Johnson, Mark (1999) *Philosophy in the Flesh*. University of Chicago Press, Chicago.

Langer, Ellen (1997) *The Power of Mindful Learning*. Da Capo Press, Boston.

Langer, Ellen J. (2014, 25th anniversary edn) *Mindfulness*. Da Capo Press, Boston.

MacIntyre, Alasdair (1981) *After Virtue*. Duckworth, London.

Maturana, Humberto & Varela, Francisco (1992) *The Tree of Knowledge: The Biological Roots of Human Understanding*. Shambhala, Boston.
McGilchrist, Iain (2010) *The Master and his Emissary: The Divided Brain and the Shaping of the Modern Mind*. Yale University Press, New Haven Conn.
Mill, John Stuart (1972, originally 1859) 'On Liberty' from *Utilitarianism, On Liberty, and Considerations of Representative Government*. Dent, London.
Morrison, Robert (1997) *Nietzsche and Buddhism: A Study in Nihilism and Ironic Affinities*. Oxford University Press, Oxford.
Ñanamoli, Bhikkhu & Bodhi, Bhikkhu (1995) *The Middle Length Discourses of the Buddha: A New Translation of the Majjhima Nikaya*. Wisdom Publications, Boston.
Nissoka (undated) *Bodh Gaya: Its Significance in the 21st Century*. Windhorse, Cambridge.
Pinker, Steven (2011) *The Better Angels of Our Nature*. Penguin, London.
Plato, trans. Hugh Tredennick (1993) 'Phaedo' from *The Last Days of Socrates*. Penguin, London.
Popper, Karl R. (1959) *The Logic of Scientific Discovery*. Routledge, London. https://doi.org/10.1063/1.3060577
Popper, Karl R. (1994) *Knowledge and the Mind-Body Problem*. Routledge, London.
Price, A.F. & Wong Mou-Lam (1969) *The Diamond Sutra and the Sutra of Hui Neng*. Shambhala, Boston.
Ross, Lee, Greene, David, & House, Pamela (1977) 'The False Consensus Effect: An Egocentric Bias in Social Perception and Attribution Processes'. *Journal of Experimental Social Psychology* 13(3): 279–301.
Sagan, Carl (1987) CSICOP Keynote Address (this seems to survive only as a quotation from an oral address).
Sangharakshita (1967) *The Three Jewels*. Windhorse, Glasgow.
Sangharakshita (1983) *Going for Refuge*. Windhorse, Glasgow.
Sangharakshita (1985) *The Essence of Zen*. Windhorse, Glasgow.
Sangharakshita (1986) *Alternative Traditions*. Windhorse, Glasgow.
Sangharakshita (1987a, 6th edn) *A Survey of Buddhism*. Tharpa Publications, London.
Sangharakshita (1987b) 'Buddhism, Sex and the Spiritual Life'. Interview in *Golden Drum* No. 6, August–October 1987.
Sangharakshita (1988a) *The Religion of Art*. Windhorse, Glasgow.
Sangharakshita (1988b) *The History of My Going for Refuge*. Windhorse, Glasgow.
Sangharakshita (1989) *The Ten Pillars of Buddhism*. Windhorse, Glasgow.
Sangharakshita (1990a) *New Currents in Western Buddhism*. Windhorse, Glasgow.
Sangharakshita (1990b) *Vision and Transformation*. Windhorse, Glasgow.
Sangharakshita (1990c) *A Guide to the Buddhist Path*. Windhorse, Glasgow.
Sangharakshita (1990d) *My Relation to the Order*. Windhorse, Glasgow.
Sangharakshita (1991) *Facing Mount Kanchenjunga*. Windhorse, Birmingham.
Sangharakshita (1992) *The FWBO and 'Protestant Buddhism'*. Windhorse, Glasgow.
Sangharakshita (1993a) *Forty-three Years Ago: Reflections on My Bhikkhu Ordination*. Windhorse, Glasgow.
Sangharakshita (1993b) *The Priceless Jewel*. Windhorse, Glasgow.
Sangharakshita (1994) *Who Is the Buddha?* Windhorse, Glasgow.

Bibliography 245

Sangharakshita (1995) *Ritual and Devotion in Buddhism: An Introduction.* Windhorse, Birmingham.
Sangharakshita (1996) *The Rainbow Road.* Windhorse, Birmingham.
Sangharakshita (1997a) *In the Sign of the Golden Wheel.* Windhorse, Birmingham.
Sangharakshita (1997b) 'Buddhism without Beliefs?' *Western Buddhist Review* Vol. 2. http://www.westernbuddhistreview.com/vol2/buddhism_without_beliefs.html
Sangharakshita (2003) *Moving against the Stream.* Windhorse, Birmingham.
Sangharakshita (2009a) 'What Is the Western Buddhist Order?' https://www.sangharakshita.org/interviews/What_is_the_Western_Buddhist_Order.pdf
Sangharakshita (2009b) 'Conversations with Bhante, August 2009'. https://www.sangharakshita.org/interviews/CONVERSATIONS_FEB_2018_REVISED.pdf (accessed 2018).
Sangharakshita, ed. Karen Stout (2009c) *The Essential Sangharakshita.* Wisdom, Boston.
Sangharakshita (2012) *The Purpose and Practice of Buddhist Meditation.* Ibis Publications, Ledbury.
Sangharakshita (2017) 'A Note on "Disciple": A Postscript to "What Is the Western Buddhist Order?"' https://thebuddhistcentre.com/adhisthana-kula/urgyen-sangharakshita-discipleship-postscript-what-western-buddhist-order (accessed 2018).
Sangharakshita (undated) *Mind Reactive and Creative* (booklet). Windhorse.
Siegel, Daniel (2010) *Mindsight: Transform Your Brain with the New Science of Kindness.* Oneworld, London.
Siegler, Ilene, Brummett, Beverly, Martin, Peter, & Helms, Michael (2013) 'Consistency and Timing of Marital Transitions and Survival During Midlife: The Role of Personality and Health Risk Behaviors'. *Annals of Behavioral Medicine* 45(3): 338–47. https://doi.org/10.1007/s12160-012-9457-3
Simon, Robin W. (2002) 'Revisiting the Relationships among Gender, Marital Status, and Mental Health'. *American Journal of Sociology* 107(4): 1065–96. https://doi.org/10.1086/339225
Storbeck, Justin & Clore, Gerald (2007) 'On the Interdependence of Cognition and Emotion'. *Cognition and Emotion* 21(6): 1212–37. https://doi.org/10.1080/02699930701438020
Subhuti (1986) Paper given to the conference on the ordination process for men, published in *Shabda* September 1986 (this is no longer made publicly available by Triratna, but is available on http://www.ex-cult.org/fwbo/SubQuote.htm).
Subhuti (1994) *Sangharakshita: A New Voice in the Buddhist Tradition.* Windhorse, Birmingham.
Subhuti (1995) *Women, Men and Angels.* Windhorse, Birmingham.
Subhuti (2017) 'Women, Men and Angels: A Personal Statement'. https://thebuddhistcentre.com/adhisthana-kula/women-men-and-angels-personal-statement-subhuti (accessed 2018).
Taylor, Donald and Doria, Janet (1981) 'Self-serving and Group-serving Bias in Attribution'. *The Journal of Social Psychology* 113(2): 201–11.
Thorne, Barrie & Henley, Nancy (eds) (1975) *Language and Sex: Difference and Dominance.* Newbury House, Rowley Mass.

Vajragupta (2010) *The Triratna Story*. Windhorse, Cambridge.
Vishvapani & Cittapala (1999) 'A Comment on the Refutation of the FWBO's Response to the FWBO Files'.
http://response.fwbo.org/response-refutation.html
Wells, Jonathan (2016) 'The Eight Surprising Health Benefits of Getting Married'. *Daily Telegraph* 11 April 2016. https://www.telegraph.co.uk/health-fitness/body/the-eight-surprising-health-benefits-of-getting-married/ (accessed 2018).

Reference List of Sangharakshita's Lectures and Seminars

Listed here are Sangharakshita's transcribed lectures and seminars that are referred to in the footnotes of this book. These are all available, along with the rest of his transcribed lectures and seminars, at https://www.freebuddhistaudio.com/texts. For the most part, the transcriptions are undated. I have added dates here where I have been able to ascertain them from other sources, but in many cases I have not, or the dates are very approximate. Rather than using normal bibliographic conventions for these, I have simply referred to them by their Lecture or Seminar number in the footnotes; the list here gives the numbers with titles.

Lecture 2: The Meaning of the Dharma (1968)

Lecture 6: Buddhism and the Bishop of Woolwich (1960s?)

Lecture 7: Buddhism and the New Reformation (1966)

Lecture 10: Stream Entry (1965)

Lecture 26: Nirvana (1966)

Lecture 31: Mind Reactive and Creative (1967)

Lecture 37: Buddhism and the Language of Myth (1960s?)

Lecture 45: The Mandala: Tantric Symbol of Integration (1967)

Lecture 76: The Axial Age and the Emergence of the New Man (1969)

Lecture 82: Buddhism, Nietzsche and 'The Superman' (1969)

Lecture 84: Alienated and Integrated Awareness (1970)

Lecture 85: Individuality, True and False (1970)

Lecture 90: Is a Guru Necessary? (1970)

Lecture 91: The Individual, the Group and the Community (1971)

Lecture 106: The Cosmic Symbolism of the Refuge Tree and the Archetypal Guru (early 1970s?)

Lecture 133: The Nucleus of a New Society (1976)

Lecture 135: A System of Meditation (1978)

Lecture 137: Levels of Going for Refuge (1982?)

Lecture 148: The Way of Non-duality (1979)

Lecture 155: Fidelity (1983?)

Lecture 168: Twenty Years on the Middle Way (1987)

Lecture 172: My Relation to the Order (1990)

Lecture 174: The Five Pillars of the FWBO (late 1980s?)

Lecture 177: The Meaning of Friendship in Buddhism (late 1980s?)
Seminar 61: The Door of Liberation
Seminar 118: Sigalovada Sutta (1983)
Seminar 129: The Religion of Art (1999)
Seminar 134: Aspects of the Higher Evolution of the Individual
Seminar 137: Higher Evolution of Man

Index

Abhidhamma, 75, 139
Absolute Mind, 31
absolutisation, 125, 156, 162, 165, 195, 197, 208, 234, 236
absolutism, 87, 166
ad hoc rationalisation, 38-9, 70, 142, 181
ad hominem (fallacy), 232
addiction, 25, 27, 42, 216
Adhisthana (Triratna retreat centre), 1, 2, 241
Aion (book by Jung), 147, 243
alienated awareness, **47**, 75, 79-81, 173, 189
Aloka (Triratna order member), 149
Ambedkar, Dr Bhim Rao, 9, 12
Amitabha (symbolic Buddha), 8, 84, 126
analysis, 73, 111, 139, 196, 229, 230
anarchism, 91
anatta: see non-substantiality
anicca: see impermanence
Anima/Animus (archetype), 147, 197, 203
anti-intellectualism, 76
apophasis (rhetorical device), 124
applied art: see art
Arahantship, 98 (see also enlightenment)
archetype, 45, 85, 115, 126-7, 130, 145-50, 161-2, 164, 167, 180-2, 184, 197, 236-7
Aristotle, 38-9, 57
art, 10, 19, 45, 87, **110-16**, 121
  applied art, 112
  fine art, 63, 112, 114-15
arts, the, 6-7, 30, 59, 63, 78, 84, **110-16**, 122-3, 223, 237
arupa-loka: see formless world

Arya Sangha (community of near-enlightened), 55-6, 92, 98, 162-3
asankhata: see uncompounded
asceticism, 69, 70, 150, 189-90
asymmetry of integration: see integration
austerities: see asceticism
authority
  appeal to ~ (fallacy), 129, 173, 241
  author's attitude to ~, 100
  author's ~, 225, 228
  concepts of ~ and credibility, **228**
  institutional ~, 212
  moral ~, 104
  of Buddhist tradition, 20, 40, 89, 119, 131, 144, 154, 155, 162, 201, 223, 233, 235
  parental ~, 64
  patriarchal ~, 219
  S's personal ~, 71, **167-78**, 224, 232
aversion: see hatred
Axial Age, 57, 247

Bahiya (Pali Canon character), 133-4
Batchelor, Stephen, 4, 36, 41, 73, 135, 242
'bearer of the archetype', 181
bhava tanha: see craving for existence
biases, 40, 46, 54, 57, 118, 134 (see also specific named biases)
Bible, 60
biology, 189
Blake, William, 5, 110
Blavatsky, Helena, 7
Bodhi, Bhikkhu, 36, 242, 244
Bodhicaryavatara (Mahayana text), 118
bodhisattva, 80, 84, 148

250   *The Thought of Sangharakshita*

body
    awareness of ~, 20, 48, 80
    embodied perspective, 101, 220
    in rebirth, 142
    in ritual, 117
    interdependence with mind, 80, 113
    ~ precepts, 88
    S's Platonic opposition to ~, 189–90, 194, 220
    S's relation to his ~, 7
Bowker, Julie, et al., 54, 242
brahma-viharas (positive mental states), 76
brain
    basis of awareness, 189
    hemispheres, 13–14, 47, 238
    in general, 18
    in meaning, 113
    in reactive/creative states, 25–6
    in rebirth, 142
    integration of ~, 47
    neural entrenchment, 141
    neuroscientific developments, 238
Buddha (Gautama Siddhartha), 2, 8, 19, 20, 28, 35, 40, 52, 57, 65, 67, 69–70, 127–31, 133, 135, 139, **145–50**, 151, 153, 155, 161–5, 170, 177, 179, 189–90, 204, 206, 223
    archetypal meaning of ~, 85, **145–50**, 180
    ethical behaviour of ~, 92
    ~ Refuge, 158, 162–4, 183
    symbol of enlightenment, 125, 148, 179–80 (see also Amitabha, Five Buddha Mandala, Ratnasambhava)
    visualisation of ~, 80, 84–5, 148
Buddhafield (camping retreats), 122, 177
Buddhism, Buddhist Tradition, *passim* (see also Theravada, Hinayana, Mahayana, Tibetan, Zen)
Buddhism without Beliefs (book by Batchelor), 36, 245
Buddhist Society (London), 8, 10, 72, 102
Bunting, Madeleine (journalist), 4, 203, 210, 212, 242

Burmese Buddhism, 152

Canki Sutta (Pali Canon), 35
causality, causation, 67–8, 137
celibacy, 11, 39, 41, 208–9, 212, 217
charity, principle of, 123, 175
children, 7, 20, 41, 58, 101, 106, 122, 155, 193, 198–9, 216, **218–21**
China, 152
Chintamani (Triratna Order Member), 149
Christ, Jesus 65, 148
Christianity, 2, 19, 60, 65, 72, 147, 152, 233
Churchill, Winston, 105
cognitive dissonance, 207, 211, 224
communities (residential), 20, 107–8, 195, 217, 220
conditionality (*pratitya samutpada*), 23, 28–9, 73, 127–8, **132–7**, 138–9, 162, 222, 237 (see also niyamas, positive nidanas, spiral, twelve links)
confirmation bias, 59, 142, 175–6, 187, 203
conflict, 27, **42–6**, 55, 67, 76, 87, 91, 105, 109, 118–20, 137, 142, 155, 163, 183, 193–5, 207–8, 211, 228, 235, 237
Confucianism, 152
Confucius, 57
conscience (*ottapa*), 158
conservation (of tradition), 177–8
conservatism, 41, 108
consumerism, 51
Cosmic Going for Refuge, 160–2
couples, 198, 214, 216–17
covetousness: see craving
craving (*tanha*), 27, 29, 51, 69, 89, 92, 123, 132–3, 135, 137–9, 206, **207**, 208
craving for existence (*bhava tanha*), 207
creative and reactive mind: see mind reactive and creative
creative mind, **24–7**, 30–1, 70, 107, 132 (see also creativity, mind reactive and creative)
creativity, 5, **24–7**, 29–30, 32, 50, 54, 57, 67, 73, 83, 111, 115, 120–2,

Index 251

133, 149, 151, 154, 156-7, 171, 176, 188-9, 193, 222-4, 240 (see also creative mind, mind reactive and creative)
credibility, 103, 161, 175, **228**, 232 (see also authority)
critical thinking, 14, 169, 184, 224, 237, 239-40
Critique of Pure Reason (book by Kant), 7, 22
Croydon (Buddhist Centre), 104-5, 211

Dalit, 9, 12
dana: see generosity
Daoism, 152
death
    in general, 27, 143
    of Ambedkar, 9
    of S, 3, 9, 167, 174, 178, 182, 233
    parinirvana, 124
    spiritual ~, 44, 79-80, 83
decision-making, 21, 103, 108-9, 174
defilements (*klesas*), 92, 124
delusion (*moha*), 27, 72, 92, 128, 135, 165, 208, 237
democracy, 5, 18, 20-1, 35, 51, 55, 57, 62, 94, 105-6, 108-9, 173-4, 190, 191, 218, 223-4 (see also liberal democracy)
deontological ethics, 212
depression, 42
desire: see craving
determinism, 32
devotional practices: see ritual
Dewey, John, 30, 55
Dharma (teaching), **19-21**, 33, 129, 153, 170, 172, 177, 195, 226, 236
    dharma-niyama (level of conditionality), 139
    Dharma Refuge, 158, 162-4, 183
dharmachari/dharmacharini (title), 40
Dharmapala, 18
Dharmapriya (S's earlier name), 8
Dhivan (Thomas Jones, Triratna Order Member), 139, 243
dhyana (meditative absorption), 43, 49
dialectic, 236

Diamond Sutra (Mahayana text), 8, 16, 127, 166, 244
Dilgo Khyentse Rimpoche, 41
discipleship, 4, 96-7, 100, 108, 131, 144, **168-9**, 174-6, 187 (see also guru)
dogma, 15, 27, 34-5, 41, 87, 123, 140, 142, 154, 207, 221-2, 226-32 (see also absolutisation, biases, metaphysics)
domain dependence (bias), 49, 224
doubt (*vicikiccha*), 64
dreams, 45
dukkha: see frustration
Dudjom Rimpoche, 41
Dunlop, Mark, 210, 212

Earth Goddess, 148
education, 12, 14, 34, 51, 58-9, 76, 113, 192, 224, 240
effective going for refuge, 35, **158-160**, 163, 172, 240
Eightfold Path: see Noble Eightfold Path
El Greco (artist), 110
embodied meaning, 14, 113, 137, 238
'embodiment of the ideal', 181
emotion, 12, 44, 47-8, **75-8**, 79-81, 111, 115, 118, 166, 230, 239
empiricism, 130
Emptiness, 36, 171
Endo, Shusaku, 60
English Sangha Trust, 10
enlightenment (*nirvana/nibbana*), 19-21, 23, 28-9, 31, 36, 39, 43, 45-7, 50, 55-6, 67-8, 73, 80, 88, 97, **123-31**, 132-3, 136, 142, 143, 145-8, 150-3, 157, 158, 159, 162-5, 171, 197, 206-7, 223
Enlightenment, the (18th century), 57
epistemology, 95, 128-9, 153
equality, 94, **97-9**, 109, 190-1
Essential Sangharakshita, The (book), 245
eternalism, 66, **68-70**, 154
ethics (*sila*), 19-20, 30, 64, 69, 72, 78, **87-93**, 114-15, 122, 205-6, 209, 212, 215, 223 (see also Five Precepts, Ten Precepts)
European Buddhist Union, 237

even-handedness, 131, 154, 178
evolution, 2, 29, 33, 160, 237 (see also Higher Evolution)
experimentation, 11, 120-2 (see also science)
extended family: see family

faith (*saddha*), 9, 35, 76, 130, 133, 150, **164-6**, 168-9, 180, 225, 229, 236
fallacies, 46, 192 (see also specific named fallacies)
false dichotomy, 75-6, 166, 174, 226-7, 230
false speech (fourth precept), 88, 93 (see also Five Precepts, Ten Precepts)
false views (precept), 36, 89 (see also Ten Precepts)
falsifiability, 27, 38, 60
family, 5, 18, 39, 110, 216, 218, **219-21**, 224
  extended family, 219
  nuclear family, 216, 219
feedback loops (open and closed), 15, **26-7**, 29-30, 82-3, 108, 128, 132, 137, 172, 190, 222 (see also mind reactive and creative)
feminism, 186, 191, 202
fertility, 193
fidelity, 95-6, 209
fine art: see art
five aggregates (*skandhas*), 124
Five Buddha Mandala, 148
Five Precepts, 88, 93, 158 (see also ethics, killing, taking the not-given, sexual misconduct, false speech, intoxication)
fixed self: see non-substantiality
Fordham, Frieda, 147, 243
'form' (in art), 111
form of life (Wittgensteinian), 111, 160, 229
formalism, 40, 88, 97, 153, 156, 159-60, 188
formless world (*arupa-loka*), 189
Forty-three Years Ago (book by S), 39, 244
Four Noble Truths, 36-7 (see also frustration, impermanence, non-substantiality, craving,

enlightenment, Noble Eightfold Path)
Four Sights (of Buddha), 149
freedom
  from constraints, 135, 219-20
  political ~, 10, 58-9, 191-2, 222
  psychological (inner) ~, 32, 125, 153
freewill, 32
friendship, 1, 48, 78, **94-101**, 107, 109, 122, 130, 135, 168-9, 198, 212, 215, 223, 240 (see also spiritual friendship)
  horizontal friendship, 96
  vertical friendship, 96-7, 99-101, 223 (see also guru, discipleship)
Fromm, Erich, 117
frustration (*dukkha*), 29
Future Dharma Fund, 77
FWBO (Friends of the Western Buddhist Order), 10-12, 16, 35, 51, 62-3, 94, 115, 121, 148, 195, 199, 203-4, 211 (see also Triratna Buddhist Community)
FWBO Files (critical website), 16, 203-4

Galileo, 38
Gautama: see Buddha
gender, 100, 167, 197, 224 (see also sex)
generosity (*dana*), 76-8, 89
gestalt, 73
Gilbert, Paul, 238, 243
global warming, 30
God, 60, 65, 67, 87, 128, 137, 145, 147-8, 206
Going for Refuge, 35, 151, **158-64**, 165, 172, 223, 230
Gotama: see Buddha
gravitation (metaphor), 136
Great Mother (archetype), 147
Greece, 110
Greek love, 214
Grossmann, Igor, 48-9, 199, 243
group (as general phenomenon), 21, **54-60**, 63-4, 66, 68, 75, 84, 101, 104-5, 118-21, 150, 168, 172-4, 183, 199-201, 219, 229
group pressure, 121
group repression, 183

Index

groupthink (bias), 54
Guardian, The (newspaper), 203, 210–12, 214, 242
Guhyaloka (retreat centre), 200
guilt, 32, 60, 207, 217
guru, 20, 96, 100, 108, 153, **167–9**, 170, 173, 179–82, 240 (see also friendship/vertical, discipleship)
Guru Yoga (meditation practice), 85, 179

hatred (aversion), 27, 89, 92, 123, 135, 137
health, 2, 208, 218, 246
Hegel, Georg, 128
heresy, 60
Hero (archetype), 147–8
hierarchy, 4, 97, 99, 159, 189, 206, 223
Higher Evolution, 53, 160, 248 (see also evolution)
Hinayana Buddhism, 155, 157
Hinduism, 8–9, 19, 72, 152
history, 57–60, 99, 156, 170, 186, 191–3, 219
　feminist views of ~, 191–3
　of democracy, 99
　religious ~, 60
homosexuality, 5, 51, 203, 205, **212–15**
horizontal friendship: see friendship
humanism, 233

iconographic painting, 149
idealisation, 52, 60, 78, 96–8, 100–1, 114, 122, 124, 135, 181–4, 223, 233, 235
ignorance, 27, 56, 139, 178 (see also delusion)
image
　Buddha image, 145–9
　use of S's image, 85, 167, **179–84**, 224
imagination, 27, 48, **115**, 121, 148, 164, 190
impermanence (*anicca*), 136
India, 5, 8–10, 12, 18, 72, 87, 152, 194
individualism, 18, 21, 51
individuality, 5, 7, 21, 34, **51–61**, 62, 64–5, 67, 73, 83, 94–5, 97–8, 102, 105, 107, 111, 119–20, 135, 149, 150–1, 154, 156, 165, 171–3, 176, 183, 188, 191, 193, 209, 220, 222, 240 (see also group)
individuation, 42 (see also integration)
Industrial Revolution, 57
ingroup bias, 54
insight, 17, 19, 29, 55, 76, 82, 98, 109–10, 127, 132–3, 136, 141, 150, 159, 161, 165, 193, 225–6, 232, 239 (see also wisdom)
institutions, 102, 104–5, **106–9**, 122, 177–8, 220, 240
integration, 5, 15, 21, 36, **42–50**, 52, 55, 59, 62, 64–5, 67, 70, 73, 76, 79–80, 83, 85, 89, 90, 93–5, 97, 100, 102–4, 106–7, 109–11, 113–14, 118, 126, 130, 136, 142, 144, 146–51, 154, 159, 165, 169, 171, 176, 178, 180, 223, 230–2, 237, 240, 241
　aesthetic v ethical ~, 114
　~ and archetypes, 146–8
　~ and *dhyana*, 43
　~ and friendship, 94–5, 97
　~ and non-duality, 46
　~ and positive emotion, 79–80
　~ and use of power, 103–4, 106
　arts aiding ~, 111
　as ethical goal, 89–90
　asymmetry of ~, **48–9**, 55, 103–4, 106, 114, 130, 136, 142, 159, 169, 180, 215, 232, 240–1
　~, confidence and decisiveness, 64–5
　degree of ~ for ordination, 48, 103, 106, 159
　emotional ~, 36, 76, 79–80, 118, 230–1
　individuality and ~, **52**, 55, 61
　institutions fostering, ~ 102
　Jungian sources, 42, 44, 146–7
　lack of ~ assumed to deflect criticism, 100
　~ of meaning, 113
　~ of opposing beliefs, 178, 230–1
　~ reducing violence, 59
　potential ~ symbolised (enlightenment), 85, 126, 149
　requiring acceptance of prior conditions, 188

social and psychological ~, 109, 113
temporary ~, 49–50, 55, 97
use in Triratna, 48
intoxication (fifth precept), 88, 93
Isaiah, 57
Islam, 72
Italy, 110
Itivuttaka (Pali text), 134

James, William, 141, 243
Japan, 152
Jaspers, Karl, 57
Jerome, Saint, 5
Johnson, Mark, 14, 113, 126, 137, 190, 238, 243
Judaism, 72
Jung, Carl, 2, 42–3, 45, 146–7, 197, 243
Jungians, 233

Kaccanagotta (Pali canon character), 66
Kahneman, Daniel, 238, 243
Kalama Sutta (Pali text), 35, 36
Kalimpong, 9, 41
kalyana mitrata: see spiritual friendship
Kamalashila (Triratna order member), 79
kama-loka: see world of desire
Kant, Immanuel, 7, 227
karma, 39, 69, 73, **138–42**, 143–4, 223, 235
Kashyap, Jagdish, 9
Kegan, Robert, 52, 95–6, 236, 243
kibbutzim, 221
killing (first precept), 88–9, **90–1**, 93
klesas: see defilements
Kuhn, Thomas, 33–4, 238, 243
kusala: see skilfulness

Lakatos, Imre, 33–4, 38–9, 238, 243
Lakoff, George, 14, 113, 126, 137, 190, 238, 243
Langer, Ellen, 238, 243
language (in general), 4, 100, 119, 126, 129, 135, 146, 190, 228–9
law
  human ~, 87
  natural or causal ~, 19, 138, 140

lay ethics, 93, 205 (see also Five Precepts)
leadership, 4, 102, 104, **173–5**
Lear, King, 174, 178
levels of Going for Refuge, 159
liberal democracy, 18, 21, 35, 51, 55, 57, 94, 105, 109, 223–4
Liberation Unleashed, 83
lineage, 85, 179
linear thinking, 48, 87, 120, 144, 149, 151, 223
Lingwood, Dennis (S's original name), 7
literature, 110
liturgy, 119, 121
love mode, 91, 94, 103 (see also power)
loving-kindness (*metta*), 79, 81, 89, 94, 182
loving-kindness meditation (*metta-bhavana*) 79, 81, 94, 182
loyalty, 95–6 (see also fidelity)
LSD (drug), 11
lying: see false speech

MacIntyre, Alastair, 87, 243
Maha Bodhi Society, 18, 72, 102
Mahamati (Triratna order member), 177, 213–15
Mahayana Buddhism, 8–9, 82, 115, 118–19, 125–6, 145–6, 148, 150, **155–7**
Mahler, Gustav, 241
mandala, 44–5, 50, 209
mantra, 84, 119, 179
Mara (symbol of evil), 146, 148
marriage, 5, 49, 101, 192, 198, 205, **216–19**, 224
masculinist, 202
materialism, 166, 231
Maturana, Humberto, 238, 244
McGilchrist, Iain, 14, 238, 244
meat, 90
mechanism (view), 33, 231
media, 58
meditation, 1, 6, 8, 14, 20, 42–50, 72–3, 76, 78, **79–86**, 88–9, 94, 115, 122, 134, 143, 152, 179, 182–3, 195–6, 200, 210, 223, 239–40
  achievement of integration in ~, 43–4, 48–50

alienated awareness in ~, 47
awareness of conflict in ~, 42, 46
Guru Yoga, 85, 179
mindfulness ~, 20, 79–81
positive emotion in ~, 76, 78–81, 94, 182
Refuge Tree visualisation, 85, 179
sadhana practice, 84–5
samatha and *vipassana*, 79–80, **81–4**
S's system of ~, 43–4, **79–86**
single-sex and ~, 195–6
subtle direction in ~, 134
visualising S in ~, 85. 179, 183
men's wing (of Triratna), 200–1
metaphor, 29, 97, 113, 125–6, 136, 161
metaphysics, 10, 23, 28, 31, 46, 52, 66, **67–8**, 70, 128, 136, 231
metta-bhavana: see loving-kindness meditation
Middle Way, 1–2, 14–15, 21–2, **62–71**, 73–4, 78, 89–93, 96, 109, 120, 122–4, 127–8, 130, 149–50, 154–8, 161–2, 171, 173, 176–7, 183, 189–90, 201, 204, 206–8, 217, 222–5, 236
~ and feedback loops, 127–8
~ and individuality, 51–2
~ and nirvana, 123–4
author's view of, 1–2, 14–15
embodiment and ~, 189–90
emotional balancing, 96
~ in Buddha's life, 150, 177
~ in moral judgement, 78, 89–93
not just Buddhist, 109
practical ~ in S's thought, 62–6, 73, 122, 222–3
S over-stressing transcendence, 74, 176–7
skilfulness expressing ~, 206
theoretical ~ in S's thought, 66–71, 223
tradition v ~, 120, 130, 154–5, 162, 207
Middle Way Philosophy, 1–2, 15, 242
Mill, John Stuart, 51, 55, 244
mind reactive and creative, 15, **23–32**, 62, 128, 132–3, 135, 222 (see also conditionality, feedback loops)
Mind Reactive and Creative (S's talk and book), 15, 23, 245, 247

mindfulness, 44, 47, 75, 79–81, 95, 117, 190, 237, 238 (see also meditation)
mindfulness of breathing (meditation), 44, 79, 81
miracles, 146
mitras (Triratna commitment), 99–100, 237
modernity, **18–22**, 33–4, 38, 41–2, 58–9, 62
monastic formalism, 40
monasticism, 10, 16, 20, 31, **39–40**, 52, 62–4, 88, 102–3, 158, 201
monastic-lay distinction, 31, 93, 154
monogamy, 208–9, 212, 216, 218 (see also marriage)
moral observance, 72 (see also ethics)
moral rules, 64 (see also ethics)
morality: see ethics
Morrison, Robert (Sagaramati, Triratna Order Member), 53, 244
Mucalinda, 146, 148
mundane, 92–3, 112, 128
myths, 148

Nagarjuna, 66
Nagpur, 9
natural law: see law
Neo-Platonism: see Platonism
Nepal, 8, 152
neuroscience, 3, 18, 24, 30, 76, 238
New Age, 122, 152
New Society, 107, 247
Nichiren Buddhism, 152
Nietzsche, Friedrich, 53–4, 244, 247
nihilism, 66, 68–70, 154
nirvana: see enlightenment
nirvana fallacy, 39, 192, 218
niyamas (levels of conditionality), 138–9
no self: see non-substantiality
Noble Eightfold Path, 20, 72–6, 78, 88, 122
non-duality, 46, 61, 68
non-substantiality (no-self, *anatta*), 52–3, 69, 171
nuclear family: see family
Nyingma (Tibetan school of Buddhism), 41

objectivity, 2, **3**, 4, 158, 237, 239
obsession, 27, 42, 44, 82, 94 (see also craving)
ocean (metaphor), 145–6
ontology, 128 (see also metaphysics)
Order, Triratna Buddhist (formerly Western Buddhist), 1–2, 7, 10–12, 14, 40, 62–3, 71, 84–5, 93, 99–108, 110, 115, 121, 148–9, 158, 163, 167, 169–78, 185, 201, 205, 210, 214, 221, 223–4, 234, 235–6, 240–1
ordination
   S's ~ as bhikkhu, 8–9, 39
   Triratna (WBO) ~, 20, 40, 48, 71, 79–80, 84–5, 101, 104, 107, 158–9, 179, 196, 240–1
organisations: see institutions
ottapa: see conscience
over-intellectualism, 77

pacifism, 91
Padmaloka (Retreat Centre), 105, 200–1
Padmaraja (Triratna Order Member), 104, 211
Padmasambhava (bodhisattva figure), 84
paganism, 122
Pali commentaries, 139
Pali Canon, 8, 28, 35, 66, 74, 88, 123, 132, 139, 145–6
parable of the raft (from Pali text), 153
parents, 7, 62, **63**, 70, 90, 101, 106, 181, 219 (see also family)
patriarchal oppression, 191, 193
Perfect… (S's translation of *samyag/samma*), 75 (see also Noble Eightfold Path)
perfection, 74, 232
philosophy, 10, 13–14, 33, 38, 74, 123, 129–30, 143, 227, 229, 238
Pinker, Steven, 58, 193, 244
Platonism, 74, 126–7, 129, 189–90, 194, 197, **206–8**, 220–1
poetry, 12, 110, 115, 148
political, 10, 18, 51, 95, 98, 99, 104, 174, 193, 220, 223
politics, 8, 10, 18, 24, 30, 36, 51, 87, 95, 98–9, **103–6**, 108, 174, 193, 220, 223

Popper, Karl, 27, 29–30, 33, 38, 55, 238, 244
positive emotion, 44, 79–81, 94
positive nidanas, 30, 133 (see also spiral)
power
   motive, 148, 180, 207, 236
   socio-political ~, 5, 58, 60, 88, 90–1, 94–5, 97–9, **102–9**, 113, 121, 136, 174, 191–3, 211, 214
power mode, 90–1, 94
pragmatism, 153–4, 173
prajña: see wisdom
prapanca: see proliferating thought
pratitya samutpada: see conditionality
preceptors, 99, 104
Preceptors' College (of Triratna Order), 105–6, 108
prescription, 78, 85–6, 120, 152, 183 (see also ethics)
presidential system (for Triratna centres), 108
primacy effect (bias), 120
professionalism, 87
projection (psychological), 97, 100, 124, 180–1, 183, 208, 241
proliferating thought (*prapanca*), 82–3
promiscuity, 208–9, **212**, 214–15, 217–18
provisionality, 5, 15, 17, **33–41**, 46, 64, 67–8, 70, 73, 78, 83, 103–4, 107–8, 111, 119–20, 142, 144, 149, 151, 153–4, 156, 159, 171, 176, 188, 191, 201, 222, 225, 230–1, 235–8
psychology, 3, 5, 14, 18, 21, 24, 42, 49, 54, 57, 62, 76, 147, 238
puja (ritual), 76, **118–20**, 121
Pure Land Buddhism, 152
Pure Land of Amitabha, 126

rationalism
   absolute a priori, 129 (see also Platonism)
   over-emphasis on reason, 230–1
Ratnasambhava (symbolic Buddha), 77
reactive mind, 21, 23–4, 27, 31, 42, 132 (see also mind reactive and creative)

reactivity, **25**, 26–30, 32, 82, 133, 188–90, 207, 222 (see also mind reactive and creative)
Reality, 45, 47, 65, 68, 123, 127–9, 135–6, 150 (see also metaphysics)
reason, 36, 60, 62, 68–70, 75–7, 112, 120, 129, 133, 143, 164–6, 171, 185, 218, 230
rebirth, 28, 39, 44, 83, 85, 131, 138, **142–4**, 207, 223, 235
reductionism, 33–4, 65, 166, 231
Reformation, 60, 247
Refuge Tree, 85, 179, 247
refuges, **162–3**, 164, 183–4
relativism, 11, 74, 87, 154, 166, 172
religion, 18–19, 21, 24, 36, 57, 87, 117, 146, 152, 155
Religion of Art, The (book by S), 110, 244, 248
reproductive processes, 190
resources of meaning, 112
retreats, 71, 115, 122, 195–6, 200, 202
revelation, 130, 148, 162
Rhys Davids, Caroline, 139
right livelihood, 20
Right Livelihood businesses, 107
rites of passage, 119
ritual, 48, 64, 76, 78, 115–16, **117–22**, 130–1, 156, 158, 173, 179, 183, 223
Robinson, John (Bishop of Woolwich), 65
Rohingya Muslims, 152
Roman Catholic Church, 154, 211
Romantic love, 94
rupa-loka: see world of form

saddha: see faith
sadhana, 79–80, 84–5 (see also meditation)
Sagan, Carl, 36–8, 244
samadhi: see meditation
samatha: see meditation
samsara, 27, 31, 127, 130, 132, 137 (see also conditionality, Wheel)
Sangha (community), 10, 17, 56, 102, 158, **162–4**, 170, 172–3, 176, 183, 222 (see also spiritual community, Arya Sangha)

Sangharakshita, *passim* (see also Lingwood, Dharmapriya)
Sarnath, 8
Satan, 148
Schindler's List (film), 114
scholasticism, 156
Schopenhauer, Arthur, 128
science, 5, 14, 18, 21, 27, 29–30, **33–8**, 41, 62, 69, 87, 226, 231, 237–9
scientific method, 21, 34, 222
Scorsese, Martin, 60
scriptures, 8–9, 16, 17, 115, 118, 146, 237 (see also Pali Canon)
secularism, 18, 21, 236
Self (archetype), 147–8, 150
seven factors of enlightenment, 23, 28
Sevenfold Puja, 119 (see also puja)
sex
  sexual activity, 100, 167, **203–15**, 221
  sexual difference, 40, 185–202, 216–18
  sexual abuse, 167, 203, 212, 215
  sexual distraction, **196**, 198
  sexual identity, 197
  sexual misconduct, 5, 49, 88–9, 93, **205**
  sexual polarisation, 196–7
  sexual relationships, 195, 203, 208–10, 214 (see also sex/sexual activity)
sexuality, 192, 196, 214 (see also homosexuality, sex)
Shadow (archetype), 44, 147–8, 204
Shinto, 152
shrine, 119, 179, 181–4
Siegel, Daniel, 25, 42, 245
Sigalovada Sutta (Pali text), 220, 248
Sikkim, 9
single-sex environments, 195–202, 216, 224
single-sex idea, 195–202
six element practice, 79–80
skandhas: see five aggregates
skilful means, 11, 155
skilfulness (*kusala*), 11, 28, 38, 139–41, 155, 206–7
slavery, 99
social proof (bias), 39, 54

social sciences, 194, 221
solitary retreats, 54
solitude, 197
soul, 67, 69
South Africa, 200
space, 4, 12, 68, 127, 136
speech precepts, 89, 91 (see also false speech)
spiral (positive conditionality), 28–9, 133, 139 (see also positive nidanas)
spiritual androgyny, 197, 208
spiritual aptitude, 186–7, 190–1, 198, 216, 224, 235
spiritual community, 54–6, 107, 119, 162, 196, 216–17, 238 (see also Sangha, communities/residential)
spiritual death, 44, 80
spiritual friendship (*kalyana mitrata*), **94–101**, 168, 214
spiritual hierarchy, 97
spiritual practice, 45, 72, 99, 110, 112, 118, 131, 163, 170, 241
spiritual rebirth, 44, 79, 83, 85
straw man (fallacy), 192
stream entry, 56, 98, 135–6, 141, 159, 162, 171
study (practice), 14, 53, 117, 170, 182, 195–6, 199, 239–40
Subhuti (Triratna Order Member), 48, 71, 155–6, 161, 185–7, 189–97, 199, 210, 214, 220, 237, 245
supererogation, 163
surveillance, 59
Survey, Order, 16, 58, 185, 191, 221
Survey of Buddhism, A (book by S), 9, 12, 29, 62, 66, 68, 127–9, 144, 153, 157–8, 164, 185, 221, 244
Sutra of Golden Light, The (Mahayana text), 148
Sutra of Hui Neng (Mahayana text), 82
symbolism, 44, 146
synthesis, 5, 229–30
systems theory, 30, 137

taking the not-given (second precept), 88–9, 93
Tara (bodhisattva figure), 84, 179
Taraloka (retreat centre), 201
technology, 58–9
temporary integration: see integration
Ten Pillars of Buddhism, The (book by S), 88, 90–1, 206, 234, 244
Ten Precepts, 87–9, 91, 93
theft: see taking the not-given
theology, 74
Theravada Buddhism, 9–10, 16, 39–41, 72–3, 82, 138, 145, 155–7
Three C's (Triratna institutions), 107
three fetters, 64
Three Jewels, 40, 158, 162–3, 183 (see also refuges)
Three Jewels, The (book by S), 141, 244
Threefold Path, 88 (see also Noble Eightfold Path)
Threefold Puja, 118 (see also puja, ritual)
Thus Spake Zarathustra (book by Nietzsche), 53
Tibetan Buddhism, 27, 41, 72–3, 84–5, 138, 156, 179, 181
time (in general), 67–8
~ and karmic operation, 140–1, 143
continuity over ~, 95
enlightenment and ~, 125, 130, 145
giving and spending ~, 77, 220
tolerance, 60
traditional society, 10, 58, 191, 194 (see also modernity)
traditionality, 119–21
Trailokya Bauddh Mahasangha (Indian FWBO), 12
transcendental, 66, 92, 125, 127–8
transcendental path, 37, 163
travel, 59, 192
Triple Gem: see Three Jewels
Triratna Buddhist Community, 1, 4, 6, 9, 11–12, 14, 21, 41, 48, 50, 54, 57, 63, 70–2, 75, 77, 79, 81, 84–5, 93–4, 96–7, 99–108, 110, 115, 118–20, 149, 158, 167, 170, 173–4, 176, 179–80, 182, 184–5, 191, 194–5, 199–201, 211–15, 218, 221–2, 227, 233–41 (see also FWBO)
Triratna centres, 104
trustees, 104–6

truthfulness, 91 (see also false speech)
Tversky, Amos, 238
twelve links (*nidanas*), 23, 27, 29, 132–3 (see also conditionality, Wheel)
twelve *nidanas*: see twelve links
Twenty Years on the Middle Way (talk by S), 62, 70, 90, 223, 247

Übermensch (concept of Nietzsche), 53
Udana (Pali text), 133, 134, 243
uncompounded (*asankhata*), 134–5
upasaka/ upasika, 40
US constitution, 103

Vajradaka (Triratna Order Member), 79
Vajragupta (Triratna Order Member), 10, 104, 200–1, 246
Vajrayana Buddhism, 155–7
Varela, Francisco, 238, 244
vertical friendship: see friendship
Vessantara (Triratna Order Member), 79
Vimalakirti-Nirdesha (Mahayana text), 148
vipassana: see meditation
Virgin Mary, 148
Vision and Transformation (book by S), 73, 77, 91, 244

visualisation, 79, 80, 83–5, 179 (see also meditation)

welfare state, 51
Western philosophy, 32
Wheel of samsara, 27–9, 31, 132–3, 136, 245 (see also twelve links)
White Lotus Sutra (Mahayana text), 148
Windhorse Trading (Triratna business), 108
Windhorse Trust (Triratna business owner), 108
wisdom (*prajña*), 20, 42, 48–9, 82, 88–9, 146, 199
Wise Old Man (archetype), 147–8, 150
Wittgenstein, Ludwig, 229
Women, Men and Angels (book by Subhuti), 185–94, 195, 245
women's wing (of Triratna), 191, 200–1
world of desire (*kama-loka*), 189
world of form (*rupa-loka*), 189
World Tree, 146

yanas, 155–6
YMBA (Young Men's Buddhist Association), 9
yoga, 7, 72, 83

Zen Buddhism, 16, 82, 84, 152

www.ingramcontent.com/pod-product-compliance
Lightning Source LLC
Chambersburg PA
CBHW062011220426
43662CB00010B/1282